THE
PROVING
GROUND

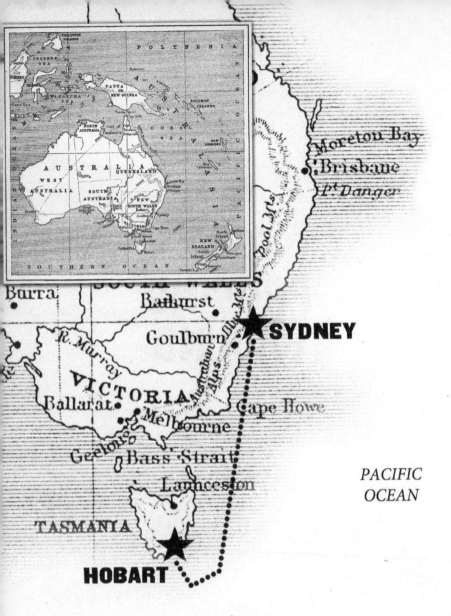

**SYDNEY TO HOBART
RACE COURSE**

THE PROVING GROUND

The Inside Story of the
1998 Sydney to Hobart Race

G. BRUCE KNECHT

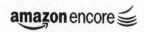

Published by AmazonEncore
P.O. Box 400818
Las Vegas, NV 89140

ISBN-13: 9781612181431
ISBN-10: 1612181430

For Elizabeth

Race Boat Diagram

Starboard = Right Side of the Boat
Port = Left Side of the Boat
Bow = Front Part of the Boat
Stern = Back Part of the Boat

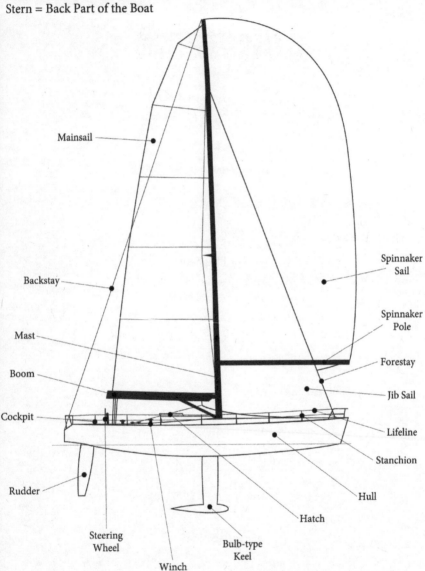

Mainsail

Spinnaker Sail

Backstay

Spinnaker Pole

Mast

Boom

Forestay

Jib Sail

Cockpit

Lifeline

Stanchion

Rudder

Hull

Hatch

Steering Wheel

Bulb-type Keel

Winch

CONTENTS

PROLOGUE

Larry Ellison was lying in his bunk, calculating the likelihood that he would die.

He was, thanks to his stock in his company, Oracle, one of the wealthiest men in the world. But right now, he was seasick and miserable, and the NASDAQ seemed very far away.

One day earlier, he had seen what was coming. Looking at one of the two laptop computers used on his boat, he saw a satellite-generated image of a cyclone-like cloud pattern. Gripped with the same surreal feeling of disconnectedness he sometimes had when he was flying a plane on instruments, he asked Mark Rudiger, the yacht's navigator, "Have you ever seen anything like this?"

Almost imperceptibly, Rudiger shook his head.

"Well, I have," Ellison declared, his voice rising in bewildered outrage. "It was on the Weather Channel — and it was called Hurricane Helen. What the fuck is that doing here?"

Ellison's yacht *Sayonara* had been struggling ever since. Steep forty-foot waves were sucking *Sayonara* up terrifying crests and then releasing it into deep troughs. Going up felt like riding an elevator during an earthquake; going down felt as though the elevator's cable had snapped. The boat's hull was made from two skins of carbon fiber surrounding a core of foam. Carbon fiber is a synthetic material with incredible strength for its weight, but Ellison knew that structural elements were beginning to fail. Several of the bulkheads, critical to maintaining the integrity of the hull, were no longer even attached. Large oval blisters had developed on the hull's inside surface near the bow, indicating that the carbon skin had separated from the foam interior and that the two surfaces were grating against each other. Ellison knew that at some point the hull would become so weak that it would collapse like a paper bag against one of the waves. He also knew that *Sayonara* was too far out at sea to be reached by helicopter and that if he ended up in the water, he was unlikely to survive long enough to be rescued by another vessel.

By every standard but his own, Ellison, who looked younger than his fifty-four years, lived the life of dreams. On most days, he directed his company of 37,000 employees without even showing up at the office. He preferred to keep in touch by phone and e-mail from *Katana*, his 240-foot power yacht, or from his elegantly simple Japanese-style house in Atherton, California, where a pond was filtered like a swimming pool to ensure that the water was always crystal clear.

But Ellison was motivated by a kind of deeply rooted ambition that would never be satisfied. He was born to an unwed mother who gave him up for adoption. His adoptive father repeatedly told him he would never amount to anything. Since then, Ellison's successes had only expanded his appetites. Although he carried himself with the bouncy manner of an adolescent who has just won an athletic championship, his dark brown eyes appeared coldly focused and constantly calculating. In a rarefied form of keeping up with the Joneses, much of the calculus involved his greatest rival, Microsoft's Bill Gates. It was a rivalry that, in Ellison's mind at least, went far beyond business and money. Ellison, who wrote short stories, played the piano, and piloted stunt planes in addition to winning sailing regattas, was constantly seeking to portray himself as more talented and more broadly gauged than Gates.

To Ellison, life was an experiment, or a contest, with a singular purpose: determining just how good he could be. Speed was an overriding theme. In addition to *Sayonara*, Ellison had a collection of high-performance planes and cars. With its 18,500-horsepower engine, *Katana* could charge through the water at thirty-five miles an hour. Ellison had given a lot of thought to his endless quest to go fast. "There are two aspects of speed," he told friends. "One is the absolute notion of speed. Then there's the relative notion — trying to go faster than the next guy. I think it's the latter that is much more interesting. It's an expression of our primal being. Ever since we were living in villages as hunter-gatherers, great rewards went to people who were stronger, faster."

Ellison had entered the Sydney to Hobart Race because it is one of sailing's most challenging contests. The danger had been part of the appeal. But as he lay in his bunk and looked around the cabin, where some of the world's best sailors were lying on heaps of wet sails and retching into buckets, he was having second thoughts about his compulsive need to win.

Sayonara burrowed deep into each oncoming wall of water. Then, as if remembering it was supposed to float, it bobbed straight up to the wave's crest. At that point Ellison began to count — "one one thousand, two one thousand" — as the bow projected out of the wave's other side, again seeming to defy the natural order of things, until such a large section of the seventy-nine-foot vessel was hanging freely that gravity brought it down. That motion seemed to continue forever, although he had only reached "four one thousand" when the cycle ended with a violent crash.

This, he kept saying to himself, would be a stupid way to die.

PART I

THE CALM

Physically and culturally, the harbor is the center of Sydney, never more so than the day after Christmas, when the start of the 630-mile race from Sydney to Hobart, a city on the east coast of Tasmania, causes it to become an enormous natural amphitheater. Virtually everyone in Sydney watches the start, either in person or on television. Parks, backyards, and rooftops overflow with thousands of spectators, most of them with drinks in hand. The harbor itself is crowded with hundreds of boats and is noisy with air horns and low-flying helicopters.

No place is busier than the source of all the excitement, the Cruising Yacht Club of Australia. The club was founded in 1945, the same year it sponsored the first Sydney to Hobart Race. The CYC's home is an undistinguished, two-story brick building on the bank of Rushcutters Bay, just a couple of miles east of downtown Sydney. Its pretensions, to the extent it has any, are related to "the Hobart," as the race is usually called, rather than to social distinctions. Sailing has always played an important role in Australian life. It's not surprising to hear policemen and taxi drivers describe themselves as yachtsmen. On an island as big as the United States but with a population of less than 19 million, access to the waterfront has never been limited to the rich. The CYC's founders wanted to make sure it stayed that way, and in 1998 its

2,500 members paid annual dues of just $250, a tenth of what they were at some yacht clubs in the United States and Europe.

But although the CYC was modest in dues, it was not so when it came to its race. The main bar, which opens onto a large deck and a network of docks, is adorned with photographs of evocatively named Hobart-winning yachts: *Assassin, Love & War, Ragamuffin, Rampage, Sagacious, Scallywag, Screw Loose,* and *Ultimate Challenge.* In the slightly more formal bar on the second floor, a plaque carries the names of forty-three men who had completed at least twenty-five Hobarts. Although women had been competing regularly since 1946, none had yet earned a place on the plaque.

The CYC's race draws the biggest names in sailing as well as prominent figures from other fields. Rupert Murdoch competed in six races, and his fifty-nine-foot yacht *Ilina,* a classic wooden ketch, came in second in 1964. Sir Edward Heath, the former British prime minister, won in 1969. Three years later, Ted Turner shocked other skippers by brazenly steering his *American Eagle* through the spectator boats after the start of the race — and then going on to win it. In 1996, Hasso Plattner, the multibillionaire cofounder of SAP AG, the German computer software giant, won in record-breaking time.

The very first race took place after Captain John Illingworth, a British naval officer who was stationed in Sydney during World War II, was invited to join a pleasure cruise from Sydney to Hobart, Australia's second-oldest city and at one time an important maritime center. Only if it's a race, he is said to have responded. It was agreed, and Illingworth's thirty-nine-foot sloop *Rani* beat eight other yachts to win the first Hobart in six and a half days. Until the 1960s it usually took four or five days to complete the course. In the following decades, the average time required shrank to three or four. Plattner's *Morning Glory* took just over two and a half days in 1996. The quickening pace reflected two of the biggest changes in competitive sailing: first, the move away from wooden boats, which were constructed according to instinct and tradition, to ones designed with the help of computers and built from fiberglass, aluminum, and space-age composite materials, and second, the transformation of what had been a purely amateur sport to one with an expanding number of full-time professionals.

For most of its history, sailing had proudly resisted the move to professionalism that had transformed many sports. But even Sir Thomas Lipton — whose five spirited but unsuccessful America's Cup campaigns, which stretched from 1899 through 1930, earned him an almost saintlike reputation — understood the value of sponsorship. The publicity engendered by his prolonged pursuit of the Cup did much to make his tea a popular brand in the United States.

Since then, the level of competition has steadily risen, requiring increasing amounts of time and money. In 1977, Ted Turner spent six months and $1.7 million preparing his winning America's Cup campaign. The only compensation he gave his crew was room and board. In 2000, five American contenders for the Cup planned to spend the better part of three years and more than $120 million preparing for the contest. Patrizio Bertelli, the head of the Italian fashion house Prada, provided the syndicate representing his country with a $50 million budget.

Ellison, who planned to compete for the America's Cup in 2003, expected to spend at least $80 million. He would pay many members of his crew upwards of $200,000 a year for the more than two years they would train together. Ellison, who intended to sail on the boat — at least some of the time as its helmsman

— would also take advantage of computer-based performance analyses and boat building technologies that had been unthinkable even a few years earlier.

Turner, who had sailed on *Sayonara* for several races, was of two minds about what has happened to the sport he once dominated. During one race, he told Gary Jobson, his longtime tactician, "There are so many computers. Whatever happened to sailing by feel?"

As one of the computer industry's pioneers, Ellison had no such qualms.

Ellison, who won the Hobart in 1995, had two goals for the 1998 race. First and foremost, he wanted to take the record away from Plattner. After Bill Gates, Plattner was Ellison's most important competitor in the software business, and sailing had intensified their rivalry and added a deeply personal dimension. "It's a blood duel," Ellison would say, without the slightest suggestion that he was anything but deadly serious. He boasted that his yacht *Sayonara*, which didn't race in the Hobart the year the record was set, had never lost to Plattner's *Morning Glory*. Ellison and Plattner were not on speaking terms, but they had found other ways to express themselves. During one regatta, Plattner — incensed by what he felt was unsportsmanlike behavior by Ellison — dropped his pants and "mooned" *Sayonara*'s crew. Ellison's other goal was to beat George Snow.

Snow, a charismatic Australian who had won the Hobart in 1997, and Ellison could hardly have been more different from each other. The crew on Snow's yacht, *Brindabella*, was almost all amateur. On *Sayonara*, with the exception of two guests — one of them Lachlan Murdoch, Rupert's eldest son and heir apparent — everyone was a professional. Ten of Ellison's twenty-three crewmen were members of Team New Zealand, which had won the America's Cup in 1995 and planned to defend it in 2000.

Ellison had always been upsetting traditions and bucking the odds. After his mother decided she couldn't take care of him, he was adopted by an aunt and uncle. Ellison never got along with his adoptive father, Louis Ellison, a Russian immigrant who took his name from Ellis Island and worked as an auditor. Growing up in a small apartment on the South Side of Chicago, Ellison wasn't interested in school or organized sports or anyone telling him what to do. "I always had problems with authority," Ellison would explain. "My father thought that if someone was in a position of authority that he knew more than you did. I never thought that. I thought if someone couldn't explain himself, I shouldn't blindly do what I was told."

After dropping out of the University of Illinois at Urbana-Champaign and then the University of Chicago, where he learned to write computer software, Ellison drove a beat-up car to California. Although he had little trouble getting hired, staying so was a different story. He stumbled through a raft of computer-related jobs until he heard about a new kind of software that could store and quickly manipulate large databases. Seeing its potential, he launched a business in 1977 that would become Oracle. The company doesn't produce the kind of software that consumers buy or even know much about, but every organization that stores significant amounts of data needs it. For most of its first decade, sales doubled every year, so quickly that Oracle appeared to be on the verge of going totally out of control. Ellison's personal life was equally rocky. He married and divorced three times, and he broke his neck in a surfing accident.

In 1990, Ellison was almost booted out of his own company after Oracle disclosed that some of its employees had booked millions of dollars of sales that hadn't actually materialized. But by the mid-1990s it seemed that Ellison's high-stakes, step-skipping management style was entirely appropriate for an industry that was changing faster than any traditional organization could. Ellison was confident that no company was better suited than his to capitalize on the burgeoning Internet. After all, the first generation of e-commerce blue bloods — Amazon.com, eBay, and Yahoo! — all relied on Oracle software. Thanks to them, and their gravity-defying stock prices, Ellison believed that the value of Oracle's shares would also explode. And he thought that would enable him to achieve his ultimate ambition — to replace Bill Gates as the world's richest man.

Ellison had always been interested in sailing. As a child, he imagined being able to travel to exotic places on the yachts he saw on Lake Michigan. Soon after he moved to California, he bought a thirty-four-foot sloop, although he gave it up because he couldn't afford it. In 1994, Ellison's next-door neighbor, a transplanted New Zealander named David Thomson, suggested the idea of building a maxi-yacht. The largest kind of boat permitted in many races, maxis are about eighty feet long. Ellison said yes, but he imposed a couple of conditions. First, he wanted it to be the fastest boat of its kind. Second, he wanted Thomson to do all the work. Thomson was a private investor affluent enough to live in Ellison's neighborhood, but he wasn't in a position to spend 3 or 4 million dollars for his own maxi. Deciding that it would be fun to oversee the design and construction of Ellison's boat, Thomson readily agreed to his terms.

Typically, when someone decides to build a boat, he or she wants to be involved in the plans, but Ellison made it clear that he didn't want to know about the details. When Thomson walked over to Ellison's house with a set of engineering drawings, they spent only a few minutes talking about the boat before Ellison turned the conversation to his newest plane, which they discussed for more than an hour. Thomson did send Ellison occasional e-mail updates. At the end of one, Thomson, who had heard that Ellison was going to the White House for a state dinner honoring the emperor of Japan, asked about the protocol for such an occasion. "What will you wear? Do Americans bow to the emperor?" At the end of the e-mail, Thomson wrote, "Have a great time. Sayonara."

Seconds after he pushed the SEND button, he sent another e-mail: "Sayonara. That's not a bad name for a boat."

Ellison didn't answer Thomson's White House etiquette questions, but to the name suggestion, he punched out an instant reply: "That's it."

Sayonara was completed in Auckland in May 1995, just a few days after Team New Zealand won the America's Cup — a victory that the tiny nation commemorated with four ticker-tape parades and an outpouring of nationalistic pride rivaling the celebrations that followed World War II. Thomson had recruited almost half of *Sayonara*'s crew from the winning squad, and they flew to San Francisco for *Sayonara*'s inaugural sail shortly after the last parade. Thomson hired Paul Cayard to be the boat's first professional skipper. Cayard, who was the lead helmsman for Dennis Conner on *Stars & Stripes*, the boat that lost the Cup to the Kiwis, had competed in a total of five America's Cup regattas and in 1998 won the around-the-world Whitbread Race. To round out the crew, Cayard recruited several other members from *Stars & Stripes* to sail on *Sayonara*, creating a dream team of American and Kiwi yachtsmen.

When they met on *Sayonara*'s deck in Alameda, across the bay from downtown San Francisco, the newly assembled crewmen were impressed by what they saw. Everything on the boat was black or white except for the red that filled the *o* in *Sayonara*'s name painted on the side of the hull. White hulls typically have a dull finish, but *Sayonara*'s reflected the shimmering water like a mirror. The 100-foot mast, which bent slightly toward the stern and tapered near the top, was black, as were the sail covers, winches, and instruments. Like most modern racers, *Sayonara* had a wide stern and a broad cockpit, on which stood a pair of large side-by-side steering wheels. *Sayonara* was narrower than most other maxis and, at twenty-three tons, lighter than most of its peers. The unpainted interior was carbon-fiber black. While there is nothing pleasant about a windowless black cabin, paint has weight, and the lack of it only emphasized the commitment to speed.

The front third of *Sayonara* was an empty black hole except for long bags of sails. There was a similar-looking black cavern in the back of the boat. Only the center section was designed to be inhabited by sailors, and even there the accommodations were spartan. Pipes, wires, and mechanical devices protruded from the walls, and nothing was done to cover them. Just as David Thomson had promised, *Sayonara* was a pure racing machine.

Within three years, *Sayonara* had become virtually invincible, winning three straight maxi-class world championships as well as the Newport to Bermuda Race, America's most prestigious offshore race. Ellison couldn't have been more pleased. "I could have bought the New York Yankees, but I couldn't be the team's shortstop. With the boat, I actually get to play on the team."

Getting to know the crew was part of the fun. Ellison discovered that many of them shared his interests in planes and fast cars, and he enjoyed being with men who were driven and competitive but wanted nothing from him beyond the chance to sail on *Sayonara*. Ellison was so pleased by his crew and so confident of their abilities that in 1997 he arrived at the maxi championship regatta, which was held in Sardinia, with Rolex watches for every crewman. They had been engraved SAYONARA. MAXI WORLD CHAMPIONS. SARDINIA 1997 long before the racing began.

During that regatta's penultimate race, Hasso Plattner's *Morning Glory* was winning until the halyard that held its mainsail broke and the sail collapsed. Seizing on the opportunity, *Sayonara*, which had been in second place, took over the lead. For the rest of the race, it "covered" *Morning Glory*: whenever *Morning Glory* tacked, *Sayonara* also turned so that it always stood between its opponent and the finish line, making it virtually impossible for Plattner to regain the lead, even after his crew rigged a new halyard. Covering is standard racing procedure, but it infuriated Plattner. Even worse, by winning that day's race, *Sayonara* clinched the championship. Ellison didn't have to sail on the last day to win the regatta, and he decided not to. Plattner considered Ellison's behavior unsportsmanlike. "I have only the worst English words to provide for them," Plattner said later.

Ellison and his girlfriend, Melanie Craft, a romance novelist, had arrived in Sydney a week before the 1998 Hobart. After Melanie heard that a major storm might coincide with the race, she thought the Hobart was one challenge Ellison could live without. Just hours before the start, she and Ellison walked from their hotel along the perimeter of the harbor and into the lush Royal Botanic Garden. There she tried, as she had several times before, to talk Ellison out of going on the race.

"It's idiotic," she said just before they got into a car that would take them to *Sayonara*'s dock. "There's no reason you have to do it. It's much too dangerous."

"It's not a dangerous race," Ellison replied. "It's hard. It's demanding, but only a couple of people have died since it started. There's a perception of danger — that's one of the reasons it's such a cool race — but it's actually not. There's nothing to worry about."

Later, Ellison would think back and wonder why he hadn't listened to Melanie. But by then it would be too late.

2

The Hobart is far from the sailing world's longest blue-water contest, but it has a reputation for being one of the most treacherous. Bass Strait, the 140-mile-wide stretch of water that separates Australia's mainland from Tasmania, is one of the world's most turbulent bodies of water. The two landmasses were once attached, and today the gap is much shallower than the oceans to the east and west. When waves that have been building for hundreds of miles pass over its shallow bottom, they tend to break like surf on the beach.

Many yachtsmen believe that every seventh Hobart is subject to a special curse. Particularly severe storms savaged the fleet in 1956, 1963, 1970, 1977, and 1984. In 1977, fifty-nine yachts dropped out of the race. In 1984, 104 out of 150 boats retired in gale-force winds. The pattern appeared to end in 1991 — or maybe was just delayed until 1993, when only thirty-eight out of 110 starters made it to Hobart. Regardless, some of the sailors remembered that the original pattern would make 1998 one of the bad years.

But the potential for a dangerous storm wouldn't cause CYC officials to consider postponing the race. Like yacht clubs everywhere, it abides by the five fundamental rules set by the International Sailing Federation. Rule number four declares: "A boat is solely responsible for deciding whether to start or to continue racing."

Brett Gage, a senior forecaster at the Bureau of Meteorology, arrived at his sixteenth-floor office in downtown Sydney at four o'clock on Saturday morning, nine hours before the start of the race. As in previous years, the bureau had agreed to provide special weather forecasts to the Cruising Yacht Club, and Gage had a lot to do: he had to decide on the prerace forecast, assemble a collection of weather data into information packages for each yacht, and then rush to the CYC so he could individually brief as many skippers and navigators as possible.

His biggest complication was the weather itself: nobody could agree on what it would be. At a preliminary briefing at the CYC on Christmas Eve, Kenn Batt, another forecaster from the bureau, had described several possible scenarios but said he wasn't sure which one would actually develop. Batt and Gage based their forecasts on three global, computer-generated weather-forecasting models as well as an Australia-based model that projected only local conditions. The U.S.-based global model, which some Australian forecasters thought tended to overstate the severity of storms, was predicting an intense low-pressure system, one that could produce hurricane-force winds. The two other models, one produced by a weather center in continental Europe and the other by a center in Britain, were forecasting a much less dangerous storm. During his Christmas Eve briefing, Batt had said a low-pressure system might develop south of Australia and move north at the same time the fleet headed south or that it could fizzle out on Christmas Day. "All the computer models are saying different things," Batt had said, provoking an outbreak of laughter. "But a strong low could be in the cards, and it could kick up strong winds and a pretty big sea."

Predicting weather in any one place requires an evaluation of the patterns for the rest of the world. The three main forecasting models are based on millions of observation points spread around the globe. For each of more than 100,000 grid points, data on wind speed, barometric pressure, temperature, and humidity are gathered from weather stations and balloons as well as from drifting buoys and are combined with estimates for twenty-nine levels of the atmosphere for every grid point, creating more than 3 million data points. Information for every one of them, plus additional data from planes and satellites, is fed into supercomputers for each of the models, which make more than 20 million calculations per second for more than an hour, to produce global pictures of the shifting temperatures, pressure, and high-altitude jet streams that create weather.

The models Batt was examining predicted very different levels of barometric pressure. The discrepancies were crucial: variations of pressure are what produce wind. At any given moment, the world's atmosphere has more than one hundred regions of low pressure, and air from everywhere else is rushing toward them. The lower the pressure, the swifter the wind. In Southern latitudes, when the air approaches the center of the low, because of the earth's rotation, the wind circles in a clockwise pattern (called the Coriolis effect), creating the kind of swirling clouds familiar from satellite images. If the force is powerful enough, it develops into a "tropical cyclone" — which is the same thing as a "hurricane" in America or a "typhoon" in northern Asia.

Early Saturday morning, as Gage sipped his first cup of coffee and scanned the latest satellite photographs and computer outputs, it was clear that a low was still forming, but the models continued to disagree about its intensity. The information packages he began to put together included predictions for barometric pressure as well as for wave heights and tidal changes, a satellite photograph showing that there were hardly any clouds over Australia, and a "strong wind warning," indicating that twenty-five-to-thirty-three-knot winds should be expected. (A knot is one nautical mile, 1.15 statute miles, per hour.) But Gage knew it could be much worse, and he was afraid the race would start before he could make a definitive judgment. At 7:30 A.M. he ran into another problem: the bureau's high-speed photocopying machine broke down, forcing him to finish running off the sheets of information for the packages at the CYC.

Kenn Batt, who was helping assemble the packages and who planned to conduct some of the briefings at the CYC, remained at the bureau, hoping to obtain updated information. Batt, who was forty-eight, had been a member of the bureau for twenty-five years but had begun forecasting long before that. As a teenager growing up in Hobart, he began producing forecasts for the Royal Yacht Club of Tasmania, which he posted on a bulletin board every weekend. He knew weather and he knew sailing: Batt came from a family that had been racing for four generations, and he had sailed in seven Hobarts.

Just before 9:00 A.M. Batt received the latest output from the European and British models. They predicted lower pressure than they had before, though still not as low as the American model. Calling Gage, Batt said, "Don't hand out the packages. We're upgrading the forecast to a gale warning," which indicated expected winds of thirty-four to forty-seven knots. "We'll fax the warning through in a couple of minutes so you can incorporate it into the package."

By the time Batt arrived at the CYC, Gage had set up a table and hung weather maps from a nearby wall. During the next three hours, representatives from eighty-six yachts picked up weather packages. Some of the yachtsmen just took them and left. Others asked lots of questions. "You'll have a nice run this afternoon," Batt told one of them, "but there's a front building down south. We're not sure which way it's going, but it could develop and become really nasty. We could have a 1993 situation."

3

Lachlan Murdoch and Sarah O'Hare, his fiancée, began Saturday at Lachlan's harborside house, surrounded by lush gardens and palm trees. Although Lachlan was just twenty-seven, for the previous four years he had been the chief executive officer of News Corporation's sprawling Australian operation, which included almost two-thirds of the nation's newspapers, more than one hundred in all, as well as magazines and a movie studio. With his press-lord powers and wealth, along with robust good looks and a reputation for racing around Sydney streets on a Ducati motorcycle, Lachlan was a major Australian celebrity. When *Vogue's* Australian edition published a lengthy profile, the headline on the magazine's cover was: LACHLAN MURDOCH: THE MAN AUSTRALIA WANTS TO SLEEP WITH. Sarah also had a following. A model, she had appeared in splashy magazine advertising for Revlon and Wonderbra and had modeled for many of the world's most important designers in Paris.

Lachlan had already met most of *Sayonara's* crew during several practice sails. As a guest, he wasn't required to participate, but he had shown up for all of them, arriving early enough to help lug food and ice down the dock and separate cans of soda from their plastic holders. Lachlan had always recognized that people tended to define him in terms of his father, and he frequently tried to find ways to make the point that he didn't expect special treatment. Although he knew he would be *Sayonara*'s least-experienced sailor, he hoped to let the others know that he wanted to do more than simply stay out of the way.

The Murdochs' stock was already strong on *Sayonara*. Rupert sailed with Ellison in the 1995 Hobart, and the media mogul had also shown up for the practice sails. During one of them, he lost the end of a finger after a line he was holding pulled his hand into a block. "I'll be fine," he had said as he calmly held what was left of his bleeding digit over the side of the boat so he didn't bleed on the deck. The missing piece was put on ice and reattached at St. Vincent's Hospital a few hours later, and when he arrived at a crew dinner that night, he declared, "Right, now I'm ready to go to Hobart."

During the race itself, Rupert had spent most of the first night seated on "the rail," the outside edge of the deck, with his legs dangling over the side. When he got up and offered to serve coffee or tea, several crewmen took him up, each specifying his cream and sugar preferences. Rupert shuttled up and down the steps delivering steaming mugs until a Team New Zealand sailor named Kevin Shoebridge cut him short: "Rupert, for fuck's sake, I said no sugar. Make me another." Rupert laughed as much as anyone, and in Hobart he won more points when he slapped a credit card on the bar, declaring, "I want to get the last laugh with you guys, so let's try to put a dent in this."

While growing up on Manhattan's Fifth Avenue, Lachlan worked for company-owned papers during school vacations: first as a reporter at the *Express-News* in San Antonio, Texas, and later as an editor at *The Sun* in London. One year after he graduated from Princeton University, he became the publisher of *The Australian*, the only nationwide general-interest daily paper.

Soon after the 1998 Hobart, Lachlan expected to start spending most of his time in New York and to take responsibility for the company's publishing operations in the United States, including HarperCollins, the *New York Post*, and *TV Guide*.

But Lachlan wasn't his father's clone, and he didn't try to be. He was known to burn joss sticks in his spacious offices in Sydney and New York, and the discs sitting near a wall-mounted CD player in Sydney were cutting edge and eclectic. When Lachlan rolled up his sleeves, his left forearm revealed a striking Polynesian-design tattoo. Even when presiding over meetings, Lachlan was relaxed and unguarded, throwing his legs over the arms of couches and punctuating lots of his sentences with question marks the way teenagers do. He spoke softly in an accent that reflected his peripatetic upbringing: there were hints of Australia and England, although the dominant strain was American. Like his father, Lachlan had an informal approach to management. But while Rupert could be gruff and intimidating, Lachlan was almost always welcoming and gentlemanly. Friends used old-fashioned words like "earnest" and "gallant" to describe him.

Lachlan also had a serious appetite for adventure. In that way he was like Ellison, although their specific tastes were somewhat different. Whereas Ellison chased speed, Lachlan liked danger, the sense that he was putting himself on the edge. While at Princeton, where he majored in philosophy, he spent several hours a day climbing sheer rock faces. More recently he had discovered that his motorcycle provided the same thrill but required less time. "There are people who in their makeup need to take risks," Lachlan told friends. "Every once in a while I just have to do things that require me to make judgments about how far I can go. It's not that it's dangerous as much as it's unprotected, if you know what I mean."

Lachlan chose his friends without much regard to what they did, although he also spent time with his father's friends, a Who's Who of global business titans. In fact, one of Rupert's friends, Michael Milken, was the reason Lachlan was sailing to Hobart on *Sayonara*. Lachlan and Rupert were among the guests at the onetime junk bond king's annual Fourth of July party in 1998. As lunch was being served in the backyard of Milken's house overlooking California's Lake Tahoe, Ellison, who was also a guest, asked Rupert if he wanted to sail another Hobart on *Sayonara*. When Rupert said he couldn't, Ellison asked Lachlan. "It wouldn't seem right if we didn't have a Murdoch on board. Do you want to come?"

Lachlan jumped at the chance. "Absolutely. I'd love to."

Lachlan had learned to sail from his father, who raced small boats in his twenties and thirties. (Rupert still sailed, but it was mostly on a vast yacht designed to be comfortable rather than fast. "It's so big, it's not really a sailboat anymore," said Lachlan, who bought his own boat in 1995, which he named *Karakoram* for the mountain range that includes K2.) Lachlan sailed as much as he could. "For someone who has a job that keeps their mind kind of ticking over all the time, it's a great way to force yourself to think about something other than work." He had raced his own boat in the 1997 Hobart, and he thought he would learn a lot from crewing on *Sayonara*.

After leaving his house Saturday morning, Lachlan arrived at a restaurant near the CYC in time for a crew meeting. It was conducted by Chris Dickson, who had replaced Paul Cayard as *Sayonara*'s professional skipper a couple of years earlier. In a room where the walls and tables were painted with nautical scenes and old sails hung from the ceiling, Dickson spoke from two pages of typewritten notes, conducting the meeting as if it were a corporate planning session.

"Meals. We have three dinners, and we should figure on a three-day race. If we do it in two and a half, that's great; but we should plan on three days.

"Bunks. Larry and I have assigned bunks, so if you need us in a hurry, you'll know where to find us.

"The start. There will be a hundred and fifteen boats at the starting line. We do twice the speed as the small boats, and we don't want to have a collision. If you're not busy, keep your head down. We have to keep the noise down. The warning gun goes at twelve-fifty.

"*Brindabella*. We have to keep an eye on them. They're very strong, and it's clearly the boat we have to beat."

When he was done, Dickson introduced Roger "Clouds" Badham, a consulting meteorologist who made his living providing forecasts to yachtsmen and was so highly regarded that America's Cup contenders regularly competed for his services. Clouds, as he was called by everyone, ran through the specifics of his forecast, which called for pleasant weather on Saturday and worsening conditions thereafter. Then he looked up from his notes and spoke plainly: "It's going to be tough out there. There's a pretty good chance it could be really tough — and if it is, you could be in for a nightmare of a race."

Ellison, who had skipped the meeting so he could take a walk with Melanie, stepped onto *Sayonara* at eleven. By then Robbie Naismith and Tony Rae, two of Team New Zealand's key members, were doing a final inventory of the sails they were taking for the race. Other crewmen were replacing the floorboards, which had been removed so that a dehumidifier could suck up moisture from the bilge. Chris Dickson and Mark Rudiger were standing in the cockpit discussing tactics. The rest of the crew was milling about the deck, bantering with sailors from nearby boats and trying to relax. *Sayonara* often attracted lots of attention because of its famous owner and track record, and the crowd was even larger than normal because of Lachlan and his photogenic fiancée. After saying hello to Lachlan and Sarah, Ellison sat down in the cockpit with Dickson.

Dickson was a crucial ingredient to *Sayonara*'s success. Like Ellison, he was intense and demanding. "We have an uncompromising commitment to winning," the thirty-seven-year-old New Zealander would say of his approach to managing *Sayonara*. "We don't accept excuses for anything. We have an absolutely ruthless approach to doing the best we can."

Even back when he started winning junior championships in Auckland, Dickson's friends talked about his competitive zeal and killer instinct. Three times he was named New Zealand's junior sailing champion. In 1987, he was the skipper of *Kiwi Magic*, the first New Zealand yacht to compete for the America's Cup, held that year in Fremantle, Australia. Dickson lost only one of the first thirty-four races leading up to the selection of the challenger; but in the final round of the challenger races, he lost to Dennis Conner, who went on to win the Cup.

Since then, Dickson had competed in two other America's Cups and the 1993-94 Whitbread Race. It was in the latter that he had the most impact. In previous years, yachts had carried full-time chefs to prepare hot meals that were sometimes accompanied by wine. Dickson brought nothing but freeze-dried food and drinks that were called milk shakes but were actually synthetic concoctions designed to deliver various nutritional supplements efficiently. "By bringing America's Cup discipline to the race,

Dickson changed the Whitbread forever," said T. A. McCann, who crewed on Dickson's boat.

Dickson was famous for his capacity to intimidate the world's greatest sailors and for the way he always asked for more. Once while training for the 1987 America's Cup, his crew thought they were done for the day until Dickson said, "Let's do ten more tacks." Then there were ten more, and another ten. On an America's Cup boat, every tack — turning the boat so that the wind approaches from a different side — is hard work. The repetition of quickly cranking in the big sails was like an unbroken series of wind sprints. Tony Rae, who was trimming the mainsail and who also performed that job for Team New Zealand and *Sayonara*, still remembered the afternoon. "Everyone knew that any suggestion that we had done enough would have been rewarded with more work. In the end, we did fifty tacks."

Before he hired Dickson, Ellison had asked T. A. McCann, an America's Cup veteran who had sailed on *Sayonara* for all of its races, the kind of questions he always posed when looking for something: "Who's the best sailor you've ever sailed with? Who's the best sailor in the world?"

"It's not even close — it's Chris Dickson," T.A. replied. Like everyone who had sailed with Dickson, T.A. had suffered from his wrath, but he believed that was a price worth paying. "He's a fanatical perfectionist who has a terrible reputation for being hard on people," T.A. told Ellison, "but he's the most talented sailor alive today."

Dickson reminded Ellison of Steve Jobs, the founder of Apple Computer and Ellison's best friend. Like Jobs, Ellison said, "Dickson wants to do everything perfectly, all the time. He's so brilliant at what he does and so unforgiving of himself that he becomes unforgiving of others." But while Ellison tried to rationalize Dickson's rough edges, he was also a bit amazed. "Dickson will yell at Joey Allen," Ellison said, referring to the principal bowman on *Sayonara* and Team New Zealand. "That is unbelievable. Joey Allen is the best bowman in the world."

While Dickson would be responsible for sailing the boat and managing the crew, Mark Rudiger, a forty-four-year-old Californian who rarely cracked a smile, would make many of the strategic decisions. In the 1993-94 Whitbread Race, which Dickson would have won if his mast hadn't snapped toward the end of the contest, Rudiger was the winning yacht's navigator. Ellison considered him the world's best.

Rudiger, who usually hunched to bring his six-foot five-inch height down to other people's, began sailing across oceans in the 1960s when his parents took him out of school to circumnavigate the world. By the time he was twenty, he was back in California, where he bought a broken-down boat that he raced single-handed. While attending a maritime academy, he began learning about navigation. In years since, the role of the navigator had changed dramatically because of technological advances. With the introduction of the satellite-based Global Positioning System, or GPS, which determines location by triangulating off satellite signals, one of the most important tasks — determining a vessel's location — had become a matter of pushing a button. Navigators had begun to spend most of their time making strategic decisions about the best course to sail. Understanding the weather was one of their most crucial jobs.

The weather was what Ellison wanted to know about. "When are we going to get the bad stuff? How long is it going to last?"

"We're going to have a northerly breeze at the start," Rudiger answered, "but by nightfall, there will be a change. In fact, it's going to be a pretty aggressive change. We could get sixty knots."

"It sounds like another Hobart," Ellison quipped.

"In terms of strategy," Rudiger continued, "we have to keep track of what the current does. Tactically, we need to keep tabs on *Brindabella*. We should be able to beat them on a boat-to-boat basis, but they could beat us on tactics, so we can't let them get too far away from us."

"We have to make sure we're the first boat to get out of the harbor," Dickson added, "but we don't have to be first across the starting line. It's more important that we get a clean start. We can't have any equipment breakdowns or protests."

Ellison planned to be at the helm for the start. The crew knew that *Sayonara* performed best when Dickson was at the wheel — but they also understood that Ellison enjoyed the challenge of driving the boat and that ownership entitled him to some perquisites. In the 1995 Hobart, Ellison didn't steer at the start, and he was looking forward to doing it himself this time. "Ellison is the boss and that's it," Dickson had told the other main helmsmen one day earlier. "He'll have the helm for the start, and he'll keep it until he gets sick of it. I'll be there to give him guidance."

In fact, by most standards, Ellison had become an excellent helmsman. He had been coached by some of the world's best teachers, and his personality was well matched to the job. He was rarely intimidated, and he handled chaos better than most people did. Even Dickson had confidence in his boss's skill — or as much confidence as Dickson had in anyone but himself.

4

Rob Kothe's alarm clock sounded at 3:30 A.M. on Saturday morning. The owner of the *Sword of Orion* began the day by filling a mug with his favorite drink, Sustagen, a vitamin-fortified chocolate mix, into which he sprinkled a teaspoon of ground coffee beans. Walking into his study, he logged on to his computer and called up data from the same global weather models Kenn Batt and Brett Gage were studying. Kothe had been doing the same thing every day for several weeks, and with good reason: in ocean racing, judgments about where the winds and currents are strongest are pivotal.

A tall and gangly fifty-four-year-old, Kothe didn't have much hair on the top of his head, although he did have a broad snow-white mustache and a goatee, which extended out over a long, pointy chin. He was relatively new to sailing. He had bought his first boat in 1997 — the year he raced his first Hobart — but he believed he could make up for his lack of experience with the same sort of relentless striving that had made him a successful entrepreneur. Understanding the weather was the area where he believed he could make the biggest contribution to his crew's race, and he spent the next three hours comparing the models, printing out charts and data while straining the largest of the coffee particles from his drink through his teeth.

It was obvious that he hadn't been sailing for long. When he tried to pass himself off as an old salt, splicing nautical terms into the conversation, he ended up sounding more like a newcomer who was trying a bit too hard. The overall impression was that of a mad professor, and for that reason many CYC members called him Kooky Owner, or simply K.O. Some, in fact, had never heard his real name. For a while he tried to get the young men he recruited for his crew to stop using the name; later, he sought, again unsuccessfully, to alter the meaning by signing e-mails as "Kompetitive Owner." The *Sword*'s crew eventually shortened the name to Kooky.

Kooky had an abiding hunger for the kind of glory that winning the Hobart could bring. "I was the smallest kid in school until I was nine, and I felt bad about that," he said more than four decades later. "It gave me a point to prove." He grew up in Eden, a port city south of Sydney where his father worked as an accountant for many of the fishing fleets based there. Although he didn't sail as a child, Kooky spent a lot of time hanging around the docks and he remembered following the Hobart races. Two days before the 1954 race, when Kooky was eight, his parents gave him a new radio. "I listened to the whole race. Back then I could recite the names of everyone who had won."

Kooky had been deeply committed to adding his name to that list ever since.

Kooky was fundamentally different from other skippers. Whereas most of them had been sailing for many years, he hoped to go from novice to Hobart winner almost immediately. And although sailing is a team sport, Kooky, who knew less about sailing than everyone else on his crew, wasn't a natural leader. A true entrepreneur, most of his achievements had come from individual pursuits rather than group efforts, and his drive wasn't matched by a talent for managing others. For example, after he hired Darren Senogles, a twenty-eight-year-old sailor known as Dags, to take care of the boat, Kooky called him so frequently that Dags told him, "If you keep calling me, I'll never have a chance to get anything done."

When he recruited his crew, Kooky didn't mislead anyone about his sailing credentials. Instead, he talked about how he had flown gliders in airborne regattas over Australian deserts when he was working as a pharmacist near Canberra in the 1970s. "In gliding, you figure out what the wind is doing, and you win by learning how to take advantage of it, just like in sailing," he said. "It's the solo version of the same thing." He also described gliding as an extremely competitive sport, recalling that one of his friends had been killed in a collision and claiming that midair contact sometimes left planes with tire marks on their wings.

Since those pharmacist days, Kooky's career had evolved through a sequence of oddly logical stages. Pharmacology got him involved in animal tranquilizers, which led to tranquilizer guns. His understanding of the propulsion component inspired him to manufacture lifeline-throwing guns, which he profitably supplied to navies and merchant fleets around the world. After going through a divorce in 1992, Kooky decided his businesses were doing well enough that he could finally find the time to pursue the Hobart. For a couple of years, he crewed on other people's boats, but since his dream had everything to do with winning the race on his own yacht, he soon bought a forty-foot sloop and joined the CYC.

Before the 1997 Hobart, he told his crew — which included Dags — that he would buy a better boat if they did well. They did, and the day after they finished the race, Kooky, always an early riser, began stalking the docks to shop for a new boat at 5:00 A.M.

Before the morning was over, he had decided to buy *Brighton Star* for $220,000. It had originally been launched as the *Sword of Orion*, and Kooky decided to restore its former name.

The *Sword*'s shape was very different from that of classic sailing yachts. Its bow dropped straight down from the deck to the water. The back half of the boat was strikingly broad, creating a large cockpit area eight feet across. A seven-foot-diameter steering wheel extended from one side to the other, enabling helmsmen to have the broadest possible perspective. Like *Sayonara* and most of the fastest racing yachts, the hull was composed of strong but lightweight skins on the inside and outside, surrounding an interior of foam. The *Sword*'s skins were made of Kevlar, a synthetic material so strong that it's used to make bulletproof vests.

Kooky went to fairly extreme measures to improve the boat and its crew. The *Sword* came with a handsome barometer, which was housed in a brass case; Kooky replaced it with a plastic one to eliminate a couple of pounds of weight. He had hinges moved from one side of the cabinet doors to the other because he thought shifting the weight of the hinges toward the front of the boat might improve the yacht's handicap rating. If something broke in a race, he was pleased: "Now we can get a better one" was his usual reaction.

Beyond a demanding racing schedule — at least two races and one practice sail every week, sometimes with a professional sailing coach on board — Kooky used e-mails to badger the crew to be on the boat on time and even to exercise more and lose weight. "I've been looking closely at crew commitment," he wrote in an all-crew message a month before the Hobart. "If you want to be on the Hobart boat, this is the commitment needed: 1) You will need to be available for all races from this weekend. No weekends off. Not for discussion. However, there will be a maximum of two midweek practice sessions, possibly only one. 2) Fitness. If you are not already, start running or go to the gym. Cut the alcohol and eat better. Lard is a penalty. 3) Smoking. Last weekend I saw cigarette ash land on sails and I suffered a coughing fit from cigarette smoke. There will be no smoking during short races, from the ten-minute gun. Before and between races, smoking sites will be per long races. In long races, there will be no smoking upwind, ahead of the traveler. In long races, there will be no smoking downwind, behind the cockpit. If you are not able to meet these conditions tell me now while you still have time to find a place on another boat going south."

Kooky didn't know any other way. "I'm just an intensely competitive person," he would say. "I don't do anything by halves."

The Hobart has two kinds of winners. Larry Ellison and George Snow hoped to make it to Hobart first to win "line honors": to be the first to cross the finish line. Others, including Kooky, aspired to win the race based on "adjusted" or "corrected" time. As in golf, every yacht is given a handicap to make up for its different size, weight, and sails. Although Kooky brought an uneven set of skills to his campaign, he rated his chances at winning on corrected time at one in six.

After he finished checking the weather information on his computer, Kooky took a cab for the fifteen-minute ride to the CYC, where he arrived just after eight o'clock. The clubhouse and the docks behind it were already packed with sailors, spectators, and journalists. Kooky's first objective was to find Dags, who in addition to preparing the boat was one of the core members of the crew. Dags could hardly have been more different from his boss. While Kooky was physically and socially awkward, Dags had the wiry body of a long-distance runner and was a gifted athlete who exuded easygoing personal warmth. Though he looked like an up-and-coming corporate attorney when he wore his wire-rimmed glasses, when he was drinking beer with his contemporaries, he was exuberantly playful and seemed, if anything, younger than his age. But Dags managed the *Sword* like a seasoned executive, systematically testing equipment and attending to his "to do" list. He was also uncommonly generous. After a long day of sailing during a weeklong regatta, he stayed on the boat much longer than anyone else, cleaning up and getting ready for the next day. By the time he arrived at the house where the crew were staying, he had missed dinner. No one had thought to save any lasagna for him; rather than complaining, he began washing the dishes.

Like Kooky, Dags had high ambitions for the *Sword*, but the nature of his aspirations was fundamentally different. Dags was less interested in glory than in becoming a great sailor for its own sake. He was a bowman, responsible for changing the sails in front of the mast. Because the bow is more affected by the motion of waves than any other part of the boat, the job requires acrobatic balance and enough dexterity to manipulate a complicated array of lines, sails, and equipment. Dags was a natural.

He hoped the *Sword* would be a stepping-stone to even more competitive yachts. It was not his first boat: he started racing to Hobart when he was just fourteen, and he had already competed in ten races. Now Dags wanted to find out whether he had the skills to sail at the very highest level — in the Whitbread or the America's Cup or on a boat like *Sayonara* — and he was willing to sacrifice a lot to get there. A few months earlier, he had quit working at his father's home-building company because it was getting in the way.

Dags sailed on the *Sword* almost in spite of its owner. There's often an implicit bargain between owners and crewmen. Talented sailors want to be on high-performance yachts, which are necessarily expensive. By providing a first-class boat and covering the ongoing expense of acquiring new sails and the latest in performance-enhancing equipment, owners attract crewmen who can't afford their own boats. The other part of the equation is that much of the recognition, as well as the trophies, goes to the owners.

"He's just a glory hound — that's all he wants," Dags said of Kooky. But if the glory came from racing victories, Dags would also benefit. A few months before the Hobart, the *Sword* was the surprise winner of a major regatta. If it continued to do well, Dags would be invited to join an even better yacht.

Still, better than anyone, Dags understood that Kooky wasn't a perfect skipper and that the owner's lack of experience and follow-through were problematic. A couple of weeks earlier, Dags had asked every member of the crew to help provision the boat with food and drink and various other supplies. Kooky's task had been to refill the propane tank that was used for cooking, but when the two met on the dock on the morning of the race, Dags wasn't surprised to learn that the tank was still sitting in a locker, virtually empty. *That's typical*, Dags said to himself. *Here we are, with just a few hours before the start, and I have to run around trying to fill the propane tank instead of checking everything on the boat one last time.*

Larry Ellison paid whatever it took to get the world's best sailors on *Sayonara*. Kooky avoided making outright payments; Dags was paid to take care of the boat, but he sailed on his own time. Like many owners, however, Kooky used his buying power with marine suppliers to bolster his team. A sailmaker named Andrew Parkes started sailing on the *Sword* after Kooky told him, "I'm going to be buying a lot of sails, and I would like you to be part of my crew."

A month before the Hobart, Kooky had met Glyn Charles, an Olympic sailor from Britain, and asked him to join the crew. A boyishly handsome thirty-three-year-old with a mop of curly dark hair, Glyn had been in Australia for several weeks working as a sailing coach. Since he hoped to represent Britain in the Sydney Olympics, he was also spending time sailing small boats back and forth across the harbor in order to develop an intimate understanding of local wind patterns. Small boats were Glyn's passion. They were what attracted him to sailing, and unlike many sailors who move to bigger boats as their skills increase, Glyn reveled in the total control he could have over a small one. At the time, he was ranked fourth in the world for the Star Class, a twenty-two-and-a-half-foot two-man boat.

Although he had been planning to leave Australia on December 22 so he could spend Christmas in England with his family and girlfriend, he agreed to meet Kooky at the CYC bar ten days before the race. Kooky loved the idea of adding an Olympic-quality helmsman to his crew. Glyn didn't like ocean racing, in part because he was prone to seasickness, but he was tempted: he could add the Hobart to his sailing résumé — and also make some money. He asked for one thousand pounds. Kooky started out saying that he couldn't pay an outright fee. While it was permitted in the class in which *Sayonara* sailed, it wasn't in the *Sword*'s. A little later, though, he offered to reimburse Glyn for various expenses, including his flight to England, and to pay about a thousand pounds for some "consulting work."

Glyn was still torn. The Hobart sounded a lot like the Fastnet Race, Britain's best-known ocean race, which starts from the Isle of Wight and goes to the southwest tip of Ireland and then back to England. Glyn had sailed in the Fastnet, and had hated it. On the other hand, he was having a hard time turning sailing into a profession, so he ultimately accepted Kooky's offer.

But two days before the race, Glyn thought he had made a terrible mistake. He was hit by a stomach virus, and all he could think about was the misery of seasickness. Even though he hadn't left land, he already felt seasick. When Kooky heard that Glyn was ill, he phoned and told him, "You've got to go to the doctor and get it fixed. If it's a virus, it's going to go right through the crew."

Glyn replied, "It's only food."

"I hope you're right. If it's food, you'll be all right — but you've got to see a doctor." Afraid that Glyn wasn't taking him seriously, Kooky added, "If by eight o'clock tonight you haven't told me that you've gotten clearance from a doctor, you're off the boat. Simple as that. I can't risk it."

Later that day, Glyn called Kooky and said he'd been to a doctor and that he was okay.

On the morning of the race, Kooky asked Glyn about the specifics of what the doctor had said. Glyn had a confession to make: he hadn't actually seen a doctor. Instead, he had talked by phone to a friend who was a physician. Kooky was annoyed, but Glyn, in part because of his enthusiastic mood, convinced him that he felt much better.

By midmorning, the docks were bustling with last-minute activity. Several yachtsmen were high above the decks of their boats, sitting in bosun's chairs — small, slinglike seats suspended from the tops of masts — checking the rigging. Other sailors were disconnecting electrical cords, removing flags from the tops of masts, folding sails, and off-loading half-empty bottles of wine. Some crews were huddling in their cockpits with maps and the rules for the race. Others were putting on their team shirts and hats and asking passersby to take pictures. Some of the yachts-men were nervous, but none of them showed it.

Before the *Sword* left the dock to head toward the starting line, Kooky joined the rest of the ten-member crew for a round of rum and Cokes at the CYC's main bar. Sailors are renowned for their capacity to drink, and theirs may be the only sport in which having a drink or two before the start of competition is not merely acceptable but, for some, de rigueur. Although it was still morning, the bar was packed — and the mood was raucous, like a Saturday night in a college pub. Since girlfriends and wives were part of the crowd, there wasn't much discussion about the ominous weather forecast. Instead, most of the talk was about Christmas Day activities and the impossible pressures of simul-taneously preparing for the race and celebrating the holiday. Beyond lighthearted ribbing and challenges, there was a steady chorus of "good luck, mate" and "see you in Hobart." Kooky — who, like skippers of many of the other most competitive yachts, had banned alcohol from the *Sword* — explained his morning cocktail with a pharmacist's sense of humor. "We might as well have a small sedative to settle our nerves." Dags had two.

On most yachts, the skipper delivers a pep talk before the start of the race. After the *Sword*'s crew assembled back on the boat, the only inspirational words came from Steve Kulmar, another relatively recent addition to the crew. Although he was brought on as a principal helmsman, Kulmar, who ran a successful Sydney advertising agency, had a far more expansive idea as to the role he would play on the *Sword*. Indeed, since he considered himself the yacht's most experienced crewman, he expected to make most of the big decisions. That Kooky was the skipper seemed to Kulmar an irrelevant detail.

Kulmar always provoked strong reactions. People either loved him or hated him; he left no room for middle ground. A solidly built forty-six-year-old with closely cropped hair that was halfway to gray, he looked a bit like a stern version of Frank Sinatra. While Kulmar's eyes weren't blue, they were distinctive, usually so wide open that they looked as if they were about to burst from their sockets. In the office, where he wore Armani suits and his secretary served him oversized cups of cappuccino, Kulmar's demeanor veered between toughness and vulnerability. He could be charming and solicitous, qualities that helped his company attract a blue-chip list of clients. The way he hesitated in the middle of a thought made him sound like an intellectual, yet his haircut and intensity gave him the appearance of a military officer and a man who was always on the verge of erupting into a tantrum if anything went wrong. Those tantrums weren't pretty: Kulmar had a towering ego, and even his closest friends complained about the way he tried to seize control of every situation and how he stamped his feet when he failed to get his way.

Before the *Sword* left the dock, Kulmar addressed the crew as if it were his own. "The yacht is in great shape. We have an excellent crew, and I don't see any reason why we shouldn't win as long as we push the boat as hard as we can." His monologue included references to his past victories. In fact, he did have a great record. As a child, he had won several Australian and world championships on twelve- and eighteen-foot boats. As an adult, he had sailed in seven Fastnets and seventeen Hobarts, three of them on boats that won on corrected time. But Dags thought Kulmar's credential wielding was more than simple egotism. He thought it was part of an effort by Kulmar to take over the boat. And that, Dags thought, was deeply troubling.

Managing the crew of a racing vessel can be complicated. There needs to be a clear line of authority, but decisions must be made fluidly, based on a foundation of mutual understanding about strengths and weaknesses, methods that work and ones that don't, a common vocabulary as well as unspoken conventions for coordinating complicated procedures in sometimes challenging conditions. There's too much going on during a race for the skipper to make all the decisions, and no one person can be the expert on everything. In addition, some of the most important calls — which course to take, what sails to fly — can't be made with scientific certainty. Despite an increased reliance on high tech, most decisions in sailing are still made by human beings. The key to a successful boat is a crew's ability to express opinions freely, without worrying about potential insults or hurt feelings, and to reach consensus rapidly.

When, late in the game, Kooky recruited Kulmar and Glyn, he was more focused on the individual skills they would bring than on the effect they would have on the rest of the crew. After months of racing as a group, the original crewmen had gotten to know one another and had become comfortable working together. The addition of Kulmar and Glyn changed things.

Dags, who had sailed with Kulmar in the past, had done everything he could to highlight the downside of bringing him on board. "He's a fantastic helmsman, but he thinks he's more than that — he thinks he's a god," Dags told Kooky. "When he steps on the boat, he's going to act like he owns it."

That had a ring of truth to Kooky. When Kooky and Kulmar met at a pub to talk about sailing the *Sword*, Kulmar was half an hour late. He then enumerated his sailing accomplishments, doing so in such elaborate detail that Kooky had little time to talk about the *Sword's* existing crew. Indeed, Kulmar's tendency to play up his victories had made him unpopular in many yachting circles, where understatement and modesty is the expected norm, but Kooky, who thought his crew was short of top-notch helmsmen, pursued him anyway. For his part, Kulmar left the pub convinced that Kooky was committed to winning the Hobart, but not experienced enough to know how. Rather than viewing that combination as a negative, Kulmar thought it would enable him to run the boat without having to bear the expense of owning it.

The potential for tension between Kulmar and the rest of the crew became apparent even before the *Sword* left the dock. Kulmar said the crew should adopt a two-watch system in which half the crew was on duty at any time. The others had already agreed to a three-watch system in which one team would sail the boat while the second was on call, relaxing either on deck or below, and the third was free to climb into their bunks and sleep. In a two-watch system, half the crew would be on deck, changing and trimming the sails. The other half would be completely off-duty at any given time. With a three-watch system, it would be easier to push the boat harder, but the crew would get less rest.

"I've never done a Hobart with a three-watch system," Kulmar said. "It's just not required."

"No," said Carl Watson, a balding, forty-five-year-old yachting industry consultant who had been sailing on the *Sword* for close to a year, "we've already decided on three watches."

Watson was another crewman who had warned Kooky against adding Kulmar and Glyn. He realized that the *Sword* could use two first-class drivers, but he didn't like the idea of adding anyone — whether it was Kulmar or an Olympian — to the crew at the last minute. "Glyn might be a fantastic helmsman," Watson said to Kooky a few days before the race, "but it's a late call. He doesn't know anything about the boat — he's never been on it — and we haven't even met him."

Standing on the dock, angry that Kulmar was trying to impose changes, Watson refused to give any ground. "We're having three watches. There's a good chance we're going to get some bad weather, so we need to have more of the crew on duty."

A little later, Kulmar and Watson had another disagreement. "What's this?" Kulmar asked, pointing to a large bag that obviously contained a spare mainsail. "We don't want to take two mains. It's nothing but extra weight."

"Yes, we do," Watson said. "We're taking it. We've already made the decision."

"This is bullshit," Kulmar thundered. "It weighs far too much. It's stupid. I've done more Hobarts than anyone on this boat — and it doesn't make any fucking sense to take two mains."

"I've done exactly the same number of Hobarts as you," Watson said. "Seventeen."

"I've won more."

Watson wasn't about to back down. Like Dags, he thought Kulmar was mounting a one-man takeover, and thought the only way to stop him was to confront him at every turn. "Your job is to steer the boat," Watson said. "Nothing else. You're not the skipper."

Yachting is full of hard-charging men who are used to having their own way. On many yachts, crewmen regularly scream at one another, and it sometimes seems as if tensions will boil over into ugly confrontations; the harsh words, however, are usually deceptive. The shouting and cursing is typically about small things — the need to raise a sail faster or clean up a mess in the galley — and the outbursts are quickly forgotten. Watson, whose main role on the *Sword* was to trim the mainsail, wasn't surprised by Kulmar's aggressive behavior, but that didn't make him any less angry as he walked down the dock. Kulmar's attempt to assume control was a serious matter, and Kooky was the only person who could resolve it.

After hearing from Watson, Kooky agreed to tell Kulmar that they were going to carry two mainsails, but Kooky was unable to decide what to do about what Watson said next: "You have to tell Kulmar that he's not the skipper, that he's not going to be making the decisions — or we're going to have a real problem."

5

With a tattered chino wardrobe, a gray beard, and a pipe hanging from his mouth, Richard Winning, the owner of the *Winston Churchill*, looked as if he were from another age. In fact, he wasn't entirely comfortable with the modern world. Rather than buy a sleek new racing yacht, he had chosen to spend a quarter of a million dollars rebuilding the *Churchill*, which was constructed in Hobart out of Huon pine in 1942. Winning, who was forty-eight, was a child when he first saw the boat, and it was love at first sight. When the yacht came up for sale two years before the 1998 Hobart, he jumped at the chance to become its owner.

A classic yacht with a teak deck, brass fittings, and an oyster white hull, the *Winston Churchill* was one of the best-known yachts in Australia. It was among the nine boats that had competed in the first Hobart, and since then it had sailed in fifteen others, twice circumnavigated the world, and become an icon for a bygone era of graceful wood-hulled sailing yachts.

Life had been good to its owner. Winning ran part of the retailing company his great-grandfather had founded in 1906. It adhered to principles that seemed almost quaint, refusing to borrow money or to spend much on advertising, but business was booming. Winning, however, found little enduring satisfaction in financial success. He had the gnawing sense that he was part of a generation that has never faced the kind of challenges that men should. "All blokes want to be tested," he liked to say. "We've had it too easy."

For him, racing a distinguished old yacht with a crew that included several of his oldest friends was more than a sporting event or an escape from everyday life. It was a chance to reenter the natural world, to be a part of a great undertaking, and to do battle with a force that was bigger than any man. It was also a test in which things he considered genuine — seamanship, old-fashioned workmanship, and camaraderie — determined success. In a time when the most celebrated achievements involved technology and stock prices, Winning was more drawn to the sea than ever, in part because it still presented the same challenges it did when the *Churchill* was launched. Winning's crew shared his way of thinking. John Stanley was its most important member. Stanley had sailed fifteen Hobarts in his fifty-one years and was, like the *Churchill*, something of a legend. He had been called Steamer ever since a childhood friend said he had as much energy as a steam-powered Stanley Steamer motorcar.

Steamer started sailing dinghies when he was eleven, and the sea had held an unshakable allure ever since. He had competed in many of the world's great long-distance yacht races. In 1980 he crewed in the America's Cup for Alan Bond, the Australian rogue who won it three years later, ending the New York Yacht Club's 132-year reign and what had been the longest winning streak in any sport. In 1998, Steamer was working for Winning as a foreman in a boatyard Winning owned, although on the water their roles reversed: there, it was often Steamer who made the decisions.

Over the previous few years, both of Steamer's hips had been replaced, and he walked with the hobble of a mechanical duck. In the months before the race, one of his kidneys was removed after it was found to contain a cancerous tumor, a large melanoma was cut away from his right forearm, and asbestosis was discovered in one of his lungs. But Steamer wasn't about to let any of that get in the way of racing. He simply had to sail. Even in appearance he seemed destined for the water. With his broad mustache, sizable jowls, and barrel-shaped chest, he looked like a walrus.

As much as anything, Steamer loved sailing's history and traditions. Sometimes, after he had had a few beers, he would tell his friends that he thought modern society valued the wrong things, that there weren't enough people interested in learning how to make things or in developing the kind of sea-manship that's required for long-distance ocean racing. "All the races are getting shorter. No one has the time." One of the things Steamer liked most about long-distance sailing was how a group of men from every imaginable background, living and working together in close quarters, got to know one another in a way that just didn't happen in normal life. "Whether you're rich or poor doesn't make any difference when you're on the water," he would say.

One of the *Churchill*'s crewmen, Michael Bannister, drove a one-man garbage truck for a living. As a teenager, Bannister told friends that he was going to join the marine police or work on a ferry after he finished school. A high-school guidance counselor talked him out of those ideas, but when he was drafted to serve in Vietnam and an application asked what part of the army he would like to serve in, he wrote, "Small ships, small ships, small ships." He ended up working on an ammunition supply vessel, and upon returning to Australia, he worked as a department-store salesman for a while, then began driving various kinds of trucks. When he wasn't on the road, he was on the water.

Bannister met his wife, Shirley, at a post-regatta party at the CYC. She didn't care about his modest professional life, and she learned to live with the fact that Bannister spent at least one day of every weekend sailing. When their only child, Stephen, was younger, Bannister took him along. Stephen was born three days apart from fellow crewman John Dean's son, Nathan, and the two boys spent countless weekends playing on the beach while their fathers raced. Bannister and his son were extremely close; when Stephen was older, the two of them sailed together competitively.

Bannister had been looking forward to the Hobart for months, and he couldn't wait to get started.

Just before 9:00 A.M. Saturday morning, Geoffrey Bascombe was swimming past the *Winston Churchill*, which was tied to a dock just outside the CYC clubhouse. Like its owner, the *Churchill* looked out of place and time.

Bascombe, with an enormous body, bulbous nose, and a two-foot-long beard, presented an altogether different image. He hadn't weighed himself in more than a decade but knew he was somewhere over three hundred pounds, the reason his friends called him Mega. A former navy sailor who made his living taking care of boats, he had just finished scrubbing the bottoms of four yachts to ensure that they were free of speed-hindering grime. Now that the work was done, he stopped paddling so he could admire the *Churchill*, which he had seen many times before but always from greater distances.

Mega's eyes were drawn to an area of the port side near the bow, where he saw a vertical dark line. It was about a foot long and ended just above the waterline. Swimming closer, he was shocked to see what looked like a serious flaw on a yacht that obviously had been meticulously maintained. It looked as if some of the caulking, which is supposed to fill the spaces between planks to make a wooden boat watertight, was missing. The gap was about as wide as the width of a pencil, and when Mega peered inside, he saw what appeared to be a black rubbery compound.

As soon as he emerged from the water, Mega walked toward the *Churchill's* dock, anxious to tell its crew about what he had seen. He knew missing caulking could be the result of shifting planks. With wooden boats, some movement is inevitable, but too much can be catastrophic because it could spring a plank. Mega spoke to two men whom he assumed were members of its crew. "There's some caulking missing," he told them. "You should make sure the owner knows about it."

Richard Winning had been the first member of his crew to arrive at the CYC, but he heard nothing about what Mega Bascombe had seen.

6

Larry Ellison took *Sayonara*'s wheel twenty minutes before the start — and disaster struck almost immediately. Four grinders, the muscular crewmen who cranked two bicycle pedal-like contraptions with their arms to provide the force needed to pull in the huge sails, realized it first. When Tony Rae, who was responsible for trimming the mainsail, wanted to let out the sail, he eased the line by letting it slip around the drum of a winch. When he wanted to pull the sail in, he needed help from the grinders, who worked the pedals, two to a station. The men and handles sometimes moved so rapidly that they looked as if they had become a single machine. But now, as they turned the pedals, which turned the winch drum by way of a driveshaft, the grinders heard something they shouldn't have: a terrible crunching sound. Suddenly the pedals started to turn freely, obviously disengaged. In just twelve knots of wind, the driveshaft, which was made from carbon fiber, had shattered.

Ellison didn't know what had happened, but he knew he had to continue focusing on steering, particularly when Dickson left his side to investigate the problem. Although Ellison didn't show any reaction, he was worried. *Things are breaking before we even get started*, he said to himself. *That's a bad omen.*

As soon as Dickson figured out what had happened, he reacted with the kind of blistering fury for which he was famous.

"This is ridiculous and inexcusable!" he boomed. "This can't happen! Our system has failed!" Though things break regularly on most boats, Dickson considered equipment failure on *Sayonara* unforgivable, except in the most extreme weather conditions. Old or new, everything was supposed to be repeatedly tested and inspected. If something broke in a relatively light wind, someone hadn't done his job.

When *Sayonara* had been shipped to Sydney, it was accompanied by two forty-foot-long cargo containers. One was outfitted as an office and a well-equipped workshop, crammed full of tools and spare parts. The other carried the twenty-four-foot chase boat along with other gear. Shouting into a cellular phone, Dickson ordered the driver of the chase boat to rocket back to its on-land base station to fetch a replacement driveshaft. Powered by two ninety-horsepower outboard engines, the chase boat could travel at forty-five knots, but — Dickson belatedly realized — that wouldn't be fast enough to get to the workshop and back to *Sayonara* before the ten-minute warning gun at 12:50 P.M., at which point off-yacht support was prohibited. Without the driveshaft, one of *Sayonara*'s three main winches would be useless. The crew would be forced to rely on a less powerful and awkwardly located winch in the pit of the cockpit, making it more difficult for Tony Rae to see the sail and control its trim.

Returning to his position near Ellison, Dickson told him, "We'll have to trim the mainsail from the middle winch. You're going to have to tack a bit more slowly to give the crew some extra time."

"That's going to make it harder to get ahead of the crowd," said Ellison. "Maybe I should be more aggressive at the start to make sure we get out in front from the beginning."

Still furious, Dickson nodded.

The start is often the most exciting part of a race — and it can be decisive. Races that are hundreds of miles long are sometimes won by just a few minutes. The first boats to get ahead enjoy uncongested water and air currents that aren't blocked by other boats. The farther back they are in the fleet, the more yachts are forced to tack back and forth to avoid collisions. Every tack has a cost: it takes a minute or more for the crew to retune the sails and for the yacht to regain optimum speed.

A good start also provides an important emotional boost. Getting the most out of a yacht requires constant attention, an undying eagerness to raise and lower sails and to tweak dozens of lines that change the shape of the sails. The benefits from the constant recalibrating are often so slight as to be virtually imperceptible. When spirits are high, so is the motivation. No one complains about lugging another sail to the deck and folding up the old one. But if nothing seems to work, the mood sinks and no one works as hard. The fun is gone, and so is the point.

The start of the Hobart is particularly challenging. Most races that have a large number of boats have several, staggered starting times, each for a different class of yacht. The Hobart has just one starting time, even though the fleet includes a vast array of shapes and sizes, from maxis like *Sayonara* and *Brindabella*, which accelerate so quickly that they seem to have some sort of invisible propulsion system, to tubby thirty-five-foot sloops, which travel about half as fast. The experience level of each helmsman also varies, from America's Cup veterans to weekend sailors, some of them terrified about setting out on their first Hobart.

The starting line was defined by a boat (from which the starting gun would be fired) at one end and a buoy at the other. Running north to south, the line was about half a mile long and stretched across almost the entire width of the harbor at one of its narrowest points. As Ellison guided *Sayonara* back and forth behind the line, the wind was blowing at just over ten knots from the northeast. Looking for openings, he felt as if he were driving an Indianapolis 500 car around the track while trying to avoid dozens of careening taxicabs.

With less than ten minutes to go before the start, Dickson pointed to another boat and said, "I think you should go above this yacht by at least twenty feet," meaning that he wanted Ellison to turn closer to the source of the wind so *Sayonara* would pass on the upwind side of the other boat.

"I can do that, but do I have a choice? Maybe we should duck under him."

"No, that would leave us in too much congestion. Your gap is above."

On land Ellison rarely deferred to anyone, but he allowed Dickson to make many of the most important decisions on *Sayonara*. In fact, Ellison couldn't even see much of what was in front of his boat because his view was obscured by sails. He had to rely on Joey Allen, who was perched at the bow and was using hand signals to send information about other boats.

After the gun signaling that five minutes remained before the start, every yacht attempted to close in on the line. It was as if a hundred pacing panthers were confined to an ever shrinking cage. They turned back and forth, testing one another, searching for an advantage, each trying to stake out territory. When there was just a minute left, Brad Butterworth, *Sayonara*'s tactician and one of its primary helmsmen, counted down the seconds, loud enough for Ellison and everyone in the cockpit to hear. Ellison's eyes darted in every direction, searching for traps and openings in the impossibly concentrated field while also watching the wind's direction and the shape of the sails.

Sayonara was close to the line. A bit too close. Tony Rae eased the mainsail so it spilled wind and *Sayonara* lost some of its speed. That meant *Sayonara* wouldn't have a flying start, but at least it wouldn't be stuck behind any other boats. With five seconds left, the grinders brought in the sails, and the boat surged forward.

A blast from a cannon — a replica of one that was on board *Endeavour* when Captain Cook reached Australia — announced the start of the race. *Sayonara*'s sails were brought in, and it crossed the line seconds later. There was screaming on many boats, but Ellison's crew was almost silent as he executed a near perfect start.

Many yachtsmen assumed that Ellison's money was the key to *Sayonara*'s success — and money certainly played a role. Ellison happily spent six-figure sums for a single regatta, replacing $50,000 sails the way tennis players buy a new can of balls. *Sayonara* sailed in only five or six major races a year, but since they were scattered all over the globe, the yacht had to be shipped between continents on cargo ships. For each trip, everything that was attached to the hull — the mast, rigging, winches, steering wheels — was removed and packed so that a kind of giant padded sock could be slipped around the boat. The hull was then lifted onto a ship, where it rested in a custom-made steel frame. The packing procedure required a week's labor from six people — as did the reassembly at the other end. Bill Erkelens, a member of *Sayonara*'s sailing crew, and his wife, Melinda, who together worked as the boat's full-time managers, oversaw the transportation. They also kept up-to-date with yachting regulations, arranged for the crew's transportation, and took care of maintenance. It all cost money, and every month they sent a summary of expenses to one of Ellison's assistants for his approval.

But the money represented only a small part of the story. Every maxi-yacht owner is rich. What set *Sayonara* apart from its peers was the quality of the crew, the way its members had learned to work together, and Ellison's ability to retain them race after race. To some extent it was self-perpetuating: everyone likes being on the winning team. But the real key to *Sayonara*'s success lay in the degree to which its crewmen specialized in their jobs. On many boats, decisions about tactics and the trim of a sail are second-guessed as a matter of course. Second-guessing on *Sayonara* was unusual. Ellison had come to appreciate the skill of his crew, and he rarely overruled them.

Dickson encouraged crewmen to develop sharply defined roles — and to take total responsibility for them. Joey Allen, the bowman, also selected the equipment he used. Whenever a change was made to the rigging, Allen was consulted. If he wanted to move a fitting or try a different kind of pulley, Bill Erkelens would arrange for it. If Allen later wanted to go back to the old one, that was fine, too.

Immediately after the start, T. A. McCann, who was responsible for raising and lowering the sails in front of the mast, began providing commentary on the wind. Looking for ripples on the water, he tried to divine the velocity and direction of the wind that would be encountered over the next sixty seconds. Seeing where the breeze or a gust disturbed the surface of the water is easy, but judging the strength and direction of the wind, which many sailors call "pressure," is an acquired skill of great subtlety. "Steady pressure for the next twenty, and then we're going to get a big puff," T.A. called out. "Ten seconds to the puff. Ten, nine, eight ..."

The goal was to help Ellison and the sail trimmers anticipate what would come next so as to create a seamless operation in which every change was reacted to rapidly and optimally. There was intelligence at every level. *Sayonara*'s grinders, most of them built like linebackers, may have looked as if they were selected only for their brawn, but they were all talented yachtsmen. Though they listened to T.A. and the sail trimmers, they also watched the wind and sails themselves, so they would be better prepared to act.

Communicating on a maxi-yacht is difficult, so Dickson insisted that anyone who didn't have vital information to convey keep quiet. T.A. was the only crewman who was expected to do much talking, and even he tried to be economical, occasionally asking, "Am I talking too much?" A few minutes after the start, when someone on the rail shouted about an approaching gust, T.A. quickly shut him down. "Hey, I'll make that call. Let's relax. We've done this millions of times. Let's stick with the system."

7

On the *Sword of Orion*, Steve Kulmar was at the helm for the start, and Glyn Charles was at his side, suggesting tactics. Kulmar had already determined that he wanted to be on the southern end of the starting line, and he was heading in that direction.

Dags was at the bow, shouting warnings about yachts Kulmar couldn't see. "Look out," Dags yelled. "*Nokia* is coming at us again."

The Racing Rules of Sailing, as specified by the International Sailing Federation, determine who has the right-of-way on a racecourse. A boat that is on a port tack — meaning that the wind is approaching the boat from its port, or left, side — must change course if it's on a collision course with a boat on a starboard tack. The convention is based on the now archaic notion that the starboard side is inherently superior. In centuries past, senior shipwrights constructed that side, leaving the port side to apprentices. Captains made a point of boarding their vessels from the starboard side. Naval artillery salutes typically had an odd number of blasts because they were fired from alternate sides of the ship, with the first and last guns both coming from the starboard side. While some of those traditions have been forgotten, the supremacy of boats sailing on starboard tacks remains absolute.

The rules are more complicated when two yachts are both on the same tack: the windward boat, the one that's closer to the source of the wind, must yield to the downwind vessel. The rules are clear, but inevitably they aren't enough to prevent collisions or controversy.

Everywhere *Sword* went, *Nokia*, an eighty-three-foot maxi-yacht, the biggest boat in the race, appeared to follow. Kulmar thought it was deliberately shadowing him, hoping to get a better start by following his example. Kulmar may or may not have been flattering himself, but one thing was suddenly very clear: with less than a minute left before the start, *Nokia* was on a collision course with the *Sword*. Both yachts were on starboard tacks. *Nokia* was the windward yacht — but it wasn't altering its course. "Go up! Go up!" Dags shouted at the big boat, trying to cause it to turn toward the wind. But *Nokia* did nothing to change direction. Its crewmen were also screaming, although no one on the *Sword* could understand what they were saying. By the time *Nokia* finally turned toward the wind, just a few yards away from the *Sword*, it was too late. *Nokia*'s sails, no longer filled with wind, began luffing, and the yacht drifted sideways toward the *Sword*. With twenty-five seconds left before the start, *Nokia*'s bow slammed into the *Sword* with a sickening crunch. The initial impact was on the *Sword*'s starboard side, near the back of the yacht. Then, since *Nokia* had more forward momentum than the *Sword*, the bigger boat scraped its way up the side of the *Sword*, doing so with the screeching sound of a train applying its brakes.

Exploding with anger, Kooky tried to push *Nokia* away from his boat, but by then *Nokia* had turned downwind again. Its sails had refilled, driving the yacht against the *Sword*.

"Take down your sail!" Nigel Russell, a *Sword* crewman, screamed at *Nokia*. Seeing no response, he reached into his pocket and brandished a knife. "Take your sails down — or I'll fucking cut them down!"

When the two boats finally separated, Kooky raised a red protest flag and Dags rushed to assess the damage. Two years earlier he had been on a boat that abandoned the Hobart after it had been damaged near the starting line, and he was appalled by the idea that the same thing could happen again. First he leaned over the starboard side to see if the hull had been pierced. It hadn't, at least above the waterline, but he saw gouges and residue from Nokia's blue paint along a fifteen-foot-long section of the Sword's hull, near where it met the deck. The most obvious damage was to two stanchions, the metal posts mounted around the perimeter of the deck to support the lifeline that was supposed to prevent crewmen from falling off the boat. Both stanchions had been bent toward the center of the yacht, and the base of the aftmost one had punched through the deck, creating a three-inch-wide hole.

Going below, Dags examined the inside of the hull. The damage to the deck near the two stanchions was obvious — he could see daylight through the hole — but it didn't look like a major structural problem. Nevertheless, it had to be fixed. Though the stanchions had no impact on the structural integrity of the yacht or the way it sailed, the lifeline they held was a crucial safeguard for the crew. Also, since the base of the stanchions and a nearby fixture were sometimes used to secure equipment and safety harnesses, the strength of the deck they were attached to was important.

While the rest of the crew focused on racing, Dags removed the screws that held the stanchions to the deck and stood on them, attempting to bend them back into shape with his weight. He reattached the stanchion that had caused the hole in the deck a few inches forward from where it had stood, trying to avoid the most damaged section of the deck. He also placed a small piece of plywood under the deck as backing. By driving the screws through both the deck and the wood, he hoped the stanchion would be as secure as it was before the crash. After nearly four hours of work, he was satisfied with the repair but annoyed that the work had made it impossible for him to sit on the rail, where his weight would have helped the boat reach its optimum speed.

For his part, Kooky was sitting in front of his onboard computer, tapping out an e-mail to race officials that described the damage and blaming it on *Nokia*, which suffered only superficial wounds. Hoping that the officials would impose a penalty on *Nokia*, Kooky wrote: "The damage to the starboard stanchions has been repaired. However, delamination occurred in a meter-long section of the starboard stern quarter."

After he finished with the stanchions, Dags inspected the mast for damage. During the collision, the *Sword*'s rigging had come into contact with *Nokia*'s, potentially creating a weakness that could bring down the mast. On the port side, about six feet up from the deck, he spotted what looked like a small bulge. "Jeez, look at this," he said to Andrew Parkes. Although the raised area was only two or three inches in diameter, it could mean the mast was damaged. A weakened mast is a disaster waiting — probably not for very long — to happen. Bearing the load of full sails in heavy winds puts the mast under tremendous stress. Even seemingly flawless masts crumble in the Hobart. Shinnying up the mast, Dags ran his fingers over the bump, but he couldn't determine anything about its cause. "Let's keep an eye on it," he said. "There's not much else we can do."

The collision had already imposed a heavy cost. The *Sword* didn't cross the starting line until about a minute after the gun. Instead of being one of the first boats to pass through the harbor, it was forced to weave its way through much slower yachts. After months of rigorous preparation, the *Sword*'s crew was playing catch-up.

8

Kenn Batt and Brett Gage arrived back at the Bureau of Meteorology's offices in time to watch the start of the race on television. A few minutes later, they examined the very latest output from the Australia-based forecasting computer model, which had just arrived. For the first time, it predicted the worst possible scenario, the one that the American model had been projecting all along. The forecasters deemed the consensus between the two models significant. If they turned out to be accurate, the center of low pressure would have substantially more intensity than what had been anticipated in the bureau's official race forecast. The more Batt looked at the data, the more certain he became that the ingredients for a dangerous, cyclone-like force — one that would be far more powerful than most yachtsmen had ever seen before — were coming together.

A cold front was moving east toward Bass Strait while warm air was flowing from the north. Both masses of air were being drawn by a region of low pressure that was also traveling east — and that appeared likely to move to a position over eastern Bass Strait just as most of the Sydney to Hobart fleet arrived there. That heavy cold air would act like a flying wedge, lifting the moist warm air upward to produce precipitation and electrical storms. And if Batt needed further evidence that the cold front was substantial, he got it in the form of a bulletin about a snowstorm in southern Australia. It wasn't unusual for snow to fall there in the winter, but this was December, which in the Southern Hemisphere meant it was the middle of the summer. Kenn Batt and Brett Gage began to get a very bad feeling.

The Hobart has three segments. In the first, boats sail down the southernmost section of Australia's eastern coast, where they are somewhat sheltered by land. During the final third, they travel along the east coast of Tasmania, where the island offers a degree of protection. In the middle segment — during which they cross Bass Strait — yachts are much more vulnerable. There is no land to block the wind or waves from the east or west. Indeed, the wind tends to funnel through the strait, and the shallower water there causes the waves to heighten.

If the models held true, Batt thought the first part of the race would be a joyride. The rush of air, like the current, would come from the north, providing a substantial but manageable tailwind. But it looked as though the intensifying storm would hit the fleet sometime after most of the yachts began crossing Bass Strait, the worst possible place to run into bad weather. When the fleet collided with the storm, Batt believed the wind would switch direction by something close to 180 degrees. The current and the waves would then be moving in opposite directions, a phenomenon that would have a dangerous multiplier effect on the waves. A one-knot contrary current can increase the average wave height by 20 percent, and two knots sometimes increases heights by 50 percent. Opposing currents also produce the kind of steep waves with high, arching backs that can damage even the sturdiest of vessels.

The main wild card was the course of polar jet streams. Predicting the exact course of jet streams, high-speed rivers of air that travel 30,000 feet above the earth's surface and change direction as they collide with one another, is difficult. But while polar jet streams generally don't extend far enough north to reach Bass Strait during the summer, satellite photographs of high-level cloud formations and weather-balloon observations suggested that one stream might do so during the race. A jet stream straddling the low would intensify it by setting off a dangerous chain reaction: the high-altitude wind would siphon the warm air out from the center of the low, further reducing the pressure at the core of the storm and speeding the rush of wind toward the low — and accelerating the system's clockwise movement.

If it weren't for the race, the meteorologists probably wouldn't have thought about making a prediction at such an early stage. But aware of the problems that could ensue if a sporting event with a global following ran into unforecasted extreme weather, they leaned toward upgrading the gale warning to a "storm warning," indicating that they believed winds would exceed forty-eight knots. After taking another look at the Australian computer output, Gage said, "If the model is right, and we go against it, it will look very bad for us."

Everyone agreed, and at 2:14 P.M., a bit more than an hour after the race began, Peter Dundar, another bureau forecaster, sat in front of a computer terminal and clicked the cursor on an icon labeled WARNINGS to bring up a page containing the standard warning language. After he entered specific details about the weather conditions, he transmitted the alert by fax to Australia's marine broadcast service as well as commercial radio and television stations, fishing boat owners, the Royal Australian Navy, rescue services, and the CYC, among others.

No one was more worried than Kenn Batt. More than a dozen of his friends were in the race, and he was so frightened for them that he felt physically ill. Sure that most of the yachtsmen had no idea what they were in for, all he could think about was how miserable he had been in the 1993 Hobart, the one in which only thirty-eight boats finished. He was convinced that this race would be much worse, so bad that some of his friends could die. With tears in his eyes, he told Gage, "It's going to be a massacre."

Gage and Batt had gone off-duty, but they stayed at the office to ring as many alarm bells as they could. Gage called Australian Search and Rescue, the government agency responsible for coordinating rescues of boats and planes at sea. "We have a priority storm warning," Gage told Andrew Burden, an officer at the agency. "If it's not as bad as this, I guess there's no harm done apart from getting a few people off holidays, but if we don't forecast it, we're going to be in for an awful amount of criticism."

A storm warning was the most serious warning the bureau could issue for the waters off southeastern Australia, though many of the Hobart competitors didn't know this. Instead, they believed the most serious warning would be for a hurricane or a cyclone. But tropical cyclones, which are common in other parts of the South Pacific, do not occur off southeastern Australia because they develop only in places where the water temperature is twenty-seven degrees Celsius or higher. Different terminology didn't mean this storm wouldn't have the kind of wind speeds that tropical cyclones or hurricanes do, however.

The bureau also circumscribed the warning. Storm warnings are theoretically open-ended — indicating forecasted winds of anything more than forty-eight knots — but the bureau included an upper limit, predicting forty-five to fifty-five knots. The bureau's forecasters would later claim that the forecast was for steady wind speeds and that sailors should have understood that gusts could exceed the predicted wind speed by as much as 40 percent. But although Hobart yachtsmen understood that gusts regularly exceed constant wind speeds, few had ever heard that gusts could be 40 percent greater. Others shrugged and decided that they wouldn't worry until the forecast said something about a cyclone or a hurricane.

While sailors recognize that wind is their power supply, few have more than a superficial understanding of the complicated forces behind it or the vocabulary of meteorology. Indeed, many of the Hobart contestants believed that the gale warning the bureau issued before the start of the race was more severe than a storm warning, even though the opposite is true.

The real danger of strong winds is the waves they produce. After centuries of study, scientists still don't fully understand waves, but they have developed formulas to estimate sea heights. Nine hours of fifty-knot wind across open ocean typically produces an average significant wave height (the average of the biggest third of all waves) of about thirty feet. But scientists also know that the patterns are regularly broken, particularly when there are strong currents and substantial variations in the depth of the sea. Sometimes, in ways that have yet to be fully understood, two or more wave crests combine, creating rogue waves, which are typically almost twice as large.

Patrick Sullivan, the director of the bureau's operations in New South Wales and a meteorologist with four decades of experience, was so concerned by the storm warning that he interrupted his Christmas vacation to drive to the office. After looking at a sequence of satellite photographs for the previous twenty-four hours, he decided that the storm warning was a bold prediction, but entirely appropriate. Although there was no question that a low-pressure system would move up the coast, he knew it would take another twelve hours or so to know whether it would be the kind of intense low that would have a tightly wound cyclonic force. Still, given the race, he agreed that the warning was the right thing to do.

He thought the warning would cause many competitors to abandon the race. He was wrong.

9

Before the starting gun fired, Richard Winning was at the *Winston Churchill*'s helm, smoking his pipe. While most yachts were jousting for position near the front of the line, Winning was surveying the scene from near the back of the fleet. The *Churchill* didn't cross the line until more than a minute after the cannon was fired. Winning was less concerned about speed and where his boat placed than Larry Ellison or Kooky. "It will be gentlemen's ocean racing," he had told his crew.

Nineteen-year-old Matthew Rynan, a generation younger than almost everyone on the *Churchill*'s crew, was disappointed. As much a kid as an adult, Rynan was a short and muscular spark plug who wore a single gold hoop through his right earlobe and a shark's tooth around his neck. His puckish face seemed to carry a perpetual half smile. Before the race, his only real concern about the *Churchill* had been the age of its crewmen. Winning's unaggressive start made him even more aware of how different he was from the rest of the crew. *Come on, old man, let's get up there,* he said silently. *This won't be any fun if we're too cautious.*

But Beaver — that was Rynan's nickname — felt incredibly lucky to be on board. Beaver's friends, most of whom didn't share his interest in boats, had been asking him when he was going to be in the race ever since he began sailing. As the *Churchill* passed through the harbor, he thought about them, one by one, and wondered whether each of them was watching.

Soon after the *Churchill* entered the ocean, it turned south. Thanks to its huge red, white, and blue spinnaker and a steady breeze from the northeast and additional help from the favorable current, the handsome yacht was moving at ten knots. Unusual for a man who didn't smile a lot, Winning was flashing a broad, childlike grin. For as long as he could remember, sailing had been his singular passion. "It's the only thing I've ever been good at," he often said. "I can't hit a ball. I've always been a water person, and virtually all of my friends are people I met through sailing." Indeed, John Dean and Mike Bannister had been sailing with Winning ever since they were teenagers racing small boats at the Vaucluse Amateur Twelve Foot Sailing Club in the late 1950s. The three of them had won dozens of trophies, sailing together and in opposition, and they'd remained friends ever since.

Steamer was wandering around the boat, checking some of the equipment he had installed. Like many sailors, he had worked the bow when he was younger. As he learned more but lost some of his agility, he moved toward the back of the boat, first to the mast, where he handled the halyards that raise and lower sails, and finally to the cockpit, where he made many of the decisions about course and sail changes. Although Steamer was a modest man who had never made much money, he had a quiet confidence in everything he did and enormous pride in the role he played in rebuilding the *Churchill*. When it first arrived at Winning's boatyard, it carried a heavy wooden mast and creaky winches, some of which barely turned. Belowdecks, floorboards were missing; the galley and toilet were unusable. Under Steamer's guidance, a new mast and boom were installed along with new fuel and water tanks, and the interior was gutted and rebuilt. The main cabin had become a handsome compartment with varnished mahogany walls and chocolate-colored cushions. It was decorated with more than thirty plaques from various races and two photographs — one of Percy Coverdale, the man who built the yacht and was its first owner, and another of the crew that sailed it with him back in 1945, when it was the third-fastest of the nine boats that sailed in the first Hobart.

Steamer had chosen several members of the crew for the Hobart, including Beaver, who sometimes drove the launch at the Middle Harbor Yacht Club, where Steamer was a member. Despite their age difference, Beaver and Steamer had a lot in common. Beaver wasn't entirely sure where his future lay except that, like Steamer, his mates were a top priority and he believed he was happier on the water than anywhere else. Indeed, although he had never sailed offshore or spent a night on a yacht, Beaver probably spent more of his waking hours on boats than on land — between racing dinghies, teaching youngsters to sail, and piloting the launch. Steamer saw some of himself reflected in Beaver, and he hoped that being part of the crew and seeing what a group of men could do when they worked together would infuse Beaver with a sense of accomplishment and purpose.

Steamer had also invited John Gibson, a longtime friend. Gibbo, a stocky sixty-five-year-old lawyer with a large nose that leaned to the left thanks to an old rugby injury, was a raconteur with a quirky sense of humor whose gregarious good nature was balanced by a willingness to display his emotions. Gibbo had sailed most of his life but he never done a Hobart, so he was thrilled when Steamer extended the invitation. "It's a great challenge," Gibbo told his wife, Jane. "At the end of the race, my biggest hope is that Steamer will turn around to me and say, 'Gibbo, are you coming again next year?'"

As they sailed south, Gibbo was trying to size up the rest of the crew, particularly Winning. Gibbo thought he had a knack for forging relationships, but he had found it difficult to engage Winning in even casual conversation during several practice sails before the Hobart. He didn't think Winning was unfriendly as much as shy. Gibbo certainly knew Winning wasn't a snob or incapable of making new friends — Paul Lumtin, another member of the crew, was proof of that. Lumpy, as he was known, was an overweight, thirty-one-year-old accountant who handled Winning's taxes. He grew up playing rugby in an unfashionable inland suburb where hardly anyone sailed. Yet, despite the differences in their backgrounds and ages, Winning had gone out of his way to turn Lumpy into a friend, particularly after Lumpy's father had died a few years earlier. Winning frequently tried to explain his love of sailing to Lumpy, eventually asking if he would like to join the crew for "twilight races" on Friday evenings. When he did, Lumpy was overwhelmed by how generous everyone was in teaching him the basics and how excited they were to share tales of past racing adventures. When he was with Winning's long-time friends, Lumpy often assumed the role of court jester, joking about his girth and his unfashionable accent. Lumpy had an ego, though. Proud of what he had learned about sailing, he was thrilled when Winning tapped him to serve as the boat's navigator for the Hobart.

Because it was a long race and everyone would need to steer at some point, Winning wanted to give everyone a chance at the wheel. Beaver was lounging on the deck when Winning asked if he would like to take a turn. The youngster accepted with obvious enthusiasm. Compared with the lightweight dinghies he usually sailed, the boat felt sluggish, but the principles were the same, and he loved the sense of power that came from controlling the big yacht.

Winning stepped down into the cabin and took a look at a sheet of weather information that had just rolled out of the fax machine. It included the storm warning and a forecast based on the increasing likelihood that the low-pressure system would be intense when it arrived over the eastern part of Bass Strait twenty-four hours later. Showing it to Bruce Gould, an investment banker, Winning said, "Jesus, what do you think of this?"

At fifty-six, Gould was a tall and thin man whose energy and forceful personality was projected by his rapid-fire, clipped sentences and the high-pitched tone of his voice. In choosing words, he frequently used ones with four letters. "Shit fight" was his favorite phrase, and he frequently managed to insert it two or three times into a single sentence. Gould had grown up in Hobart and still remembered seeing the *Churchill* at the end of one of the early races when he was a child. For him, the arrival of the yachts from Sydney was the biggest event of the year, and it gave rise to a lifelong obsession. In 1967, when he was twenty-four, he had been on the first Australian yacht to win the Admiral's Cup, and he had sailed in thirty-one Hobarts.

Looking at the forecast, Gould declared, "Bloody hell! It looks like we're in for a bit of a caning."

Not long after that, the spinnaker pole popped off the sail. Like other sails, the balloon-shaped spinnaker was attached to the top of the mast by a halyard. One of the sail's other corners was held by a line controlled from the cockpit. The third was secured by a line attached to the end of a pole that reached horizontally out from the mast. Under pressure from the wind, the pin holding the line to the pole had slid open. Now someone was going to have to sit in a bosun's chair and pull himself along the pole and toward the corner of the sail, which was situated over the water. Once there, he would have to put the line back through the pin. Steamer knew that Beaver would be perfect for the job, so he explained the procedure to him. The whole idea terrified Beaver, who was afraid he would fall out of the chair and into the water, although he was not about to admit to his fears or refuse to do the job.

It's not easy to avoid responsibilities on a boat. First of all, since everyone is confined to such a small place, there's no place to hide, and it's easy to see just how much of a contribution each crewman is making. To varying degrees, yachtsmen tend to specialize in a particular function; but on boats smaller than *Sayonara*, the around-the-clock need to steer, adjust sails, and navigate means that everyone should know something about everyone else's job so they are prepared to pitch in at any time. There are also many mundane chores such as preparing meals and washing dishes. The best approach, Steamer had suggested to Beaver, was to avoid any calculation as to whether you are doing your fair share. Try to do more than that, he said — and if everyone else does the same, everything will get done. Despite his fear, Beaver was eager to prove himself. Pulling himself away from the boat, he made a point of not looking down at the water. It didn't take long to put the line back where it belonged.

When he stepped out of the bosun's chair, he was proud of himself and also a little bit amazed. "I can't believe you got me to do that!" he exclaimed to Steamer.

At the same time, Beaver wondered what would come next.

PART II

EAST OF EDEN

10

Sayonara was the first boat to pass through the mile-wide gap between North and South Heads, the sheer basalt cliffs that separate Sydney Harbor from the open ocean. *Brindabella* was not far behind. As they entered the sea, where gently sloped three-to-four-foot waves and fifteen knots of wind were coming from the northeast, both maxis raised spinnakers to scoop up the maximum amount of the breeze. Ellison was still at the wheel. The race was in its infancy, but he was already thinking in terms of Plattner's record. Once the spinnaker was flying, he glanced at the "jumbo," a digital indicator mounted on the mast, which showed that the boat's speed briefly reached fourteen knots. The indicator didn't reflect the south-flowing current, which was adding another couple of knots to the speed over the ground. Ellison knew that if the favorable wind kept up for a good portion of the race, he would own the record.

To the casual observer, driving *Sayonara* looked easy. In fact, though, proficient helming requires an almost instinctive ability to get the most out of every puff of air and wave. And *Sayonara's* crew could always see how the helmsman was measuring up. Using data from previous races, Mark Rudiger had assembled a table indicating the optimal velocities for various conditions, and several copies had been taped to the cockpit. There are two main components to reaching top speed — sail trimming and steering. However, since the trimming was almost always without flaw, everyone could make an informed evaluation of the helmsman's skill by comparing Rudiger's target speed with the actual speed.

Initially, since he rated himself a pretty good airplane pilot, Ellison had thought he'd quickly become a skilled helmsman. Instead, he came to believe that steering a boat during a race was the more difficult task, requiring intense concentration, lightning-fast reactions, and an ability to simultaneously judge the impact of the wind and waves as well as the trim of the sails. "It's the integration of an awful lot of information and experience in a way that has to become automatic," he said. "Cognitive reasoning doesn't work that fast."

A few minutes after the spinnaker went up, something didn't feel right. When the wind gusted to eighteen knots, Ellison thought the air felt strangely heavy. Seconds later, the spinnaker exploded, shredding the $25,000 sail into rags. The boat instantly slowed as if its engine had run out of gas, which in a way it had. Ellison knew it could have been his fault. He had probably overloaded the sail by heading too close to the wind. With a mounting sense of frustration, Ellison realized that Dickson would have sensed that there was too much pressure against the sail and would have changed course to relieve it or requested a heavier spinnaker.

For Ellison, this was one of the costs of playing in the major leagues: he had brought together a yacht and crew in which flawless execution was the norm. It was tough to keep up. But luckily, T.A. McCann had a replacement spinnaker ready to go. "I'll go to the front of the foredeck, then Lachlan," he shouted. In most races, the crew wouldn't think of asking one of Ellison's guests to jump into a sail change at the bow. But T.A., who had been impressed by Lachlan during the practice sails, needed all the help he could get to quickly pull down the remains of the tattered spinnaker and get the new one up before *Brindabella* made up too much ground.

Lachlan was pleased to be included. He felt validated as a member of the crew, but he also knew that an overeager helper could do more harm than good. Taking T.A.'s lead, Lachlan reached up as high as he could, got a grip on the sail, and used his own weight to pull a section all the way down to the deck. Repeating the same procedure several times, he became confident that he had the right rhythm. Soon the destroyed sail was down, and Lachlan's status on the crew was firmly established.

Sayonara's new spinnaker was flying just a few minutes after the first one was doused, but *Brindabella* had made the most of the delay, cutting *Sayonara*'s lead from two hundred yards to just fifty. Ellison was annoyed with himself. "Here, Chris," he said to Dickson, "take the wheel. I'm not concentrating enough."

Sitting down next to Lachlan on the rail, Ellison changed the subject to business. Although Oracle and News Corporation were in different industries, the computer-software and media-content businesses were converging because of the Internet. Ellison was interested in how much classified-advertising revenue Murdoch's newspapers were losing to Web-based competitors. "Online classifieds are a huge threat," Lachlan acknowledged. "In five years newspapers won't have any classifieds. And for most papers, if they lose classifieds, they won't be profitable. All of our businesses are going online."

"Have you thought about getting into the online auctions? Those sites make tons of money."

"We'd like to, but it isn't easy. It's just like the newspaper business. If you're the number one site in the market, like eBay, you'll make a lot of money. If you're not number one, it'll be tough to survive."

While Lachlan and Ellison chatted, *Brindabella* continued to pick up ground. The wind and waves were building, which played to *Brindabella*'s strengths. With a seventy-five-foot hull, *Brindabella* was almost as long as *Sayonara*, but because its hull was wider and flatter, it was better suited for surfing down the fronts of waves.

As the wind reached twenty-four knots, both maxis were being carried by fast-moving waves. During one surfing run, *Sayonara* reached twenty-six knots, its fastest speed ever. On average, *Brindabella* was doing even better. When it caught up to *Sayonara* just before 3:00 P.M., the two maxis were only twenty feet apart. Half an hour later, when the wind speed reached twenty-eight knots, *Brindabella* put up a new asymmetrical spinnaker. George Snow guessed that it had about 5 percent more sail area than *Sayonara*'s spinnaker, a crucial advantage. Not long after that, *Brindabella*'s speed briefly touched thirty-one knots, the best it had ever done. Minutes later, it cut across *Sayonara*'s bow.

"It looks like we have a boat race on our hands," Dickson said to Ellison. "*Brindabella* is handling these conditions very well."

"She's just more competitive than last time," Ellison said. "They've improved more than we have improved." But with several hundred miles to go, he wasn't about to give up.

On *Brindabella*, George Snow declared, "This is as exciting as it gets."

A large and voluble man whose eyes, set beneath bushy brows, opened wide when he was talking but narrowed to slits and sometimes closed altogether when he was listening to someone else, Snow sailed for the first time when he was twenty-six. It was on

Lake Burley Griffin, a man-made lake in Canberra, his hometown, and it became an obsession. Back in the late 1970s, Snow was one of the founders of the Canberra Ocean Racing Club, which Sydney yachtsmen originally considered pretty much a joke. After all, Canberra is landlocked. But Snow and the other members were absolutely serious. The club bought a boat and kept it in Sydney, and its members began spending their weekends flying back and forth to sail. Snow's Canberra-based real-estate business had made him wealthy, and he eventually sold his interests and moved to Sydney, mostly so he could be closer to the water. "Sailing," he frequently said, "is more important than business." He enjoyed the camaraderie, but like Ellison, what Snow really craved was the challenge. "In modern life," he mused, "there isn't that much that can really test your nerves, your courage, and your ability to rely on others." Other executive entertainments simply weren't satisfying. "Golf," Snow said dismissively, "doesn't do it."

During races when he wasn't at the wheel or discussing tactics, Snow roamed the boat, engaging in an endless round of playful banter. Much of it was purely for fun, but it also served a serious purpose. Snow viewed his main job as watching out for the crew, identifying anyone who wasn't feeling well or who wasn't happy with the way something was being done. Whereas Ellison and Kooky rarely gave pep talks, Snow shared his thoughts and enthusiasm before and after every race. Just before the start of this Hobart, he had gathered his twenty-two-member crew and said, "It's a long race. There are times when you might feel good, and there are other times when you are going to feel down. That's when you have to find some strength to look after each other. If someone is struggling, don't look at him. Help him. This boat is full of champions. *Sayonara* is used to winning inshore races —

but when it comes to ocean racing, we have the best team there is. There's no reason why we can't beat them."

Brindabella raced almost every weekend of the year, but everything led up to the Hobart. Like Ellison, Snow's ultimate goal was beating Plattner's record, which stood at two days, fourteen hours, seven minutes, and ten seconds. But aside from their common goal, Snow and Ellison had little in common. Snow believed sailing should remain an amateur sport. Although three members of *Brindabella*'s crew were paid to maintain the boat between races, a necessity given its size, Snow criticized Ellison for having a "full paid" sailing crew, saying, "There's a bit of buying the team." More fundamentally, Snow didn't really accept the idea that Ellison, with his limited racing schedule and his habit of arriving at races just before the start, was truly committed to sailing. "The trouble with guys like Ellison," Snow said, "is that they aren't natural sailors."

Snow had stayed with the sport in spite of a racing history marked by terrible disappointments. In the Hobart of 1993, the year he launched *Brindabella*, Snow had a sixty-mile lead halfway across Bass Strait when the boat ran into something, possibly a whale, at two o'clock in the morning. With a damaged hull, he had to quit a race he was sure to win. In 1994, as *Brindabella* sailed up the Derwent River to Hobart, it was about one hundred yards behind *Tasmania*, the leading yacht. *Brindabella* was gaining ground until its jib halyard snapped. Even without the sail, *Brindabella* finished just seven minutes behind *Tasmania*, but to Snow, runner-up status was almost as bitter as finishing last. Losing hope, Snow told some members of his crew that the 1995 could be his "last shot." Unfortunately for Snow, it was also the first year Larry Ellison entered the race. *Sayonara* crossed the finish line first, two hours ahead of *Brindabella*, which for the second year in a row took second place. The next day, when Snow and his crew sat down at Maloney's, a popular Hobart pub, Snow was far from his jovial self. "In case you're all wondering whether you'll get a berth next year," he announced, "I'm telling you now that the *Brindabella* days are over. I'm selling her. Last year we lost by seven minutes. This year we were beaten by two hours. We're going backwards, so I'm giving up."

He eventually changed his mind, but Snow still couldn't shake his bad luck. Three hours into the 1996 race, *Brindabella* was a mile ahead of *Morning Glory*, Hasso Plattner's maxi. Propelled by a powerful tailwind, *Brindabella* was flying south at a speed that looked likely to earn the ultimate trifecta: line honors, winning on handicap, and capturing the race record. Not since John Illingworth won the inaugural race had a yacht won all three. Then another disaster: the mast broke, buckling just a few feet above the deck. Taking over the lead, Plattner went on to win line honors and set the record (although he didn't win on handicap). As *Brindabella* limped back to Sydney under motor, Lindsay May, *Brindabella*'s navigator, thought the whole crew needed counseling.

Wives and girlfriends had always been a kind of extended family for *Brindabella*. They showed up before and after races and gathered for parties. Sabrina Snow, George's wife, a tall, dark-haired Asian art scholar, was the "den mother." The daughter of an Australian diplomat, she was known as Lady Sabrina to *Brindabella*'s crewmen because of her graceful poise. Sabrina greeted the crew when they arrived back in Sydney, trying to smile and hug downcast crewmen. "You'll just have to get back out there and do it again," she told them. "There's unfinished business."

Finally, in 1997, a year when neither Ellison nor Plattner were in the race, nothing went wrong and *Brindabella* was the first boat to reach Hobart. For the next three days, Snow led his crew in nonstop celebration. "It was," he said later, "the pub crawl to end all pub crawls."

It was hard not to think about that victory as *Brindabella* passed *Sayonara*. "These show ponies may have the best boat in the world, but now we'll see what they can do in rough weather," exclaimed an elated Erik Adriaanse, a Canberra-based accountant who had sailed with Snow in a dozen Hobarts. Winning the Hobart would be great, but crushing *Sayonara* would be glorious.

Bob Fraser, Australia's leading sailmaker, was at the wheel. Several of the top-rated yachts in the race were flying his sails, but Fraser, one of Sydney's best-regarded helmsmen, always sailed on *Brindabella*. Now he concentrated on catching waves, which, since they were traveling at better than twenty knots, wasn't an easy task. As one began to lift the yacht, he yelled, "I'm going for speed," signaling that he was changing course to gain speed, like a bodysurfer taking his last furious strokes before trying to catch a ride. Then, judging that he'd achieved maximum velocity, Fraser announced, "I've got my speed — I'm going into height mode," and he steered directly down the wave. As the boat fell into what felt like a groove, the sails were eased a bit, and Fraser tried to stay with the wave as long as possible. Then he did it all over, again and again.

On *Sayonara*, Dickson had given the wheel to Brad Butterworth. The laconic gray-haired forty-year-old had been Team New Zealand's tactician when it won the America's Cup in 1995, and he planned to play the same role in 2000. Although the Kiwis took pains to emphasize that theirs was a team effort, Butterworth and Russell Coutts were the two most crucial players. Butterworth was a genius at making split-second decisions on how to best maneuver a yacht. Some of it had to do with basic sailing skills, but equally important was his strategic sense of how to outfox opposing boats. There was a psychological aspect to Butterworth's work, both in the way he evaluated other skippers and in his youthful cheekiness. Once, when he was the tactician on a yacht that was about to cross the finish line after a hotly contested weekend race, he opened a Sunday newspaper and sat comfortably in the cockpit, spreading the pages as widely as he could, to create the impression that winning hadn't been all that difficult.

He had been in two Whitbread Races, but this Hobart was the most exciting sailing he had ever experienced. Steering a maxi-yacht downwind, catching waves and reaching speeds greater than twenty knots, was always exciting. To be neck and neck with *Brindabella* added immeasurably to the thrill.

Because the spinnaker tended to drive the bow down into the water, most of *Sayonara*'s crew were stationed at the stern. With the strong wind, the crew knew that everything was heavily loaded. Another spinnaker could rip. Tackle could fail. The mast could buckle. Eyes and ears were alert for signs, and the tension was palpable. When Joey Allen asked Butterworth if he'd like a drink of water, he half jokingly replied, "No, I think I need a rum."

Dickson took the wheel again forty minutes after he had given it to Butterworth. Glancing at the waves over his shoulder, he said he wanted to try a different angle on them. "I'm going to go ten degrees lower. It takes us off course, but I should be able to catch more waves." Tony Rae, who was trimming the mainsail, accommodated the new course by letting the sail out a bit. He too had been a member of Team New Zealand in 1995, as well as two other America's Cup regattas and a pair of Whitbreads, one of them on the winning yacht. In fact, he and Robbie Naismith, who was trimming the spinnaker, were among the handful of people who had been on winning boats in both the Whitbread and the America's Cup. On *Sayonara*, Naismith and Rae had the same jobs they did for Team New Zealand: Rae was responsible for adjusting the shape of the mainsail while Naismith did the same for the jib or spinnaker. Mike Howard, a Californian who once worked as Frank Sinatra's bodyguard, was grinding the mainsail. On most maxis, two men work as mainsail grinders, but on *Sayonara*, Howard, who bench-pressed 450 pounds and almost twice as much with his legs, often did the job himself. Tony Rae and Howard had worked together on *Sayonara* for so long that they could coordinate their work almost wordlessly.

Brindabella was still in front, but *Sayonara's* bow was surging toward *Brindabella's* stern when Butterworth returned to the helm. There are rules for overtaking another boat. As *Sayonara* gradually moved ahead, Dickson stood at the stern, judging their relative positions. When he decided that the boats no longer overlapped — that *Brindabella* could turn toward *Sayonara* without causing a collision — he raised his right arm above his head and then brought it straight down, as if he were swinging a butcher's knife.

But Butterworth didn't get very far before *Brindabella* began to eat at the margin. David Adams was now at *Brindabella's* helm. When Adams had sailed a fifty-foot yacht in the solo, around-the-world BOC Challenge, in 1994-95, he won his class and slashed more than ten days off the previous record. A fierce competitor, he was concentrating on every wave and gust, trying to catch up.

"Let's harden up the sails," Adams called out as *Brindabella* drew even with *Sayonara*. Then, satisfied, he said, "Okay, we're in the groove."

Bob Fraser was standing at the stern. After *Brindabella* moved far enough ahead to eliminate the overlap, he dropped his arm in the same dramatic way that Dickson had earlier. The gesture drew a half smile from Dickson.

11

Glyn Charles was at the *Sword of Orion*'s wheel for much of Saturday afternoon as it flew down the coast several miles behind *Sayonara* and *Brindabella*. The wind was becoming more powerful, reaching twenty knots by four o'clock, and Glyn was beginning to think doing the race might have been the right decision after all. The spinnaker was up, the sky was still blue, and the boat was moving through the water at an average speed of thirteen knots.

The waves were five to six feet high, big enough for the *Sword* to ride. With its broad stern and deep rudder, it was behaving like an oceangoing surfboard. When Glyn saw the *Sword*'s speed reach twenty knots, he broke into an unabashed broad grin.

Glyn's fascination with sailboats began when he was just six. His grandfather had been in the navy and his father had owned a powerboat, but Glyn's interest in sailing was entirely self-motivated. He began by building models of classic sailboats and collecting boat-related posters, hobbies that turned his bedroom into a nautical shrine, his own little yacht club. By age ten, he was desperate for a real boat and started clipping newspaper advertisements for used sailing dinghies. He eventually persuaded his father, the proprietor of a bicycle and toy store, to buy a thirteen-foot yellow boat named *Jinx*. Glyn's sister, Merrion, remembered how he learned to use it. "He bought a book called *Teach Yourself How to Sail*, and when we first went out on the boat, it was my job to turn the pages. It didn't take long before he didn't need me — and after that, he wanted to be on the boat all day, every day."

From then on, nothing got in the way of sailing. He rode his bicycle back and forth between his family's house in Winchester and the Bosham Sailing Club on the southern coast of England, where he kept *Jinx*. It was a long ride, but he never seemed to tire of it. At age thirteen, without telling anyone, he took his little boat on a solo voyage to the Isle of Wight, crossing The Solent, one of the world's busiest sea-lanes. His parents were shocked, but they already knew not to stand between Glyn and sailing. Even then he was talking about the Olympics — and, inevitably, his need for a faster boat. Following up on another advertisement, he found himself at the home of Olympic gold medalist Rodney Pattisson. He bought Pattisson's Laser, a popular fourteen-foot boat, and at nineteen he won the British Laser championship.

By then, his parents had divorced and his father had died. Glyn, always self-sufficient and focused, became even more driven. When he decided he needed to gain weight, he created a horrible calorie-laden concoction of milk, eggs, and powdered milk and drank unthinkable quantities of it. After college, he tried a couple of traditional jobs, working for a computer company and a bank. But his sailing ambitions, by then completely focused on winning an Olympic medal, were so great that he didn't have the time or patience to maintain any sort of regular employment. Seeking to turn his passion into a business, he wrote a book about sailing tactics, *Keelboat & Sportsboat Racing*; attempted to line up sponsors; and, occasionally, sailed for money. He just missed making the British Olympic team in 1988 and 1992 but was selected for the Atlanta Games in 1996, where he finished tenth in the Star class competition. Come the 2000 Games in Sydney, he was confident that a medal would be his.

On board the *Sword*, Dags was watching Glyn's technique, trying to judge his skill. He had opposed this addition to the crew, but now that Glyn was on board, Dags wanted to get to know him. In superficial ways, the two of them were quite similar. Both had made up for being smaller than most of their contemporaries with agility and drive, and they shared a total commitment to competitive sailing. But Dags knew that many of sailing's "rock stars" were arrogant and self-centered characters who folded their arms rather than help out with humdrum tasks. Glyn did seem aloof, although that could have been because he didn't really know anyone but Steve Kulmar. Watching Glyn as he maneuvered the *Sword* to catch waves, Dags still wasn't sure what to think, but it was hard not to like someone who was having so much fun and maintaining a fantastic pace. There was also a bit of reflected glory in sailing with an Olympic yachtsman, and Dags decided that he had already realized an important achievement: he was on a top boat with a talented crew, flying down the coast of Australia in one of the world's greatest ocean races.

Adam Brown was still skeptical about Glyn. A big-boned twenty-nine-year-old with piercing blue eyes and unruly blond hair, Brownie looked like an overweight rugby player. But his physical stature was complemented by a gentle character that made him more laid-back teddy bear than grizzly. He rarely complained about anything, and his friends repeatedly remarked upon his steadfast loyalty. Brownie took sailing seriously. He had been in nine Hobarts, starting out as a grinder before moving up the ranks to become one of the *Sword*'s main helmsmen. Brownie fully understood his skipper's limitations. "Kooky's playing a big game he doesn't fully understand," Brownie told other yachtsmen. "His desire to win is so great that it's bigger than his respect for the sea." Even so, Brownie didn't hesitate to join the *Sword* for the Hobart, mostly because of his regard for the rest of the crew, particularly Dags, whom Brownie believed to be the best bowman in Australia. "The rest of the crew is so good," he explained, "that Kooky doesn't matter."

Brownie opposed adding Kulmar and Glyn, in part because it required dropping two crewmen who had been sailing with the *Sword* for months. The newcomers waltzed into important roles without the months of training that everyone else had gone through, and Brownie resented it. Certain that the boat would be making greater progress if Glyn aimed a little closer to the wind, Brownie wondered whether Glyn was as good as his reputation.

"Head up a little bit," Brownie suggested.

Glyn ignored him.

Brownie enjoyed making new friends, and though he was usually open-minded and slow to judge, he had zero tolerance for what he perceived to be overinflated egos and arrogance. He had never liked Kulmar for that reason, and he had already begun to assign Glyn to the same category.

Kooky knew the *Sword* was doing well, although he didn't project any sense of excitement. He spent most of his time below, seated at the nav station near the galley, gathering weather information from faxes and commercial radio stations and jotting down the wind speeds and barometric pressure reported from various on-land locations. Most owners want to steer their boats. While they may not be as effective as other crewmen, they consider it a privilege of ownership. Kooky, however, believed he was better suited to make other contributions. Getting the best possible fix on the weather was his top priority.

He heard about the storm warning from a government radio station immediately after it was issued. Unlike many of the other competitors, he fully understood what it meant, although he wasn't really alarmed by the prospect of forty-to-fifty-five-knot winds. That would be more than the average Hobart, he thought, but not by much. What did concern him was the lack of precise information about the storm's trajectory. But for now there was nothing to do but keep going.

By late afternoon, the wind was howling, and the *Sword*, still powered by the spinnaker, continued to travel rapidly south. That was the good news. The bad news was that since the wind had picked up to thirty knots, the boat was under enormous pressure. Everything was designed to withstand severe loads of one kind or another. However, the interaction of the gear with waves and wind involves endless permutations, and the most sophisticated computer analysis couldn't predict where things would come apart. Dags believed it was just a matter of time before something broke from the strain.

Trouble was not long in coming. Sailboats tend to turn into the wind in a strong breeze. Sometimes the wind is so powerful that it also pushes the boat onto its side. If it's pushed far enough over, the rudder is no longer in the water. At that point, the boat has broached and gone out of control. In the early evening, a whip of wind knocked the *Sword* too far. It didn't matter how hard Glyn turned the wheel to force the boat in the opposite direction. It had no effect. With no steerage, the yacht could have been capsized by the wind and waves. As the deck slanted, crewmen grabbed at anything they could to keep them from falling overboard.

The *Sword* returned to a more upright position before it got into real trouble, but even then Glyn couldn't control the boat. "I still have no steerage!" Glyn called after the *Sword* righted itself. The yacht was totally out of control.

Dags knew exactly what had happened. The broach had caused the steering cable, a steel wire that connects the steering wheel to the rudder, to snap. After the same thing had happened a couple of months earlier, he had stowed a spare cable in a locker near the steering mechanism. While some of the crew rushed to take down the spinnaker in a frantic attempt to slow the boat, Dags scrambled below and replaced the broken cable. When the repair was completed, less than ten minutes later, calm returned to the *Sword*.

The first scheduled radio check-in — or "sked," short for "schedule," during which the updated weather forecast was provided and every yacht was required to report its position — began not long after the repair was completed, at 8:05 P.M. For the rest of the race, skeds would take place at 3:05 A.M. and 2:05 P.M. The odd times were to allow a short period of silence, beginning on the hour, during which any yachts in distress could be heard. The first sked began with a weather forecast. For the first time, the fleet was officially told about the storm warning. Like Kooky, some skippers had heard about the warning from radio stations; but for others, this was the first they had heard of it. However, many of them thought it sounded almost like a routine announcement, and it failed to make much of an impression on most yachts. Like Kooky, many of the competitors considered forty-to-fifty-knot winds to be only marginally greater than the norm.

What did impress Kooky was the amount of ground the *Sword* had made up since the start: only twenty boats were in front of him. Kooky was also encouraged when he heard that several yachts had broken steering cables and that one of them had dropped out of the race as a result. "See," he gloated, "we're ready for anything."

After the sked, Kooky mixed himself a glass of Sustagen and ground coffee beans and joined the rest of the crew in the cockpit for dinner: chicken curry served on small plastic trays. As they ate, bolts of lightning began to flash through several dark clouds that had formed ahead of them. The bolts were only partly visible and didn't appear to reach down to the ocean, but they worried Kooky, who knew that the electricity reflected the intensity of the coming weather system.

Dags was also concerned about the weather, but now that the *Sword* had survived the hurtling down the coast, he was much less worried about the mast. If it had been damaged, he was sure it would have already collapsed. That, he felt, was reason enough to celebrate. In spite of Kooky's alcohol ban, Dags had tucked a bottle of rum into the bottom of his duffel bag. Brownie had brought two large bottles of Coca-Cola, and he knew exactly what Dags meant when he asked, "Should we prepare the on-deck medical kit?" Once they fetched their bottles from below, Brownie took a gulp of Coke and poured as much rum as he could into the plastic bottle. Assessing their day, Dags and Brownie were reasonably satisfied. Except for the crash with *Nokia*, everything had gone very well. They had pushed the boat as hard as they could and had picked up a lot of ground on their competitors. But they were also aware that a dramatic shift in the weather could change everything.

12

Just before dusk on *Sayonara*, T. A. McCann passed out plastic trays of sushi and bottles of water, followed by Snickers bars. Sushi was Ellison's favorite food, and he insisted on having it as the first meal of every long-distance race.

During the 1995 Hobart, T.A., who had developed an interest in nutrition when he was a student at Purdue University, volunteered to provision the boat with food. He bought most of it at a camping supply store. Initially, he thought he had done a great job. On the first night of the race, when he made himself a midnight snack of instant noodles, Ellison got out of his bunk and asked if he could have some. "These are fantastic," he raved. Hearing Ellison's praise, Rupert Murdoch had some, too, and he deemed them "the best noodles I've ever had." T.A. loved the idea that two envelopes of instant noodles, costing $1.29 apiece, could bring such pleasure to a pair of billionaires. But the next day, after he passed around bags of freeze-dried turkey tetrazzini, the honeymoon was over.

"I can't eat this shit!" Ellison bellowed. "You've got to be kidding: it's fucking dog food!"

For the 1998 Hobart, Ellison spent ten thousand dollars to provide better grub. For six days before the race, Kerry Stanfield, a professional caterer and the wife of *Sayonara* crewman Justin

Clougher, took over a Sydney apartment and used fresh ingredients to prepare meals that could be put into Seal-A-Meal bags and flash frozen. Dinners included shrimp scampi with garlic and wine, beef bourguignonne with roasted Red Bliss potatoes, and, for T.A, a vegetarian, meat-free lasagna. For breakfast, there were frittatas with mushrooms and shallots as well as bacon-and-egg sandwiches. With the exception of Snickers bars, which he loved, Ellison didn't like foods that had a lot of fat or sugar, so Kerry used plenty of vegetables and other healthy ingredients. Before the start, T.A. placed the food in two lockers in the center of the cabin that were cooled by dry ice, making sure that the first-to-be-eaten meals were on top. It still wouldn't be elegant dining. The bags would be dropped into hot water, and the contents would be consumed directly from the bag without plates or utensils — but Ellison believed it was the best he could do.

Sayonara's galley, after all, was a tiny area near the front of the cabin, about ten feet from Ellison's bunk. The stove consisted of four small burners that were held in a spindly contraption that looked as if it were made of metal hangers. Plastic jars, which hung from the wall, contained Lipton tea bags, Ghirardelli hot chocolate mix, and Nescafe. A cabinet opposite the stove held a jar of shelled pistachios, Pringles, and a mix for a lemon-lime drink that came from a ShopRite somewhere, alongside several rolls of electrical tape and a plastic bottle filled with hydraulic oil. On top of the cabinet were a dozen lid-equipped coffee mugs.

Mark Rudiger ate his sushi at the nav station, a nook near the rear of the cabin where most of *Sayonara*'s electronic equipment was housed. He was sitting on a bench in front of a slanted desk, on which he placed the food. The desk had notches near the highest part that held two laptop computers. Part of the desk could be lifted to access a pair of three-ring binders. Inside, typewritten pages, each one covered in plastic, contained the performance data Rudiger had collected from previous races, the handicap ratings for other boats in the Hobart fleet, the race rules, and instructions on how to use the satellite-based e-mail system. Mounted on the wall facing Rudiger were radio equipment, a radar screen, a list of times for the radio skeds, a telephone handset, and a monitor that provided the same information displayed on the jumbo on deck. A black pipelike tube projected down from the ceiling directly over his head, although it bent forward and disappeared in a hole that went though the center of the wall that Rudiger faced. The tube contained the driveshaft from the winch that controlled the mainsail, but it brought to mind a periscope, completing the impression that Rudiger's realm could have been on a submarine. Since he had to provide around-the-clock guidance, Rudiger was unlikely to sleep more than half an hour at a stretch. And his breaks were few and far between. When he visited the cockpit for some fresh air at about 10:00 P.M. and saw bolts of high-altitude lightning across half the horizon, he thought about disconnecting the radios from the antenna but decided he didn't want to risk missing any weather information over the radio. When it started raining, he had an even more immediate concern: the driveshaft over his desk started leaking. It had happened before, but there had never been such a substantial flow of water. Worried that it would damage the electronics, he tried covering the shaft with rags, but that only delayed the dripping. When he opened the desktop, he saw that the compartment holding the three-ring binders was full of water.

"There's water pissing on me all the time," he complained to Justin Clougher. "Can you do something to stop it?"

Clougher used duct tape to fashion a makeshift funnel, but it failed to capture all the water. Badly damaged was the single-sideband radio, which Rudiger had been using to receive weather faxes. The digital barometer survived the water damage, though, and now Rudiger watched the plummeting atmospheric pressure. Shortly after darkness set in, he noted that it went from 1008 to 930 millibars in less than four hours, a decline so steep that the graphic depiction reminded him of his favorite ski slope at California's Heavenly Valley.

By midnight, most of the yachts in the race had lowered their spinnakers because of the worsening weather. But *Sayonara's* was still up. The yacht's speed varied according to the gusts and waves, but it occasionally touched twenty-five knots, an exhilarating pace at any time, but particularly at night. Brad Butterworth and Graeme "Frizzle" Freeman, who were taking turns at the wheel, both recognized that the spinnaker was close to its breaking point. When a gust of wind reached forty knots, Frizzle, who had sailed in twenty-four Hobarts, said, "We're at our limit. We have too much sail up."

Joey Allen and T.A. had already discussed how to take down the spinnaker. But *Brindabella* was still nearby and its spinnaker, illuminated by a light at the top of its mast, was obviously still flying.

Suddenly everyone heard a bang from the bow. Ellison, who was sitting in the cockpit, originally thought the spinnaker pole had broken near where it was connected to the mast, but he saw that the pole and the mast were still joined. Realizing it wasn't the distinctive cracking sound of disintegrating carbon fiber, he was sure it couldn't be the pole or the mast. Bewildered, he screamed, "What the hell happened?"

T.A., who was near the front of the cockpit, rushed forward. The twenty-eight-foot carbon-fiber pole hadn't broken, but the two-foot-long metal fitting at the end had been ripped away by the power of the sail. The spinnaker was still flying, but now that it was no longer attached to the pole, the crew couldn't control it. Seconds later, the swinging pole sliced through the middle of the sail, shredding it as if it were tissue paper. Back in the cockpit, T.A. said, "I can't believe it. The end has just pulled out of the pole."

"Get rid of the spinnaker — get the pole down," Butterworth yelled. While the tattered sail was pulled onto the deck and into the hull through a hatch near the bow, the spare spinnaker pole was carried up from below and attached to the mast. Despite the wind, Butterworth wanted to put up another spinnaker. But controlling it was difficult with the gusty wind, and after it collapsed and then suddenly filled with a particularly strong blast of air, the sail blew into pieces. Now three of *Sayonara*'s four heavy-weather spinnakers had been destroyed. Robbie Naismith and Joey Allen wanted to raise the last one. "We can't do that," said a crewman named Zan Drejes. "We'll blow it up, and have nothing to use for the next four hundred miles." Drejes prevailed, and Butterworth assumed that *Brindabella* would take the lead.

Before long, however, spinnakers were irrelevant. For most of the day, the wind had come out of the northeast. During the evening, it began shifting so that it came from the northwest, and during the early morning the direction continued to shift toward the west until it would have been impossible to fly a spinnaker.

Although *Sayonara*'s crew was worried about *Brindabella*, which had disappeared into the darkness, Mark Rudiger was thrilled by *Sayonara*'s rate of progress. Shortly after one o'clock in the morning, he climbed up to the deck bearing incredible news. "For the first twelve hours of the race, our average speed over the ground was almost nineteen knots. At this point, we're thirteen hours ahead of where *Morning Glory* was the year it broke the record."

"That's crazy — that's fantastic!" Ellison blurted. *But something about this isn't right*, he said to himself. The way the spinnaker pole came apart had deeply unnerved him. And the worsening weather wasn't making him feel any better. When the wind direction first began to shift, he had thought they were passing through a front, but things were only getting uglier.

The continuing shift in the wind's direction eventually caused Butterworth to decide he needed to turn the boat. Rather than coming about by turning the bow through the wind, he planned to jibe, turning so that the stern would pass through the wind. To begin the maneuver, the grinders brought in the mainsail so that the massive boom and sail wouldn't slam from one side to the other with too much force when the boat came about. Then, at the bottom of a trough between waves, when the wind was weakest, Butterworth turned the wheel hard, putting *Sayonara* on the other tack so the wind hit the opposite side of the sails. His execution looked perfect, but when the boat turned through the wind, one of the battens, a fifteen-foot-long strip of carbon fiber that fit into a horizontal pocket in the sail to help it maintain its shape, had slipped out and caught on the backstay, which connected the top of the mast to the stern. The snag tore the pocket as well as the sail. Since the rip didn't pass through the part of the sail that was reinforced with Kevlar, it didn't look serious. However, the leech line (a cord that held the back edge of the sail taut) had been severed, and without it, the back of the sail was flapping. The flogging was sure to damage the fabric, in the same way a strand of wire weakens if it is repeatedly bent back and forth.

* * *

Early Sunday morning Lachlan was sitting on the rail near the stern. Each time the bow started going down a wave, the stern soared upward, jerking Lachlan toward the sky — so violently that it made him think of a cracking whip. Since he wasn't wearing a safety harness, he was using both of his hands to grasp the lifeline. When a particularly steep wave sent Lachlan's body upward, his grip was so tight that it caused the skin between his first and second knuckles on the inside of his right hand to peel away. The damaged skin looked as if it had been burned. Although it wasn't a debilitating injury, it was painful, particularly when it came into contact with salt water. Lachlan put on sailing gloves, but he still felt stinging pain whenever he grabbed something.

Ellison was lying on his bunk, feeling sorry for himself. *The crew is being paid to be here*, he said to himself. *I'm paying. That makes me really stupid. If I could push a button to get off this boat, I'd do it.* His mind, in fact, was taking him to other places — mostly Antigua, where *Katana* was waiting for his arrival. Ellison was thinking of how differently he would be spending his time if he were there, ordering up great food, shooting baskets on the deck where he had replaced the helipad with a basketball court, or sitting in the sun reading a novel.

Everyone was concerned about the strain on the yacht. T.A. was looking at the hairline cracks that had developed along the base of the carbon-fiber pedestal that held the central winch. Since the starboard winch was already incapacitated, the line that controlled the mainsail was wrapped around the central winch. Carbon fiber has incredible strength, but when it does fail, it does so all at once. Examining the cracks with a flashlight, T.A. was afraid it would be torn from the deck. "You don't want to be downwind of this thing," he said to Justin Clougher. "If you're there when it goes, you die."

Catching glimpses of faces in the darkness, Clougher imagined that everyone was thinking the same thing: "What's going to break first?" There were many possibilities beyond the winch and the damaged mainsail. Part of the rigging or the mast itself could snap. Everything was designed to stand up to fairly substantial peak loads, but the boat had never been under so much pressure for such an extended period. The winds that had propelled them thirteen hours — *thirteen hours* — ahead of record time might have been a Midas-like curse.

Frizzle wanted to reduce some of the forces by reefing the mainsail, a step that had been taken on *Sayonara* only once before. The sail had 1,900 square feet of surface area, and pulling it down and securing a portion of it to the boom was difficult even in calm conditions. With the wind putting enormous pressure against the flapping sail, it was easily capable of knocking a man into the water. But the crew agreed that it would be even more dangerous not to reduce the mainsail's size. Frizzle carefully turned *Sayonara* into the wind. When the sail was no longer filled, the flapping intensified. Hearing it from below, Ellison thought it didn't even sound like a sail anymore. It made a crackling noise that reminded him of breaking fiberglass.

From the cockpit, Robbie Naismith was handling the lines that controlled the sail. The rest of the crew had to contend with the rocking deck and the constraints of their tethers as they wrestled the extra sailcloth down to the boom and tied it there. When it was secure, Frizzle turned away from the wind, putting an end to the worst of the noise. The mainsail was then 20 percent smaller, but Frizzle believed the yacht was still overpowered, so he asked Joey Allen to replace the jib with a storm jib, a tiny triangle of a sail.

When it was Brad Butterworth's turn to take the wheel again, the mainsail was his greatest worry. It was the only one they had. Although *Sayonara* had never carried two mains, Dickson had discussed taking a second one before the race but ultimately decided it would add too much weight. Butterworth had hoped that conditions would ease, reducing the tension on the damaged sail. But after the 3:05 A.M. sked, Rudiger told him that the wind was likely to strengthen and that more than twenty boats had retired from the race. Afraid the sail would be mortally damaged, Butterworth ordered that it be completely lowered and tied to the boom. The operation, which usually required a few minutes, took half an hour. In the dark, no one could tell how bad the damage was.

After the sail was secured, Joey Allen said, "This sucks. There's no way *Brindabella* isn't going to pass us now."

Steve Wilson, another member of Team New Zealand, said, "Yeah, well, I just hope we have a working mainsail to hoist tomorrow."

George Snow was also nervous about his mainsail. As on *Sayonara*, *Brindabella* had reefed the sail. However, the crew couldn't tie the lowered portion to the boom, so about ten feet of sail was left to flog. When Snow saw that a tear had developed in the back of his mainsail, he said, "We're going to have a problem with that." Seeing that *Sayonara*, which was several miles farther south but visible because of a light on the top of its mast, was sailing without its mainsail, he added, "The bloke who repairs his mainsail first is the bloke who's going to win the race."

13

Early Sunday morning, a lighthouse at Wilson's Promontory, a point of land that extends far into Bass Strait and is the southern-most tip of the Australian mainland, reported average winds of seventy-nine knots with gusts of ninety-two knots. The lighthouse's anemometer, high above the water and affected by terrain that tends to funnel the wind, always provides readings greater than what exists near the surface of the water. Still, the promontory is one of the only weather observation points in the area. When Clouds Badham heard about the wind reported there, he delved into the records he had accumulated since he began providing forecasts for Hobart competitors more than twenty years earlier. He saw that the wind at the promontory reached seventy-nine knots only once or twice a year, always during the winter. According to his files, gusts had never before exceeded ninety knots.

Extraordinary weather was affecting much of southeastern Australia. It was snowing in places that had experienced a heat wave two days earlier. Clouds knew that the extreme temperature change was a bad sign because it suggested that a polar jet stream was arching over the storm.

Drawing a weather chart at his home south of Sydney, where he was close enough to the beach to hear the pounding waves, he became convinced that the fleet would experience winds significantly greater than the forty to fifty-five knots that the weather bureau had predicted. Indeed, given the readings from the promontory, Clouds believed that the wind was already blowing at least fifty-five, that the barometric pressure at the center of the storm was continuing to fall, and that the wind would only strengthen. Some of the weather bureau's forecasters, he suspected, didn't understand just how important the seemingly small differences were for boats at sea. Anything up to fifty knots, he believed, was difficult but manageable; sixty knots was another world. The power of the wind increases disproportionately to its speed. In mathematical terms, the force of the wind equals the square of its speed. Therefore, an increase from fifty to sixty knots, a 20 percent increase in speed, amounts to an increase in power of more than 40 percent.

Clouds believed the center of low pressure, which was moving in an easterly course across Bass Strait, would intersect a line between Sydney and Hobart early Sunday afternoon and affect the area for the following twenty-four hours. In preparing to draw his map, Clouds suspected that wind speed would vary within the area and that the worst conditions would be concentrated in a narrow section at the system's western side. That was exactly what happened in the 1979 Fastnet Race, in which fifteen sailors died. Following that race, weather forecasters concluded that they had failed to predict maximum wind speeds because their computer models dealt in averages and that the actual speeds varied substantially in different bands of the storm. On his map Clouds drew an elliptical circle around where he believed the winds would be strongest. It was about fifty miles long and thirty miles wide. He believed that the yachts in the middle and back of the fleet would fall within the circle and that they would be hit by a deadly combination of powerful wind and hull-breaking waves. He estimated that the worst would come in a twelve-hour period beginning at 3:00 P.M. Sunday, and that it would knock more than half the fleet out of the race.

The most recent sked had been at 3:05 A.M. on Sunday morning, but the forecast that was broadcast then was based on observations from several hours earlier, before the low had intensified. The next sked wasn't until 2:05 P.M. Worried that skippers in the race would be making decisions on the basis of grossly inadequate forecasts, Clouds tried to call cellular phones on two of the yachts he had given prerace forecasts to. Both were new and relatively untested, and Clouds feared their crews didn't know how much the boats could take. He knew that providing outside assistance during the race violated the rules, but he did it anyway because he was sure most of the yachtsmen would soon be more focused on surviving than on racing.

Both calls went unanswered.

14

The *Sword* maintained its rapid pace through Saturday night and into Sunday morning. By the 3:05 A.M. sked, it was about thirty miles behind *Sayonara* and *Brindabella* but ahead of all but seven or eight other boats. By then, however, Glyn, who was at the wheel, realized that the wind, which had gusted up to thirty-eight knots, had become too much of a good thing. "Let's reef the main," he said. "We can always put it back up later." It was a good call: not long after that, the wind increased to a steady forty-five knots.

At 4:30 A.M., the wind speed suddenly dropped to less than twenty knots. Thinking that the worst of the storm was over, Kulmar said, "Let's shake the reefs out of the main."

Brownie disagreed. "It's just a lull. It won't last."

"Come on. We're in a fucking boat race. We can't be messing around."

Kooky, who had just come on deck, agreed with Brownie and saw the disagreement as an opportunity to put Kulmar in his place. "No!" he declared. "We're not going to put up the fucking main. It's my fucking boat — and we're not putting it up!"

Fifteen minutes later, a rain front swept past the *Sword*, and the wind rapidly built back up to close to fifty knots. At the same time, the wind shifted to come from a more westerly direction.

The boat was still moving through the water at thirteen knots, but it had become a much more uncomfortable ride. The waves were bigger, and they were turning the crowded main cabin into a bumpy amusement-park ride. Nausea and exhaustion were inevitable by-products. Only Sam Hunt appeared unaffected. Rather than lying in a bunk, he was on his knees, moving wet sails and other gear to reduce the general level of disarray. Unlike everyone else, Hunt still had an appetite, and just after 5:00 A.M., he rummaged through one of the food lockers until he came across something he didn't like.

"There's bananas on the boat! What are they doing here?"

Just twenty-four years old, Hunt had already completed six Hobarts. He was the youngest member of the crew, but his outburst sprang from a great nautical tradition — superstitions about things that shouldn't be brought or done on boats. Rooted in real disasters and legends of uncertain provenance, they retain relevance because of a great unalterable reality: even the most experienced mariners aren't always the masters of their destiny, and their survival is sometimes subject to forces beyond their control, or even understanding. People who pride themselves on being coldly rational on land are disinclined to tempt fate at sea. Whistling, for example, is prohibited on some boats. Whistlers aren't working, according to one theory, and the wind gods show their disdain for idlers by cursing them with bad weather. Some sailors believe yachts shouldn't be given names that are disrespectful of the sea's might. They say naming a boat *Ocean Conqueror* or *Wave Walker* would be asking for trouble. The reason for the fear of bananas isn't entirely clear. Some say a fishing boat that sank was carrying a large quantity of them. Whatever the reason, Hunt was loudly insisting that these bananas had to go — fast. He was absolutely serious.

"Can't we at least let people eat them?" Kooky asked with a sarcasm that Hunt didn't catch.

Hunt pitched the offensive fruit over the side and resumed his search for food. Before long he was confronted by another potential horror — a suspicious-looking brown cake. "What sort of cake is this?" he asked. Kooky, whose girlfriend had baked it, knew exactly what it was. He had been afraid that Hunt would discover it. Not the slightest bit superstitious himself, Kooky thought Hunt's fears were absurd and he considered lying. In the end, deciding it wasn't worth fibbing or fighting, he watched his banana cake disappear into the dark.

By dawn on Sunday, the *Sword* was east of Eden, the coastal town where Kooky grew up. Eden is twenty-five miles north of the Australian mainland's southeastern corner and has the last protected harbor near the racecourse before Tasmania. Like much of the fleet, the *Sword* was still sailing at a pace that would, if maintained, smash the race record, but Kooky worried that the wind direction would continue to change until the *Sword* was sailing into a head wind. There were a few blue patches in the sky, but they were only partially visible through a layer of haze that was turning everything into cold shades of gray. The only sharp contrast was in front of the boat, where the sky was black.

15

When Lumpy stuck his head out the *Winston Churchill*'s hatch just after dawn on Sunday, he was overwhelmed, unable to put what he saw into any kind of perspective. The waves were as tall as houses, close to thirty feet. He had never seen anything like this — not even close — but he wasn't experienced enough to know how extreme the conditions really were or to gauge the appropriate level of fear, so he tried to make an assessment by judging the anxiety levels of the *Churchill*'s most veteran sailors. Seeing how calm Steamer was, Lumpy delivered a little lecture to himself: *Well, if Steamer isn't scared, there's obviously nothing to worry about. It's like a roller coaster: it's scary, that's what it's intended to be, but it can't be really dangerous because people hardly ever die sailing to Hobart.*

On the other hand, several of the crew were seasick, and no one felt well enough to eat or drink much. Bruce Gould, who was one of the *Churchill*'s main helmsmen, was so worried about his flagging energy level that he tried to force himself to eat one of the bran muffins his wife had packed for him, but he managed only a couple of nibbles. When Gibbo took a bite of an apple, he retched almost immediately and again after he had a sip of water. Exhausted and unable to see very well, as he had lost one of his contact lenses the night before, he felt handicapped and was approaching even simple tasks with cautious unease.

The boat had broached during the night, and they had reefed the mainsail so that they could be more "comfortable," as Steamer put it. What Steamer called "comfortable" was very different from the usual definition. To him and other ocean racers, who make a habit of speaking about extreme weather with almost absurd understatement, it meant only that the boat remained on the safe side of being overpowered by the wind or waves. It certainly didn't mean that the boat was a nice place to be. With the constant pitching movement and occasional downpours of rain, being anywhere on the *Churchill* was miserable.

By late morning, the wind had reached a steady forty-five knots and was coming from the southwest. The arching waves, which were arriving from almost the same direction, now resembled an evil army. And as the wind continued to build, or as Steamer said, "freshened," it failed to meet even his definition of "comfortable." Steamer believed they had entered a tightly wound cyclone within which it was impossible to know where the wind would come from next. Worried about sudden wind shifts, he asked Michael Bannister and John Dean to take down the regular jib and replace it with the storm jib, the smallest sail in the *Churchill*'s wardrobe. A little later, the mainsail was removed. Although the *Churchill* was then powered by only a small jib, plus the pressure of the wind against the hull and rigging, it still had enough momentum to mount the waves. They had put on the brakes, but thanks to the increasingly ferocious wind, it was as if they had done nothing.

* * *

Sunday was John Dean's forty-seventh birthday, and he was beginning to think it wasn't going to be a good one.

Dean had been born in Watson's Bay, an idyllic village on the south side of Sydney Harbor near South Head. Located on a peninsula, with the harbor on one side and ocean on the other, it was the perfect place for anyone who liked to swim, surf, or sail. Ever since he was a kid, Dean had loved all three, and he'd never wanted to live anywhere else. His parents didn't have a boat, but at age six he jumped off a dock down the street from where he lived and swam to an eight-foot-long sailing dinghy that a neighbor was taking out for a sail. Dean had never sailed before, but from that day on, he went out whenever he got the chance.

Dean grew up to be a handsome man with a rakish mustache. When the woman who became his wife met him at a cocktail party, she thought he looked like Steve McQueen. From their first date, she understood that sailing would always be a top priority with him, a fact that became particularly clear just a few months after they were married in 1978. At four o'clock in the morning on the day after Christmas, Dean received a phone call. After hanging up, he told his wife that he was going to help a friend prepare his boat for the Hobart, which would begin later that day. John and Penny were planning to go to a party in Watson's Bay to watch the start of the race, and he said he would meet her there. But when she arrived at the party, Penny couldn't find her husband. Finding his brother, Warwick, she asked, "Where's John?"

"See that boat," Warwick said, pointing to *Apollo*, a sleek fifty-seven-footer that was leading the fleet out of the harbor and went on to win that year's race. "That's where John is."

Dean, who worked in the printing industry, later claimed that it was a last-minute decision after another crewman dropped out. Penny didn't quite believe him, though, particularly after she learned that he had packed a bag before he left home. Although he never pulled that trick again, he sailed almost every weekend, and he did everything he could to make sure that his teenage sons, Nathan and Peter, enjoyed the sport as much as he did. But right now, wet and tired, John Dean was worried.

16

When Brownie took the *Sword of Orion*'s wheel at 8:00 A.M., a black cloud stretched all the way across the horizon in front of the *Sword*, like a wall between worlds. An hour later, when it seemed as though the *Sword* was getting near the cloud, Brownie said the mainsail should come down. It had already been reefed, so the only thing left was to remove it entirely. Dags, sitting near Brownie, agreed, but there was a complication. The vang, a metal support that connected the bottom of the boom to the base of the mast, had broken sometime during the night. Normally, when the mainsail was taken down, the boom would be propped up by the vang. Without it, either the boom had to be detached from the mast and stowed below or the back end of the boom had to be lashed to the deck so it didn't swing freely across the cockpit. Given the conditions, Dags decided it would be better to tie it down, so he lashed it to the port side of the deck.

Afterward, he watched for big waves. When he saw one, he used his shoulder or a linked arm to help Brownie stay in position at the wheel. Brownie had attached himself to two tethers, each of which was fastened to a different place on the deck; but even with them, plus help from Dags, he sometimes lost his footing as he was thrown from side to side and on occasion almost over the top of the wheel. With the biggest waves, Brownie also had a hard time turning the wheel, so sometimes Dags helped him with that, too. Talking over the shrieking wind was difficult. The half-shouted communications focused on one thing, the worsening weather and the looming black cloud.

"I've never seen anything like that," Brownie said. "Is it a front? What's it going to be like when we go through it?"

"I have no idea," Dags replied, "but it can't be good."

The shape of the sea was also changing. The waves were farther apart from each other but much larger, some of them thirty feet high. The overall pattern was also becoming more irregular, and every half an hour or so, a particularly large wave moved in a direction that was somewhat at odds with the others. The great cloud still looked like a single mass, although it had begun to reveal dark gray vertical ribs extending down to the sea. "It's going to be a helluva downpour when we go under that thing," Brownie said. It was hard to imagine worse than what he was already dealing with. Just seeing through the onslaught of wind-borne salt water was difficult. Except for turning his head sideways and squinting, there was no way to shield his face, so his eyes were burning. The only way to relieve the sting was to open them wide and pour a bottle of fresh water over his face.

Powered by just the storm jib and the wind against the hull, the *Sword* continued to move quickly. Because of the danger that a man could be thrown overboard, no one was on the rail, though. Everyone had agreed that until they passed through the black cloud, only two people should be on deck. Not that the cabin was a comfortable sanctuary. Everything was wet, it was too loud to talk without raised voices, and the air reeked of vomit. Standing was difficult, both because of the turbulence and because it added to the feeling of nausea. Most of the crewmen were lying in bunks or on the floor of the cabin. Kooky, still at the nav station, was tuning in to commercial radio stations, continuing his search for information about the weather. He wanted to plot his own weather map, but he still didn't know where the low was. He hadn't been on deck for several hours, so he hadn't seen the black cloud, but given everything he had heard, he was even more convinced that it was part of a powerful cyclone. When Dags went below, Kooky told him, "I don't know what the fuck we're going into, but one thing's for sure — these aren't the conditions the weather bureau was forecasting."

Steve Kulmar, more nervous than he had ever been in a lifetime of ocean sailing, had lost his gung-ho aggressiveness. Indeed, he was beginning to wonder if they should abandon the race. It was the steplike increases in the wind's strength that scared him.

"In seventeen Hobarts, I've never seen anything like this," he told Kooky. "In 1993, we had a steady forty-knot wind and there were gusts of seventy-five and eighty — but the gusts were brief and there weren't these big waves."

A little later, he added, "We should think about going back."

"We can't do anything until we know where the low is," Kooky replied.

The very idea of quitting was repulsive to Kooky. Beyond that, leaving the race might be more dangerous than continuing. The *Sword* was already south of Eden, the nearest port. At this point, turning back would have required the *Sword* to sail away from the waves, which, now that they were so large, would have been perilous. On the other hand, finding shelter along Tasmania's eastern coast meant crossing Bass Strait. Without knowing where the storm was centered or where it was moving, Kooky thought it was impossible to evaluate the options.

For Kulmar, who never had much respect for the *Sword*'s owner, the idea that Kooky was making the big decisions seemed absurd. Going on deck to have another firsthand look at the conditions, Kulmar sat next to crewman Simon Reffold, who was helping Brownie. The *Sword* had already begun to be enveloped in the dark cloud.

"This is really dangerous," Kulmar told Reffold. "Kooky isn't telling us what's going on with the weather, and I'm not confident. I think we should probably pull the pin right now."

"I don't know about that," Reffold said. "But we have to get more information. That's for sure."

Turning to Brownie, Kulmar said, "This isn't sailing. Don't you think we should be thinking about dropping out?"

Brownie was extremely competitive, much more of a bull-headed stalwart than a quitter, but ever since he took the wheel, he had been moving toward the idea that the *Sword* should abandon the race. The fear he saw in Kulmar's face — his brow was furrowed as if he were watching a horror movie — only raised his level of anxiety. Brownie wasn't sure anyone else could handle the wheel. Glyn seemed too seasick to drive, and Brownie thought Kulmar was reluctant even to be on deck.

"Absolutely," said Brownie.

By late morning, the *Sword*'s anemometer was indicating sustained wind speeds greater than fifty knots. After the wind gusted to more than seventy knots, Brownie turned to Kulmar. "Why don't you go down and talk to Kooky?"

A minute later Kulmar confronted Kooky again. "I'm very uncomfortable. I've never seen anything like this, and we don't have a choice: we need to retire."

"We can't. We have to know more about what's going on with the weather."

"Look," Kulmar said, "I have no confidence in the forecast. We're running out of drivers. The wind keeps trending up. The farther we go, the worse it gets. We shouldn't be here. Maybe we'll just retire temporarily. If the wind dies down, we could get back in the race."

Kooky remained unconvinced. "The problem is, where do we go? If we go north, the waves will be behind us. If we go south or west, we're going to have shallow water and steeper seas. If we go east, we'll be farther from land."

Standing nearby, Dags overheard the conversation. He thought dropping out was a terrible idea, a massive overreaction. Kooky was sure that Dags would not be in favor of abandoning the race, so when Kulmar was out of earshot, Kooky confided in him. "I don't care what Kulmar wants. We're going to keep racing. He's not the only guy on the boat."

"I knew he'd want to quit," Dags said. "But he's not making decisions. You are. And it doesn't make any sense to quit."

Kooky wasn't reacting against Kulmar's proposal simply because it came from him or because of his own desire to win the race. "We don't know where the storm is centered or where it's going," he said to Dags. "We could end up going back into it again."

Kulmar couldn't hear what Kooky and Dags were saying, but he accurately guessed the substance. Kulmar respected Dags's skill as a bowman, but he thought Dags was too young and inexperienced to fully understand the risks they were facing. *We have a serious chain-of-command problem*, Kulmar said to himself. *We have an owner who has done exactly one Hobart — and instead of listening to me, he's chosen a twenty-eight-year-old to be his confidant.*

* * *

During the early afternoon, the worsening weather caused four of the most competitive yachts in the race to initiate an unusual series of radio conversations with Lew Carter, a longtime CYC member who coordinated the skeds from aboard *Young Endeavour*, a 144-foot naval vessel that was sailing with the fleet. At 12:35 P.M., a yacht called *Doctel Rager*, which was about twenty miles southwest of the *Sword*, gave its position, and said it was being buffeted by fifty-to-sixty-knot winds with gusts up to seventy.

Announcing weather conditions was almost unprecedented. In most races, competitors would head to where the strongest breeze was reported. But as Clouds had predicted, racing was becoming less important than surviving. Within an hour after *Doctel Rager* called in, three other yachts — *Secret Men's Business, Wild One,* and *Terra Firma* — announced that they were experiencing similarly extreme conditions. At 1:32 P.M. *Wild One* said it was abandoning the race. Seven minutes later, *Secret Men's Business* announced that it too was retiring.

Kooky didn't hear any of those transmissions. He was on a different channel, asking a Coast Guard station for any updated weather information. During the conversation, he heard about the ninety-four-knot wind that had been recorded at Wilson's Promontory, but nothing about where the low was. "The information I have isn't any good," he told Kulmar. "I still want to wait for the two o'clock sked."

On deck, Brownie continued to get plenty of firsthand insight into the weather. When Dags, who had returned to the cockpit, spotted a forty-foot wave, he screamed, "Bad wave — this one is huge!"

Brownie reminded himself of what he had to do: carve into the wave, maintaining enough speed to make it over the top, but not so much that the yacht charged off the peak. Not making it over the top would be the worst disaster, but he also had to avoid crashing into the trough on the other side with hull-cracking momentum. Brownie's execution was flawless, but he knew he had been wrestling with the waves far too long and that he wouldn't be able to handle many more like that one. Yet no one offered to relieve him.

Just before the 2:05 P.M. sked, Andrew Parkes came on deck to give Dags a respite. "This is bullshit," Parkes said to Brownie. "What are we doing this for?"

"I agree," Brownie said. "We should be out of here."

Below, Kulmar was continuing to press his case — and Kooky was continuing to resist. "I hear what you're saying, but we still don't know where to go," Kooky said. "And how do we know it won't let up?"

In fact, although Kooky wasn't saying so, he was beginning to lose his resolve. Aware that two senior members of the core crew, Brownie and Parkes, wanted to abandon the race, Kooky was silently struggling with a decision. Knowing that Kulmar would seize on any ambivalence, he was trying to preserve his options a bit longer — but even as he talked about staying the course, he was much less sure. When the *Sword*'s lightweight barometer came loose from its bracket and flew halfway across the cabin and smashed, he forgot his posturing. "We don't need it. We already know we're in trouble."

Kooky hoped two things would happen during the two o'clock sked: first, that the official forecast at the start of the broadcast would provide better information about the low; second, that some of the big boats, which had already entered Bass Strait, would share what they were experiencing. Neither happened. The forecast said only that the low was in the eastern part of Bass Strait — and none of the yachts that reported before the *Sword* said anything about their weather. In fact, the most alarming information was the lack of it. *Brindabella* was among several yachts that didn't respond when their names were called. That probably meant their radios weren't working — an all-too-common problem in rough weather — but it could also mean that yachts farther down the track were in serious trouble.

As the sked continued down the alphabetical list of yachts, Kooky was watching the digital readout of the wind. From fifty knots at the start of the sked, it had climbed to sixty-five. Then it touched seventy-three knots, and a few minutes later, seventy-eight. By the time the S's came up, forty-five minutes after the sked had started, the wind was back down to sixty-five, but Kooky was still alarmed.

"Are you going to tell them what we're getting?" Carl Watson asked.

"Yes, I think it makes sense."

The sked is a tedious process in which each yacht reports its latitude and longitude to Lew Carter, who repeats the coordinates for confirmation. Kooky plotted some of their positions on a map. As he did, he realized that the *Sword* had continued to gain on the rest of the fleet and that only six or seven yachts were farther south than it was.

But when the *Sword* was called, Kooky's tone was somber. "I just want to tell you about the weather we're experiencing down here."

Carter responded, "*Sword of Orion*, I would appreciate that for ourselves and all of the fleet, over."

"We have fifty-to-sixty-five-knot westerlies with gusts to seventy-eight knots, over."

Incredulous, Carter asked, "Gusts of seventy-eight knots?"

"Seventy-eight knots!" Kooky affirmed.

Toward the end of the sked, *Yendys*, which was only two miles from the *Sword*, confirmed Kooky's report.

"He's not lying. We're getting the same wind conditions."

During the sked, Lew Carter, who had played the same role during thirteen previous Hobarts, reminded skippers that it was

Larry Ellison's maxi-yacht, *Sayonara*, leads the fleet through Sydney Harbor.

Yachtsmen inspect their rigging before the start.

Sayonara is unloaded from
a Russian cargo ship several
days before the race.

The Cruising Yacht Club
of Australia is located on
Rushcutters Bay,
just a couple of miles
from downtown Sydney.

Larry Ellison, the world's second-richest man, views life as a contest aimed at determining just how good he is.

Rupert and Lachlan Murdoch after Rupert completed the 1995 Hobart on *Sayonara*. The end of Rupert's right index finger had been severed in an accident on the yacht.

Chris Dickson, a veteran of the America's Cup and the around-the-world Whitbread Race, was *Sayonara's* professional skipper.

With Ellison at the wheel, *Sayonara's* spinnaker explodes just after it left Sydney Harbor.

Sayonara and *Brindabella* fight for the lead during the first day of the race.

News Ltd. / Alan Pryke

Peter Bentley / PPL

Rob Kothe (right), the *Sword of Orion*'s owner, was relatively new to sailing, but he desperately wanted to win a Hobart. Steve Kulmar, a successful advertising executive, was one of the *Sword*'s main helmsmen.

News Ltd. / Bob Finlayson

Carl Watson, a forty-five-year-old marine consultant, had sailed in seventeen Hobarts before he joined the *Sword*.

Glyn Charles, a British Olympic sailor, was a late addition to the *Sword*'s crew.

News Ltd. / Jennifer Weisbord

G. Bruce Knecht

Richard Purcell, a tough-minded construction contractor, aboard the *Margaret Rintoul II*.

Darren "Dags" Senogles, the *Sword*'s twenty-eight-year-old bowman, was also responsible for maintaining the yacht.

The "new" *Sword of Orion*. Adam Brown is sitting on the rail closest to the back of the boat. Rob Kothe is next to Brownie.

The *Winston Churchill* leaves Sydney Harbor.

Richard Winning, who derived little satisfaction from his financial success, rebuilt the *Churchill* to prepare it for what he called "gentlemen's ocean racing."

John "Steamer" Stanley, who had sailed in fifteen Hobarts, played a major role in rebuilding the *Churchill* and assembling its crew.

Percy Coverdale built the *Winston Churchill* and was its first owner.

The *Churchill*'s crew in 1945, when it was one of nine yachts to compete in the first Hobart.

John Gibson, a gregarious sixty-five-year-old lawyer who joined the *Churchill*'s crew for his first Hobart.

News Ltd. / Michael Klein

Paul Lumtin, a thirty-one-year-old accountant, was the *Churchill*'s navigator.

News Ltd. / Tracey Haslam

Michael Rynan, a nineteen-year-old known as Beaver, had never spent a night at sea before he sailed on the *Churchill*.

Michael Bannister, who operated a one-man garbage truck, was fifty-two when he joined the *Churchill*'s crew.

John Dean planned to celebrate his forty-seventh birthday while racing to Hobart on the *Churchill*.

Brindabella, George Snow's seventy-five-foot maxi-yacht, was *Sayonara*'s main competition.

Snow — who proclaims that "sailing is more important than business" — and his wife, "Lady Sabrina."

Larry Ellison, who hopes to take the wheel during the America's Cup in 2003, steers *Sayonara*.

Sayonara's crewmen sit on the rail as the wind speed increases.

Roger "Clouds" Badham, one of the world's most respected marine forecasters.

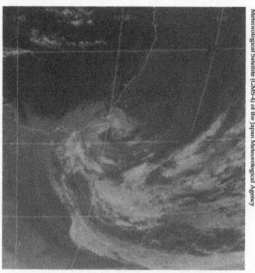

The cyclonic cloud formation Ellison saw on a computer screen. Australia's southeastern coastline is visible through the clouds.

Sayonara after its damaged mainsail was lashed to the boom.

Officers at Australian Search and Rescue plan the largest operation in the agency's history.

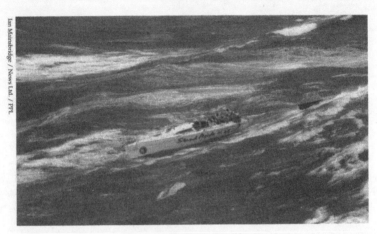

The crew of *Stand Aside*, which was dismasted after a steep wave hurled the yacht into a 360-degree roll, wait to be rescued.

An air force plane searches for a yacht that had broadcast a Mayday.

Helicopter pilot Paul "Tanzi" Lea rescued sailors from the disastrous 1979 Fastnet Race in Britain as well as from the 1998 Hobart. He thought conditions were much worse in 1998.

Brian "Dixie" Lee was responsible for getting his helicopter's cable to yachtsmen.

Petty officer Shane Pashley, thirty-four, joined the navy when he was sixteen.

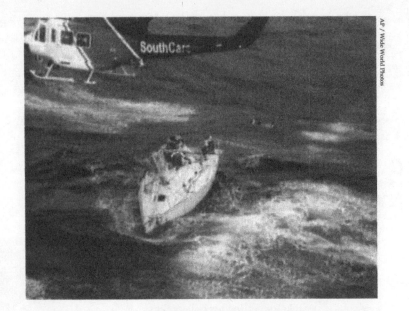

A civilian helicopter
prepares to lower a
cable to another dis-
masted yacht.

A sailor is
lifted to safety.

The sun emerges as *Sayonara* approaches Hobart.

Larry Ellison kisses his girlfriend, romance novelist Melanie Craft, after arriving in Hobart.

A memorial service replaces the usual postrace celebrations.

The son of one of the yachtsmen who died.

Relatives of one of the deceased sailors at the memorial service.

Following the memorial service, a floral wreath was set adrift for each of the sailors who were lost.

their decision whether to continue racing. "The CYC is not responsible for any damage or injury either ashore or at sea," he said. "I ask all skippers, before proceeding into Bass Strait or wherever you're proceeding, to give it your utmost consideration as to what you're doing. And talk about it with your crew."

Carter's warning had an impact. Almost twenty yachts abandoned the race soon after the broadcast. But on the *Sword*, decision making was further delayed because Kooky took on a new assignment, acting as the radio relay for *Team Jaguar*, a sixty-five-foot maxi-yacht that had lost its mast. After the dismasting, its second in as many Hobarts, the crew turned on the engine, which worked only briefly because a line that was hanging over the side wrapped around the propeller shaft. Several crewmen were injured, and without the mast-mounted antenna, its radio signal was too weak to reach Lew Carter. Kooky, who could communicate with both *Young Endeavour* and *Team Jaguar*, offered to relay information to Carter. Kooky knew that whenever a boat is in trouble, nearby vessels are expected to provide any possible assistance. *Team Jaguar* was clearly in distress, and it required Kooky's full-time attention for more than an hour.

On the *Sword*, no one suffered more during that time than Brownie, who had remained at the wheel. Although he didn't anger easily, he was furious, bewildered that no one had offered to relieve him. He was so cold and exhausted that he began pounding on the deck for attention. Even then, there was no reaction. Every minute was an ordeal. His arms were burning with pain, and he knew he was putting everyone at risk by continuing.

Finally, Kulmar appeared on the deck and took the wheel. Brownie had been steering for more than five hours. His muscles were trembling, as was his lower lip, which had turned blue. After Brownie staggered below and sat at the foot of the steps, Kooky thought he was suffering from hypothermia. Or worse. "He's going into shock," Kooky declared. "For Christ's sake, give him something to drink."

But Brownie had enough energy left to vent his fury. "What the fuck is going on down here? This is fucking crazy. It's time to go home."

Once again, Kooky repeated that he had to know where the low was before making a decision, adding that he was stuck on the radio with *Team Jaguar*, too busy to do anything else. Brownie climbed into one of the aft bunks and surrounded his body with a sleeping bag. He held back from telling Kooky what he really thought: *You don't have a clue about the danger we're in. You won't even put your head out on deck — and you're making a mistake that could kill all of us.*

Kooky didn't say everything he was thinking, either. Even though it's the skipper's job to look after his crew's well-being, Kooky blamed Brownie for potentially disabling himself as a helmsman by staying at the wheel for too long.

Thirty minutes after Kulmar took the wheel, Glyn got out of his bunk and told Kooky he wanted to drive. He was still seasick, but he knew there was a shortage of helmsmen. Since he, unlike the other main drivers, was being paid, he felt guilty about not doing more. He also hoped that being in fresh air and having something to do would help him feel better.

Seasickness is an all-encompassing horror of nausea, weakness, and headache that can, in extreme cases, be totally debilitating. For some sailors, it's as ubiquitous as the common cold. Like the cold, there's no sure solution — short of stepping onto land. Some yachtsmen acclimate by sleeping on a boat the night before a race or by taking drugs. Other partial cures include lying down or looking at the horizon. Neither of those therapies held much promise on the *Sword*. The only place to lie down was in the cabin, but the stench of vomit there only encouraged more of the same. Though there was fresh air on deck, the horizon was barely visible.

"How are you feeling?" Kooky asked.

"Well enough to take it on — and I won't be as sick if I'm on deck."

"Okay, but take another seasickness tablet."

"I can't. They won't stay down, but I'll be fine."

After having spent most of the day in a bunk, weakened by seasickness and dehydration and perhaps by the lingering effects of his stomach bug, Glyn was clearly in bad shape. Just before he climbed up the steps to the cockpit, he vomited on Simon Reffold's shoulder.

Taking the wheel from Kulmar, Glyn stared at the waves with open-eyed amazement and asked Kulmar to talk to Kooky. "Doesn't he know that people die in these conditions? You have to do something to get us out of here."

Kulmar climbed below to face Kooky again. "We have to get out of this," he said. "This is unsailable — and it's only getting worse. We have to go back."

Kooky, who was studying a marine chart, responded, "I'll let you know."

While Dags still opposed the idea of turning around, he was troubled by the degree of contrary thinking, particularly among the lead drivers. All of them — Kulmar, Glyn, and Brownie — wanted to quit. Even more to the point, Dags worried about who would steer the boat in conditions that required the most seasoned crew members. Brownie, the only one of the three who wasn't seasick, was a wreck. Like Brownie, Dags believed Kulmar wanted to avoid going on deck. And it was not at all clear that

Glyn could do the job for long. Dags also recognized that there was an emotional component: even if it was impossible to make a truly informed judgment on how to find calmer water or avoid going back into the storm, he knew most of the crew would be comforted by the idea, regardless of its merit, that they were heading toward land.

He also realized that not everyone had as much invested in the race as he and Kooky. For Dags, the race had been his predominate focus for several months; but for the others, he knew that families and careers had greater importance. "Maybe we should go back," a deflated Dags said to Kooky. "We may end up going right back into the worst of it, but everyone's spirits are really down. Going back would give them a lift."

"You may be right," Kooky said. "The last thing I want to do is quit, but it's hard to find logic in hell. This isn't racing anymore — and it is getting worse all the time. Let's do this: if the wind gets up to sixty knots again — and stays there — we go back."

The *Sword* continued.

17

When Lew Carter called the *Winston Churchill*'s name during the 2:05 P.M. sked, it was one of the yachts that failed to respond. At the end of the sked, Carter attempted to reach each of the non-reporting yachts again, asking, "Any sightings or copy on *Winston Churchill*?"

At that point, Michael Bennett, the navigator on *Adrenaline*, got on the radio. "This is *Adrenaline* here," he said. "At the beginning of the sked, we had *Winston Churchill* approximately a mile to the west of us."

Lumpy had set an alarm on the *Churchill*'s anemometer to indicate when the wind speed reached fifty-five knots, and during early Sunday afternoon the high-pitched signal was sounding every ten minutes or so. Glancing at the gauge, Lumpy saw one gust register sixty-eight knots. The waves had grown accordingly, the average ones now as large as a four-story building. Steering had become so arduous that the main helmsmen were swapping positions after just three-quarters of an hour. Steamer and Bruce Gould were already worrying about how they would be able to see the waves when night fell.

"What are we going to do?" Gould asked Steamer. "Should we be thinking about heading toward land?"

"I don't know. It's going to be a dangerous night, but if we head toward land, the waves would be coming over our side."

Winning wasn't overly concerned about the weather or his boat, which he believed to be among the strongest in the fleet. He felt the same way about the crew. When he tried to calculate the total number of Hobarts they had sailed, he concluded that his team was one of the most experienced in the race. He believed that he — and even more so, Steamer and Gould — had sailed for so many years and through so many storms that they were prepared for anything.

Still, when he took the helm, Winning realized just how hard it was to surmount the waves. His biggest fear was a rogue wave. Rogues result from the interplay of wind, current, and other waves. Winning, who estimated that most of the waves were thirty to forty feet high, knew that rogues are often twice as tall as the average wave. With high winds, at least one out of every thousand waves is a rogue. With about three hundred waves passing every hour, he also knew that running into one was a matter of time and chance.

If he did, he knew that even an experienced crew and seasoned yacht could be no match.

PART III

THE BLACK CLOUD

18

Sayonara entered Bass Strait just before dawn on Sunday. By mid-morning, Tony Rae, who was sitting in the cockpit, was amazed that the wind hadn't died down yet. When he saw a gust register sixty-three knots on the jumbo, he realized that he had never experienced wind so strong. During *months* of Whitbread racing, the wind had never topped sixty knots.

In the cabin below, Ellison was talking to Phil Kiely, the forty-four-year-old head of Oracle's operations in Australia and Ellison's second guest for the race. When Kiely, who grew up in Sydney, was being recruited by Oracle four years earlier, the possibility of sailing on his ultimate boss's yacht was dangled before him as an enticement. The executive who hired Kiely no longer worked at Oracle, so a couple of months before the race, Kiely sent an e-mail to Ellison — whom Kiely had met only once — asking if he could sail to Hobart on *Sayonara*. He mentioned that he had completed two Hobarts on much smaller boats, and within a couple of days Ellison responded with an invitation.

On board, Ellison said, "Just think about the little boats back there. They must be having a miserable time."

Kiely agreed, but when he went on deck a little later, the clouds appeared to be breaking up. A portion of the sky was blue, but the sea remained a monochrome white-gray, broken only by occasional white streaks. Justin Clougher was captivated by the contrast between the polar sea and blue sky. Seeing that Kiely, who had sat down next to him on the rail, had his head down, Clougher gently prodded him with an elbow and said, "Don't forget to look around. When you get up to the top of a wave, it's actually quite beautiful — and you need to remember this for when you're back at Oracle, sitting through a boring meeting in your ergonomic chair."

What a bizarre thing to say, Kiely said to himself. To him, the sea looked like a bleak, inhospitable wilderness. But after a few minutes, his perspective changed. "I never thought about it that way," he said to Clougher, "but you're right: it is beautiful. It's Mother Nature in all her glory."

By early afternoon, the portion of the sky that was blue had expanded and the wind had dropped to twenty-five knots, offering Robbie Naismith and Tony Rae, both of whom had worked as sailmakers before they were selected for Team New Zealand, a chance to repair *Sayonara*'s mainsail. Starting at about one o'clock, Naismith and Rae positioned themselves on either side of the sail. Able to see each other through semitransparent Mylar, for the next two hours they forced a huge needle, followed by waxed thread, back and forth between them until they covered the length of the rip.

Just after the repair began, *Brindabella* became visible. At that point, twenty-four hours after the start of the race, it was about three miles behind *Sayonara*. By the time the sewing was completed, *Brindabella* had cut the distance in half. "They must have had some problems, too," Joey Allen said, "but they're hanging in pretty well."

The wind speed continued to drop until it was only ten to twelve knots. It felt like nothing. Once again, Ellison believed

Sayonara had passed through a front and that the worst was over. Returning to racing mode, he thought they should put up a larger jib to arrest *Brindabella's* gains. "Why don't we put the heavy number one back up," he said to Brad Butterworth, who was at the helm. Butterworth thought putting up the big jib was probably premature — that the sudden calm might not last — but he didn't feel strongly enough to object. "Okay, let's get it up."

Leaving the deck, Ellison climbed below. The thought that he had made it through the storm was an enormous relief. It didn't last long, though.

"The wind's coming back — and it's coming back strong!" he heard Butterworth scream from above. "Get the fucking jib down!"

Within minutes, the wind skyrocketed from less than fifteen knots to more than forty. As *Sayonara* was pushed over on its side, Ellison grabbed for something to hold on to and made his way to the nav station. Even with the water damage, Rudiger's instruments and computers were still working. On one of the computer screens, Ellison saw what looked like a hurricane.

"We didn't go through a front," Ellison exclaimed. "We're in the eye of a hurricane!!"

19

At about four o'clock, Kooky's requirement for giving up the race — sixty knots — was met and surpassed as the wind reached close to seventy. By then, the yacht was ninety miles from Eden. In racing terms, the *Sword* was still doing extremely well. On a corrected-time basis, Kooky estimated that the *Sword* was in fifth or sixth place. He also thought he was likely to move ahead of at least some of the other boats because the *Sword* was relatively close to the coast, which would enable it to take advantage of the more westerly breeze he believed would develop later. Even so, he told Kulmar he was prepared to give up. "It's up to the helmsmen. If they want to go back, we'll go back."

Kulmar already knew what Brownie and Glyn would say, but he quickly checked with both of them before telling Kooky it was unanimous. Kulmar wasn't really satisfied, though. *We should have done this at 9:00 A.M.*, he said to himself. *We were just twenty miles from Eden then.*

"Fine, let's do it," Kooky said.

"But where are we going to go?" Dags interjected. "We can't head directly to Eden. That would put the waves behind us."

Hunched over a map, Kooky suggested that they head to the west, which would take them roughly in the direction of Melbourne, until it was safe to turn toward Eden. Actually, he hoped it would be a temporary move. As soon as the wind abated, Kooky intended to resume racing. If the storm ended soon enough and the wind direction changed in the way he believed it would, he thought the Sword might still win the race on adjusted time.

At 4:44 P.M. Kooky announced the Sword's retirement over the radio. He hoped others would make the same decision, in part for their own good and also because it could help the Sword's competitive position if it was later able to rejoin the race.

A few minutes after Kooky's call, Lew Carter made an ominous broadcast that sounded like a legalistic disclaimer. "I just want to remind you that all those taking part in CYC races do so at their own risk and responsibility," Carter said, quoting from the race rules. "The CYC is not responsible for the seaworthiness of a yacht whose entry is accepted, or the sufficiency or adequacy of its equipment. The CYC is not responsible for any damage or injury, either ashore or at sea either to persons or yachts which might result from participating in club races. Attention is drawn to rule four. A boat is solely responsible for deciding whether to start or to continue racing."

Immediately after that broadcast, Brownie got out of his bunk and told Kooky, "I'll take the helm when we turn around."

Kooky said no. "Glyn's already on the wheel, and he can do it. He's okay with it."

Dags started the engine and then went back on deck to talk to Glyn about the new course and how to redirect the boat amid the mammoth seas. Glyn already had a plan. "I'll wait for a big wave," he said. "As soon as we're over the top, I'll turn the wheel hard as we go down the other side. There'll be less wind between the waves, and we should be able to get around pretty fast."

"That sounds good," Dags replied. "I'll use the engine to keep our momentum up. Since you'll have the wheel, I'll handle the throttle." Although putting the engine in gear would normally disqualify a yacht, it doesn't when it's used only as a safety measure. If the *Sword* rejoined the race later, Kooky would simply tell the race committee how the engine was used, and he was confident that the committee wouldn't object.

The *Sword* was traveling beneath a huge black blanket of clouds. The surface of the sea was light gray, scored by wispy veins of white. Being on deck was painful. The wind was ripping through the rigging, producing a constant high-pitched shriek that sounded like a distant human voice. And having created the waves, the wind had gone into battle with them, shaving off the foam at their peaks and creating a jet stream of moisture that looked like smoke. The droplets slapped Glyn and Dags with skin-stinging speed.

All the waves were huge, but after letting several pass, Glyn, squinting to give the salt water less of an opportunity to punish his eyes, judged one to be larger than the others. "This is the one," he shouted. The angle of the *Sword* increased dramatically as it climbed the thirty-five-foot wave. Just before it reached the top, Glyn pulled at the wheel, hand over hand. As the *Sword* passed over the crest and began to tilt forward, the rudder briefly came out of the water, rendering it useless. When it resubmerged a couple of seconds later, the *Sword* carved a tight arc as it skidded down the wave, and by the time it reached the valley, it was on a new course. Although Dags put the engine in forward gear, Glyn didn't need the help. The *Sword* had maintained forward momentum throughout.

"Great job," Dags shouted, exuberantly slapping Glyn on the shoulder. "That was perfect. Absolutely perfect."

Glyn said thanks, but nothing else. A few minutes later, Dags turned off the engine, even though he had already begun to worry about Glyn's ability to drive the boat. Rather than steering the westerly course they had talked about, he was heading north.

"How are you feeling?" Dags asked.

Glyn admitted to feeling terrible and then went on to say how bad he felt about not putting in more time at the wheel. "I haven't done my job. I've let the team down."

"No, that's not true. Shit happens. If you're not feeling well, it's not your fault. There's nothing you can do about it."

The waves were no larger than before the *Sword* changed course, but they were far more dangerous. The previous course to the south had taken the *Sword* almost directly into them. With that angle to the waves, the *Sword* wouldn't have capsized unless it failed to make it over one of them or it was struck by a rogue. The almost northerly course Glyn was steering would take the *Sword* directly to Eden, but it meant the waves were hitting the yacht from the rear or slightly to the side. That meant the *Sword* was doing exactly what Dags had desperately wanted to avoid — surfing. He thought the speed was dangerous, vastly increasing the chances that the boat would go out of control and roll upside down.

Glyn wasn't really looking at the waves. Having cinched the cord in the hood of his rain jacket so tightly around his face that he looked as if he were wearing blinders, he seemed to be paying more attention to the instruments.

Dags, not sure what to do, shouted over the wind, "Do you want me to steer?"

With his eyes focused on the compass, Glyn replied, "No, I can do it. It makes me feel better."

Almost pleading, Dags said, "But you can't steer this way. We have to go into the waves."

Glyn's visibility was also constrained by the boom. Before they changed course, it had been tied down to the port side of the deck, which had been the downwind side. On the new course, it crossed Glyn's field of vision, so Dags wanted to move it to the other side. With help from Watson and Brownie, he picked it up and moved it over the top of the wheel to the starboard side. The boom extended almost three feet past the wheel, so as it was moved, Glyn took a couple of steps backward to get out of the way. Dags then used a cord made of Spectra, a superstrong synthetic material, to lash the back end of the boom to a metal fixture screwed to the deck, not far from one of the stanchions that had been damaged during the collision with *Nokia*. Once the boom was secured, Watson and Brownie went back below, leaving only Glyn and Dags on deck. Glyn was standing on the port side of the cockpit, and Dags was just in front of him.

Glyn was obviously miserable. His jacket was equipped with rubber seals around his neck and wrists, which were supposed to keep water from getting inside, but a steady stream of water was trickling down his back and chest, causing him to tremble with cold. "This gear is worthless," he said bitterly. "I'm completely wet. I wish we could just get out of here."

Dags still didn't know what to do. He believed Glyn needed to be forcibly told to steer a different course — or he needed to be relieved. It was, Dags thought, a job for Kooky — but he was still below, seemingly chained to the nav station. He hadn't ventured on deck all day.

"You have to stop surfing," Dags insisted. "Why don't you let someone else steer?"

Glyn said nothing.

Dags wasn't the only crewman who was worried about Glyn's steering. As the *Sword* accelerated down another wave, Simon Reffold said to Carl Watson, "We're going too fast. He's putting the waves behind us." Watson agreed, and went to talk to Glyn.

Clipping his harness onto the safety line, he made his way to the back of the boat. "Glyn, your course is too low — you have to come up so we can keep the boat on track. We need to keep heading into the waves."

"Don't worry," Glyn replied without making eye contact. "I had friends who died in the Fastnet Race. I know what to do."

Watson returned below, assuming that Glyn would adopt a safer approach. But he didn't. Although Dags continued to shout warnings for the biggest waves and point to where they were coming from, Glyn appeared to pay no attention.

Less than half an hour after they had turned around, Brownie decided he had to do something. Each time the *Sword* picked up speed, he thought the boat was about to spin totally out of control. Twice, he braced himself against rides that he thought would end in capsizing. Furious, he pulled himself up from his bunk and half shouted at Kooky, "We can't steer the boat this way! We have to get Glyn to head more to the west, or we have to get someone else to steer."

Kooky, believing that Brownie was still on the verge of shock and overreacting, said, "It's okay. Glyn knows what he's doing."

"No, he doesn't," said Brownie, who was becoming even more agitated. "We have to head into the waves, or we're going to be in major trouble."

Turning away from Kooky, Brownie stood on the second step so his head reached into the cockpit. "For fuck's sake, turn into the waves," he shouted to Glyn. "You can't do this anymore."

Even though the wheel was just a few feet from the hatch, Glyn and Dags couldn't understand what Brownie was saying, so Dags slid forward in the cockpit until he was sitting near Brownie. "What the fuck is he doing?" Brownie screamed. "We have to change course. It doesn't matter where we're heading, but we can't let the waves hit us like this."

It was already too late. Before Brownie said another word, a monstrous wave — it was at least forty feet high and steeper than the ones preceding it — lifted the *Sword*. It had come from behind the yacht, slightly from the port side, and seconds after the *Sword* began to ride upward, the wave began to break. When the tumbling white water caught up to the boat, it turned the yacht sideways to the wave and made it impossible for Glyn to steer. At the same time, the torrent of white water tipped the *Sword* onto its starboard side. As it fell down the wave, the boat tipped farther on its side, so far that the mast was parallel to the surface of the sea. After the hull crashed into the trough, the momentum forced the *Sword* to capsize.

Just before Dags submerged, he looked back toward the wheel but saw nothing but turbulent water. He was connected to the *Sword* by his safety tether, which was secured to the deck at one end and to a harness wrapped around his chest at the other. Although the tether saved him from being washed away from the yacht, it then pulled him underwater. Holding his breath and trying not to panic, Dags was seized by a horrifying thought: *If I don't disconnect the tether, it will hold me here until I drown.* His hands fumbled with the clasp at the end of the tether, which was locked to his harness. He didn't need to see the clasp; he had opened and shut it hundreds of times. But in spite of his frenzied pulling and tugging, there was so much tension against the tether that he couldn't release it. Suddenly, the inverted hull, hit by another wave, began to twist, turning until it completed a 360-degree roll, still dragging Dags along by his tether. When the *Sword* returned to its upright position, he was floating in the water, still connected to the *Sword*. It was lurching side to side, giving Dags, energized with adrenaline, a chance to grab at a stanchion and pull himself back on board. Once there, he saw that the mast had fallen. The rigging — a tangled mess of metal, lines, and wires — was wrapped around the port side of the boat like spaghetti. The top half of the aluminum steering wheel had been sheared off.

Something else was missing.

Where was Glyn?

At first, Dags guessed that he was in the water, connected to the yacht but unable to hoist himself onto the deck. Then he saw Glyn's orange tether. One end was still attached to the deck, but at the other there was only frayed nylon. Glyn's clasp wasn't attached to what remained of his tether. Looking up, Dags saw a small figure in the water, thirty feet away. Frozen but then bursting, Dags emptied his lungs.

"Man overboard! Help! Man overboard!" Down below, Steve Kulmar hit the MAN OVERBOARD button on the GPS, marking the spot where Glyn had gone over.

Dags didn't take his eyes off of Glyn, but his mind raced with questions. *Can he swim to us? Should I swim after him? Should I tie a line around myself first? Can we get the boat to him? Will the engine start?*

In fact, not only was the mast gone but the rigging was under the boat, so turning on the engine, even if it did work, wouldn't have gotten them very far; the lines that were in the water would wrap around the propeller, stopping the engine. And given what had happened to the wheel, steering would have been impossible. Dags scrambled to throw a life ring toward Glyn, but it went almost nowhere against the wind. Even without a mast or sails, the *Sword* was being pushed away from Glyn, who, with only his head exposed to the wind, appeared to be almost stationary except for the way he was riding up and down the waves. He wasn't wearing a life preserver. Like everyone else on the *Sword*, he had been relying on his tether.

"Swim, Glyn!" Dags screamed. "Come on, Glyn. You can do it. Swim!"

Glyn's eyes were wide open, and Dags believed they were focused on him. He assumed that Glyn had heard his cries because he began to swim. But he took just six half strokes, using only his left arm, before he stopped. His face was locked in a grimace, perhaps because of pain or perhaps because he couldn't understand his predicament or why Dags wasn't coming to get him. Dags couldn't believe what he was seeing, either. Like yachtsmen everywhere, he had been trained not to swim after someone who had gone overboard, certainly not without being tied to the yacht by a line: the chances that a would-be rescuer could swim to his target and bring him back to safety were too small. But bouncing back and forth on the balls of his feet while keeping his eyes trained on Glyn, Dags believed he had no option but to go into the water. Brownie was the first man from below to climb on deck. "Glyn's in the water," Dags screamed. "I've got to get him. Get me a long line. I'm going in."

Although Glyn was already fifty feet from the boat, Brownie didn't have any trouble spotting him. He looked small, utterly helpless.

Finding the long lines that controlled the spinnaker, Brownie knotted them together. He tied one end to Dags and the other to the deck. Each of the lines was eighty feet long, but Brownie already had second thoughts. He was afraid that by the time Dags swam to Glyn, the lines might not be long enough to cover the rapidly expanding gap between Glyn and the *Sword*. Even if they were, Brownie worried that their weight would make it impossible for Dags to keep himself and Glyn above water. From the water, it would be difficult for Dags to even see Glyn through the waves. But Dags wanted to go. Immediately. He had been trying to strip off his foul-weather gear until he gave up, deciding that he didn't have time. Brownie knew that the extra clothing would make it even more difficult to reach Glyn.

"You won't get to him," Brownie said. "It's too late."

"No! I have to go. I have to."

Dags was breathing hard, almost hyperventilating, and tears were already rolling down his cheeks. Brownie also felt the weight of what was happening, but recognizing that two lives were in his hands, he was trying to be as rational as possible. He thought one life was probably already lost, and he was beginning to believe that Dags too would be doomed if he went into the water. After a wave increased the distance to Glyn by what looked like another twenty feet, Brownie was certain. Grabbing the chest straps of Dags's harness, he looked into his friend's eyes.

"You're not going. You'll never get there. There's no way you can get to him."

Realizing that Brownie was probably right, Dags didn't argue. He just stood near the back of the cockpit, staring at Glyn. By then, several other members of the crew were on the deck, all of them doing the same thing.

"Who is it?" Nigel Russell asked.

"It's Glyn," Brownie told him. "And there's no way for us to get him."

Glyn was already having a hard time keeping his head above water, and everyone quickly reached the same unthinkable conclusion — Glyn was going to die, and there was nothing they could do but watch. Andrew Parkes fired off two parachute flares. Given the low-altitude clouds, they were unlikely to be seen by another boat, but he hoped that Glyn would see them.

For most of the *Sword*'s crew, there was a strange sense of unreality about all of this, although not because there was anything abstract about it. They could still see Glyn, and they knew how easily they could be in precisely the same position. Steve Kulmar was more shaken than anyone. When he first came on deck, he believed Glyn was looking directly back at him. Unlike the others, who had met Glyn only a day earlier, Kulmar, who had sailed with Glyn before and introduced him to Kooky, was looking at a friend. For him, survivor's guilt arrived like a lightning bolt. *This wouldn't have happened if I hadn't asked Glyn to come with us*, he said to himself. Kulmar wasn't sharing his thoughts with anyone. In fact, he didn't utter a single word. He was withdrawing into a paralyzing state of shocked disbelief.

Just ten minutes after the roll, it was becoming more difficult to see Glyn. His head submerged into each of the passing waves, and it seemed to be taking him longer to get back to the surface.

"I can't see him anymore," Dags cried out. "We're losing him."

20

Richard Winning had never seen a bigger wave. It was a few minutes after five o'clock, almost exactly the same time that the *Sword* capsized, and he was looking at a curling mass of water that appeared to be twice as high as the preceding waves. Winning thought it was at least eighty feet tall. But it was the shape of the wave that really concerned him. All the waves that had been pummeling the *Churchill* had been steep and muscular. But now, from his perspective at the helm, it looked as though he was heading toward a monumental version of a beach wave that was about to break.

There was nowhere to hide.

Winning grasped the wheel not only to steer but to stay on his feet. Cocking his head sideways to the more than fifty knots of wind, he tried to preserve his vision against the airborne salt water. Winning believed that there was a proper procedure for everything — all he had to do was follow it. Yet halfway up the wave, the slope seemed impossibly vertical, and Winning realized that even flawless helmsmanship might not be enough. The wave began to break well before the *Churchill* reached the peak. The leading edge of the roiling white water poured over the boat. The *Churchill* stopped moving forward, lurched backward, and then was spun by the rush of water until it was parallel to the wave. Caught in the breaking water, the yacht was hurled onto its side, so far over that the mast was horizontal as the *Churchill* slid down the face of the wave. White water engulfed the deck and the yacht fell farther on its side — now more than ninety degrees over, so far that the top of the mast went below the surface of the water.

Winning desperately tried to hang on to the wheel, but as the *Churchill* approached the trough, he knew he was no longer on board. The water pounding against his body seemed to be coming from every direction. At first, the motion and the noise overwhelmed his senses, but then he felt the tug of his safety tether. If it failed, he knew he would be lost. Even if the tether held, he could drown; he believed that this was the most likely outcome.

But seconds later, the *Churchill's* heavy keel did exactly what it was designed to do. As it righted the yacht, Winning was hoisted out of the water, and the next thing he knew, he was dangling from the *Churchill's* backstay, a cable running between the top of the mast and the back of the boat. John Dean, who had been standing on deck next to Winning, was in the same position. While they were being tossed about in the water, their tethers had obviously become entangled, and now the two men found that their tethers had wrapped around the backstay. Winning, his feet hanging three feet above the deck, was amazed to see that the mast was still standing, but he knew his yacht was foundering. Things were so chaotic that he and Dean hardly had time to realize that, although no longer in the water, they were in perhaps an even more dangerous situation. Lashed to the backstay they resembled heretics fastened to a stake. If the boat capsized, they would be held underwater. In a daze, Winning cried out for help.

"Steamer! We're in a lot of trouble here!"

Steamer knew. He had been lying in a bunk in a small cabin near the stern when the *Churchill* collided with the enormous wave. When he felt the yacht begin to fall, he tried to get up. He was immediately thrown to the floor, and then three portholes on the side of the cabin imploded, admitting a torrent of water. The blast of seawater pinned him to the floor, stuck under the table that normally held navigational charts.

The other crewmen were in the main cabin. For them, the *Churchill's* descent down the wave ended with a crash so loud that it sounded as if their boat had struck another vessel. As they picked themselves up from where they had been thrown, they were shouting in pain and confusion. Evidence of the *Churchill's* downfall appeared in a kaleidoscope of images. The floorboards, heavy nine-foot-long planks, had been knocked out of place, exposing the bilge, and the wineglass-shaped cavity was filling with water. Boxes of cereal, apples, and clothes were floating on the surface along with a box of Band-Aids and a life preserver.

Gibbo, who moments earlier had been stowing gear, trying to do something about the clutter that had accumulated since the race began twenty-eight hours earlier, was launched from one side of the cabin to the other, where his head met an exposed bolt. Standing, he realized that the warm fluid on his forehead was blood. His mind was racing: *What should I do?* Assuming that the mast had collapsed — rendering the boat impossible to sail — his first thought was that he should turn on the *Churchill's* big diesel engine, which would power the bilge pump. Gibbo regularly raced his own yacht in Sydney Harbor, but among the *Churchill's* crew he was relatively junior and inexperienced. He rushed to the engine's control panel in the back of the cabin, but then hesitated. He decided he'd better not do anything until Steamer and Winning, the real decision makers, regained control.

It took six minutes for Steamer, the first man to climb on deck, to free Winning and Dean. With no momentum of its own, the *Churchill* was even more vulnerable to the waves, and the violent tossing made it hard for Steamer to stand, let alone unwind the tethers from the rigging. When the job was completed, Steamer knew exactly what he had to do.

"We've got to get the boat started," Steamer told Winning. "You go down into the coach house and turn on the engine so we can get the bilge pump going. I'll go down and turn the valves."

The *Churchill* was equipped with three bilge pumps, but two of them were hand-operated devices that didn't work very well. The engine-powered bilge pump was the one that counted. Down below, while Winning made his way to the engine control panel, Steamer turned two valves to activate the pump. But when Winning turned the key, the engine only sputtered for a few seconds and then went silent. It was too late. The main batteries were on the port side of the boat, and they were partly underwater, unable to provide enough power.

Gibbo was furious with himself. He knew that if he had started the motor minutes before, it would have continued to run — and drive the bilge pump — even if the electrical system became inundated with water.

Steamer knew some of the water was coming through the broken portholes, but he thought there had to be a much larger source. He frantically opened cabinets and emptied their contents so he could see sections of the hull where a plank might have been dislodged. He couldn't find a breach, but he was sure something catastrophic had happened below the waterline. *Maybe*, he thought, *the base of the mast punched a hole in the bottom. Or did we spring one of the planks near the keel?* Steamer knew the water level was continuing to rise, and he was becoming convinced that the boat was likely to sink, perhaps very quickly. Scooping up several life preservers, he carried them onto the deck, where most of the crew had assembled in the cockpit.

"How bad is it?" Winning asked.

"It's going to go," Steamer responded. In a calm matter-of-fact tone that seemed entirely at odds with the circumstances, he added, "We need to get the life rafts up on deck."

Bruce Gould was attempting to steer the broken vessel, but the waves were doing most of the driving, sometimes spinning the *Churchill* around so much that all Gould could do was surf the waves rather than head into them. He knew it wasn't the best course, but the *Churchill* had taken on so much water that he couldn't do anything else.

After Steamer told Winning that he should broadcast a Mayday, Gould added, "Don't just fucking say it's a Mayday. I want them to understand that this is goddamn serious — that we're getting the life rafts on deck."

Foaming waves were cascading into the cockpit. When one wave broke over the back of the boat, sending a torrent of water down the hatch, Gould yelled, "One more like that and we're gone!"

He regretted his words instantly. He knew that fear is an infectious disease, one that can quickly degenerate into debilitating panic. Therefore, he didn't say anything more as he considered a formidable list of worries. If they did launch the *Churchill*'s two life rafts, would they inflate? It was impossible to know whether the cans of compressed air would do their job. And how should the rafts be launched amid massive waves? Could everyone get from the big boat to the rafts without being washed away or slammed against the *Churchill*'s hull?

Down below, all Gibbo could do was wait. The *Churchill* had taken on so much water that the bilge was almost full. Convinced that they wouldn't be in danger of sinking if he had only followed his initial instinct and turned on the engine, he was desperate to make sure he didn't waste any more opportunities. As if preparing for a trip, he tried to think of things that might be useful if they ended up on a raft. He came up with two ideas — his safety tether and a knife. He was already wearing his safety harness, so he attached both ends of the tether to the harness.

Lumpy didn't know what to do. After a sleepless night, he had been passed out on a starboard bunk when the boat crashed and launched him across the cabin. When he picked himself up from the floor, he saw a book he had borrowed from his sister-in-law, *Tommo and Hawk*, floating next to a sneaker. Worried more about his sister-in-law's reaction to the damaged book than anything else, he placed the swollen volume on a bunk, spreading its covers, hoping to start the drying process. He then looked for his foul-weather gear, which he found near the bow. By the time he crawled through a small passage that connected the main cabin to the small cabin where Steamer had been and which housed the *Churchill*'s navigational equipment and radios, Winning was already there, trying to use the radio.

Most of the electrical equipment wasn't working. The printer was dangling by its electrical cord. One of the radio handsets was floating in the water that covered the floor of the cabin. Drawers were opened and emptied. The navigational charts and the log were gone. The GPS was mounted above the desk, well above the water, but it showed no signs of life. As bad as things were, though, Lumpy was startled when Winning said he was going to issue a Mayday and asked, "Where the hell are we?"

"I have no idea, I was asleep — and the GPS is dead."

"Bloody useless piece of equipment," Winning cursed. "Where's the handheld GPS?"

Crawling back to the main cabin, Lumpy found the portable GPS on a shelf. Turning it on and trying to shield it from the rain that was pouring through the hatch, he waited for it to acquire satellite signals and calculate a location. It failed to pick up even one satellite.

When Lumpy told him that the GPS wasn't working, Winning decided he'd better not broadcast estimated coordinates because they would cause search-and-rescue aircraft to confine their search too narrowly. "I reckon we're twenty miles southeast of Twofold Bay," he told Lumpy.

Winning still wasn't convinced the *Churchill* would sink. "When Percy Coverdale built the boat," he told Lumpy, "he put a lot of concrete in the keel. The guy who owned it before me swapped the concrete for lead." Hypothesizing that the lead took up less space than the concrete and that the leftover volume was sealed and filled with air or some kind of buoyant material, Winning thought the yacht would wallow at the surface even if it filled with water. Even so, he was worried. With overcast skies and only a few hours of daylight remaining, he realized how difficult it would be for rescuers to spot a foundering yacht — or worse, life rafts — without a more precise position. He wasn't even sure he would be able to get a message out. The high frequency radio was stuck on the channel that was used to receive weather faxes. Using the very high frequency radio, which has much less range, Winning began broadcasting.

"Mayday. Mayday. Here is the yacht *Winston Churchill* ..."

A few miles away, Gary Ticehurst was piloting the Australian Broadcasting Corporation's helicopter over another troubled yacht, *Stand Aside*, ready to film the rescue of its crew by a second helicopter. As Peter Davidson, the "designated tea bag," was lowered in a sling from the rescue chopper into the water, not far from where a sailor was sitting in a life raft tied to the yacht, a forty-foot wave slammed into him. Returning to the surface, Davidson was thirty feet from his target. Davidson fought his way back to the raft and hoisted himself onto it, but it promptly overturned and flew away, hurled by the blasting wind, leaving Davidson and the sailor flailing in the waves.

Ticehurst had covered sixteen Hobarts, but he had never seen anything like this. "Mate," he said to his cameraman, "this is award-winning stuff! You realize that, don't you? Pity we aren't going to be here. We have to get some fuel!"

Below them, Davidson finally managed to get the rescue sling over the yachtsman's head and signaled so with a thumbs-up. The two men were attached to the wire and each other, but as soon as they rose out of the water, trouble again struck. The helicopter was too far upwind, and they were launched sideways, as if fired by a circus cannon, directly into the face of another wave. As they were finally lifted toward the rescue chopper, Ticehurst checked his fuel gauge and calculated whether he could stay a little longer. Even though he was running dangerously low, he was desperate to record one more rescue, and he decided to give himself another few minutes.

Starting his second rescue attempt, Davidson touched down on the top of one wave and then bounced across the water as if he were a skipping stone. Flying almost directly over the top of the raft, he finally submerged about thirty feet away from it. It was then — at 5:21 P.M., less than half an hour after the *Churchill* crashed off the wave — that Ticehurst suddenly heard a voice over the radio. It came in strongly, although it was muffled, as if it were coming from outer space.

"Mayday. Mayday. Mayday. Here is the *Winston Churchill*."

It was Richard Winning, speaking slowly and with grave deliberation. To the cameraman, Ticehurst said, "Record, mate! Record!" Assured that a tape recorder that was built into the camera was already running, Ticehurst responded.

"*Winston Churchill. Winston Churchill.* This is the ABC chopper. Go ahead with your position, over."

Ticehurst heard shouting in the background, but he couldn't make out any words until Winning gave his position as "twenty miles southeast of Twofold Bay." Ticehurst repeated the position and asked Winning to confirm that this was an actual Mayday.

"Affirmative. We are getting the life rafts on deck. We are holed. We are taking on water rapidly."

Ticehurst relayed the information to Australian Search and Rescue. When he tried to raise Winning a couple of minutes later, there was no response. Given the strength of the *Churchill*'s radio signal, Ticehurst believed he must have been within a few miles of the yacht. But glancing at his fuel gauge, he realized he had to turn toward shore. Someone would have to find the *Churchill*, but it wouldn't be him.

21

On the *Sword of Orion*, Kooky was at the nav station, frantically broadcasting Mayday calls. He knew someone was in the water, but no one had told him who it was.

When the boat rolled, Kooky had fallen to the floor. The steps Brownie had been standing on as he spoke to Dags gave way, and Brownie as well as the steps crashed down on top of Kooky. After the boat rolled back upright, Brownie got up quickly; there was a stinging pain around his shoulder, and he realized he must have fractured it. Kooky didn't move. So disoriented that he thought he was underwater, he was lying motionless, partly covered by a bag of wet sails, holding his breath.

Carl Watson, seeing Kooky's bloated cheeks, assumed that the *Sword*'s owner was either unconscious or dead. Tapping his shoulder, Watson asked, "Are you okay?"

Realizing he wasn't underwater, Kooky released his breath and asked, "What happened? Something's wrong with my leg."

"Anything else?"

"Nothing — it's just my left leg. It must be broken."

After Watson helped him get back to the nav station, Kooky saw that his yellow computer was destroyed. Smoke was seeping out of its portals. Reaching under the desk, he pulled the emergency position indicating radio beacon, or EPIRB — a device that can transmit a distress signal and approximate position — out from its bracket, switched it on, and asked Watson to secure it to the deck. Kooky also recorded the *Sword*'s coordinates. If he could contact a helicopter quickly, he thought it might be able to pluck the missing man from the sea. But when he tried it, the main radio, the long-distance HF set, emitted sparks and a crackling noise and then died. The VHF radio, which normally had a range of fifteen to twenty-five miles, appeared to be working, but since the mast-mounted aerial was gone, he knew its signal would have little strength. But it was all he had, so Kooky tuned the VHF radio to channel 16, the international designated distress frequency.

"Mayday. Mayday. Mayday. This is the *Sword of Orion*. We have a man overboard."

After several minutes of frantic but futile calls, Kooky asked, "Who did we lose?"

Watson, who was standing in the cabin, up to his knees in water, said, "It's Glyn. There's no way to get him."

Thank God it isn't Dags, Kooky said to himself. He was horrified that anyone was lost, but not only was he much closer to Dags, he believed he needed him to keep the *Sword* afloat.

Water mixed with diesel fuel was sloshing around the inside of the cabin. Watson had already determined that the engine, which was situated just behind the steps, wouldn't start. It had been pushed off its supporting blocks, and the fuel line was cut when the steps fell.

Watson believed the *Sword* was sinking. He wanted, more quickly than the others, he wanted to shift the focus away from Glyn and onto the yacht. "Forget about Glyn," he shouted through the hatch to the cockpit. "We have to worry about ourselves."

When Dags climbed down into the cabin and saw how much water was there, he too believed the *Sword* would sink. There was no time for discussion. He quickly found an emergency aerial for the radio and mounted it on the deck so Kooky's Maydays would have a better chance of being heard. Dags then rushed to remove floorboards and open lockers so he could see more of the hull. Though he didn't find any places where water seemed to be entering, he saw that the bottom of the mast had lifted away from the brackets that were supposed to hold it in the bilge. Watching the base of the aluminum shaft move back and forth, Dags realized it could pierce the hull, creating a hole that would sink the *Sword* in minutes. The ragged metal edges from the top of the mast were also dangerous. They were hanging over the side, scraping against the hull and threatening to gouge a hole. Going back on deck with a pair of wire cutters and a hacksaw, he began to cut all the lines and wires that connected the mast to the yacht so the rigging and mast could be pushed overboard.

Kulmar wasn't doing anything. Sitting near the front of the cockpit, he appeared to be in a trance. Convinced that the *Sword* was going to roll again — and that the next one would cause the boat to sink — he didn't want to go below. He just sat near the hatch, staring into the distance.

The crew knew Kulmar wasn't himself, but they didn't realize how far gone he was. Semiconscious, Kulmar was struggling with an extraordinary sense of dislocation. At one point he felt himself rising above the boat to a place where he could see everything that was happening but wasn't playing a role in any of it. When Nigel Russell, who was helping Dags free the rigging, asked Kulmar to find a screwdriver, he made no response. "If you're not going to help," Russell growled as he went below to get the tool himself, "at least get out of my way!" Again, Kulmar said nothing.

Back on deck, Russell and Dags methodically cut through lines and wires. The hacksaw was the only device capable of getting through the metal rods that were part of the rigging, but holding the saw in place was difficult, and the whole procedure took half an hour. Russell had pushed a broken mast over the side of another boat, and he remembered how that boat had lurched when the weight was off-loaded. Therefore, as he and Dags shoved the mast over the side, Russell shouted, "Hang on, the rig's going over!" They then braced themselves.

22

After the *Winston Churchill* fell off the wave, Beaver, who had been sleeping on the floor of the main cabin, woke up lying on the stove, his head between two burners.

"My God, what happened?" he screamed.

"Don't worry," Michael Bannister responded. "We're going to be all right — whatever happens."

Seeing how much water was in the boat, Beaver didn't believe him. When he heard Winning broadcasting the Mayday, he understood just how serious the situation was. Beaver had recently passed an examination that allowed him to operate small commercial boats, and he knew what a Mayday meant — imminent danger.

Going above, Beaver sat down in the cockpit and grasped a stanchion as tightly as he could. His eyes and mind were stuck on the contrast between the size of the waves and the size of the boat until he spotted something even more frightening. The *Churchill* had wooden ribs that extended from the bottom of the hull to a foot and a half above the deck. They were separated from one another by sixteen inches. Horizontal planks were attached to the section of the ribs that reached above the deck, creating a knee-high wall that went all the way around the perimeter of the deck. Beaver saw that an eight-foot-long section of the horizontal planks was missing from the port side of the yacht near the stern. Not only was the planking gone, but the heavy ribs had been sheared away. If the roll was powerful enough to destroy the ribs, Beaver knew that planks easily could have broken loose below the waterline. And that would mean the boat was headed for the bottom.

Down below, Gibbo and Steamer were struggling to pull the two life rafts out from a shelf under the steps while maintaining their footing as the yacht bucked and turned. After they carried the rafts up and tied them to the deck, Steamer decided that the boat was still sailing far too fast to deploy them.

"We need to get the storm jib down," he shouted.

"I'll do that," Bannister said. After releasing the halyard that held up the jib, he carefully made his way to the bow and pulled down the last sail.

Gibbo, who was sitting in the cockpit several feet in front of the wheel, didn't understand why Winning and Steamer were taking so long to do what to him appeared inevitable — abandon ship. Gould knew why. Many of the most important principles of yachting are developed through experience, and one of the great lessons of the disastrous 1979 Fastnet Race was that sailors must stay with their boats until they don't have a choice. Several of the men who drowned in 1979 were on life rafts that had been launched from yachts that ultimately stayed afloat. If they had simply stayed on their boats and waited for rescuers, they probably would have survived.

* * *

"We're not going until we have to step up to the fucking raft," Gould declared. "The boat may not sink. They always find the boat. Sometimes they can't find a life raft."

By 5:45 P.M., less than three-quarters of an hour after the violent wave had struck, no one had to be told that it was time to get into the life rafts. Sections of the deck were underwater. Unable to exercise any control over the yacht, Gould released the wheel for the last time. Winning gathered up several signal flares.

"Are we going to decide who goes into which raft and who will captain them?" Jim Lawler asked Steamer.

"Don't worry about it," Steamer told him. "Let's just get our asses into a raft."

In fact, though, Steamer had already decided on one of his companions. Much more so than for the other, older men he had invited to join the crew, Steamer felt responsible for Beaver. To Steamer, the thought that the teenager might fail to make it back home was more horrible than anything else. He didn't care who else joined him, but his raft was going to include Beaver.

Lumpy was sitting next to the smaller of the two rafts, but he wasn't willing to wait any longer. "That's it — the raft is going off," he shouted against the wind. When he pushed it into the water, the raft was still uninflated, but tension against the line that held it to the yacht activated a canister of compressed air, and the raft took shape in just a few seconds. Its base consisted of two almost rectangular black inner tubes, each of them about a foot in diameter, one stacked on top of the other. An orange canopy, which extended over the top and looked like a tent, had an opening on one side about two feet wide and three feet tall. The lowest point of the opening was two feet above the surface of the water, but after Lumpy swam a few feet to the raft, he had little trouble pulling himself inside. Once there, however, he was shocked by the raft's small size. It seemed as if it had been designed for two people, not four. He also realized how few provisions it had. Lumpy didn't think to bring his wallet or camera, but he did carry the blue-and-white-striped *Winston Churchill* shirt that he and the other crewmen had worn at the start of the race. It was a handsome shirt, and Lumpy had put it back into the plastic bag it came in so it would be relatively fresh for the end of the race. He still wanted to have it.

Lumpy tucked the EPIRB, which Winning had already turned on, into the side of the raft. Although the device provided a degree of assurance, what Gould had said — "They always find the boat. Sometimes they can't find a life raft" — was running through his mind like a continuously looping tape. The only other thing he could think about was his wife and two daughters.

Just after Lumpy's feet disappeared into the raft, Beaver, his heart racing, declared, "I'm out of here — I'm going." Taking a flying leap, he landed with both arms over the side of the raft and his head partly through the opening. Lumpy pulled him the rest of the way by his underarms.

After waiting for a wave to pass, Gould dove headfirst toward the same raft. By then, the *Churchill* was leaning backward, so its stern was several feet underwater and the bow was riding about three feet above the water. Steamer and Winning were the last crewmen to leave the *Churchill*. When they did, the water was up to their knees, but both men were strangely calm.

"She was a great boat," Winning said just before he abandoned it and went to the raft that held Lumpy, Gould, and Beaver. "I'm going to miss her."

"Me, too," Steamer replied just before Winning jumped into the water.

Beaver helped Winning climb into the raft. As he did, he looked over Winning's shoulder to see the top of the mast slip below the surface. The *Winston Churchill* was gone, sinking in water at least a mile deep.

Steamer swam to the raft he had watched Beaver get in, but Lumpy turned him away. "You can't get on this one," he said. "This is a four-man raft. If you get in here, none of us are going to make it."

Gibbo swam directly toward the bigger raft, which was inflated just after the smaller one. Michael Bannister, Jim Lawler, and John Dean were already inside. Before Gibbo got there, he felt the line connecting the raft to the yacht, so he used it to pull himself to the raft. When he was just a few feet from the raft, the line became taut. Gibbo shuddered with a terrible thought: *The* Churchill *is sinking, and it's going to drag the raft down with it.* Seconds later, the line broke, producing a bang that sounded like an exploding tire. Grabbing at the canvas that surrounded the opening, Gibbo tried pulling himself inside, but he couldn't do it. The opening was too high above the water. There was no place to plant his feet, and his bulky life jacket was in the way. He knew the crewmen who were already inside would help him — and they did — but he was embarrassed that he couldn't do it himself.

As soon as everyone was in one of the rafts, which were separated by only a few feet, Winning wanted to tie them together. "There's only one EPIRB, and we have it," he said. Using a small paddle, he pulled his raft toward the other one, leaned out the opening, and tied a line between them. He knew the line was unlikely to hold, but he also knew how difficult it would be for rescuers to find a raft without a beacon. Beaver didn't say anything, but he thought connecting the rafts was a terrible idea because the tension against the line could rip a hole in one or both of them. But when the line itself snapped — within a few minutes — it caused no damage. It did, however, mean the small rafts would drift their separate ways into a roller coaster of waves, and what already felt like a very big and very lonely ocean.

23

Gary Ticehurst wasn't the only person who had heard Richard Winning's Mayday. Lieutenant Commander Neil Galletly, the captain of *Young Endeavour*, the radio relay vessel, had been listening, too. Galletly, a balding, owlish-looking man who always spoke with military precision, estimated that he was ten miles south of the position Winning had broadcast. The commander figured that he could get there at 7:00 P.M., which would give him about an hour before darkness.

Galletly immediately radioed Australia Search and Rescue — generally known as AusSAR — the government agency responsible for assisting people, ships, and planes in a vast expanse that stretches across seven time zones and includes a tenth of the earth's surface. Most of the uniformed rescue coordinators, who work in a large room on the third floor of a nondescript building in Canberra, have had previous careers as air-traffic controllers, pilots, or naval officers. From their desktop computers, they can access information about a broad array of men and equipment, including military planes and ships as well as almost ten thousand civilian pilots. During a standard shift, seven officers are on duty and the atmosphere is hushed. But by the time the *Churchill* issued its Mayday, twenty-four officers were in the room, organizing what was on the way to becoming the biggest and most complicated maritime rescue effort in Australian history, involving twenty-five planes and helicopters, six ships, and more than one thousand men and women. When AusSAR asked the navy to dispatch the *Newcastle*, a Sydney-based frigate, it reacted so quickly that it left its dock at 4:30 A.M. Sunday with just eighty crewmen, a third of its normal complement. By then, thirty-eight yachts had already abandoned the race.

When Gary Ticehurst contacted AusSAR to pass along what he had heard from the *Churchill*, Dick Jamieson, one of the rescue coordinators, jotted down every detail. He also asked Ticehurst to play the tape of his conversation with Winning. After he derived everything he could, Jamieson stamped his notes with a time clock. He then used a black Magic Marker to transcribe the most pertinent information onto a large whiteboard affixed to the wall, enabling every officer to see the details. As they looked at the entry, all of them focused on one thing — the lack of a precise position. They knew it would be almost impossible to find Winning before nightfall.

Young Endeavour provided hope. The two-masted, square-rigged tall ship wasn't an ideal vessel for a search-and-rescue operation. It wouldn't be able to conduct a box-shaped search pattern, and sidling up to a yacht or life rafts would be impossible. On the other hand, its heavy 144-foot hull made it big enough to handle the waves, and in addition to twelve navy personnel, the crew included eighteen young men from a youth sailing organization. Galletly was sure that during a search they would volunteer to climb up into the rigging to get a better vantage point, and he thought this perspective and young eyes would give him a good chance of finding the *Churchill*.

At 5:44, Galletly told AusSAR that "we intend to" alter course toward the position Winning had given, twenty miles southeast of Twofold Bay. His use of the word *intend* was deliberate: he knew it would precipitate a quicker response than a more open-ended communication — and it did. Two minutes after he radioed AusSAR, Galletly was told, "We concur. Proceed to that position until otherwise directed." At 5:48, *Young Endeavour* turned toward Winning's position.

As Galletly expected, all the trainees were eager to go up into the rigging. After he briefed them on the best technique for scanning the horizon, he described what the procedure would be if they found the target. First, *Young Endeavour* would move to an upwind position. From there it would launch one of its life rafts and let it stream toward the *Churchill* or its rafts. Once yachtsmen were aboard *Young Endeavour*'s raft, they would be pulled back to the ship.

At 5:57, AusSAR received another call about the *Churchill*. Neil Boag, the pilot of a civilian search plane that AusSAR had hired, thought he had spotted the *Churchill* at a position thirty-three miles south of the one Winning had provided. AusSAR had asked Boag to look for the yacht but hadn't given him a description.

"We're overhead a vessel we believe to be the *Winston Churchill*," said Adrian Walter, Boag's copilot. "It's in distress. It has no mast. There's people on the deck. We're overhead at this time, and there's apparently a rescue boat on its way." Walter couldn't communicate directly with the yacht, but he had overheard a radio conversation about a commercial ship that planned to tow the yacht.

"Roger," replied Tony Marshall, one of AusSAR's senior search-and-rescue officers. "And confirm that it is definitely the *Winston Churchill*?"

"Affirm," Walter said.

"Do you have an estimated time of the arrival of the rescue boat?"

"Not as yet. We can find out and get back to you with that information."

"Roger. Does it look like it's going to sink or remain afloat."

"At this stage, it looks like it will remain afloat. The only visible damage is the mast is missing. The mast is gone."

"Roger. Thank you."

By then sixteen EPIRBs were emitting distress signals, and each of them was flashing on AusSAR's computer screens. The agency rarely manages more than one rescue at a time, and when there is more than one, the targets are typically hundreds of miles apart. With limited information and so many active EPIRBs, all of them in the same area, the officers were forced to constantly weigh and shift their priorities, a kind of triage that made everyone uncomfortable because they knew how easy it would be to make a mistake.

Indeed, on the basis of what Boag's plane had reported, what AusSAR considered "a confirmed sighting," the agency told Galletly to call off his search.

The commander was uneasy. Although he thought it would be inappropriate for him to challenge AusSAR, he had a strong feeling that the new position was incorrect. He couldn't believe that an experienced yachtsman would give a position that was thirty-three miles wrong. Galletly also wondered whether it was a military plane that had sighted the yacht and whether the pilot had been thoroughly interrogated by AusSAR. Military pilots have protocols for confirming a sighting. Civilian pilots are sometimes less disciplined. "I had a gut feeling," the commander said later. "I would have given anything to have had an excuse not to abandon the search."

One of the helicopters searching for the *Winston Churchill* was a police chopper that was sidetracked by an even more pressing emergency — the yacht *Kingurra*.

Just before dusk, a wave sent *Kingurra* into a 360-degree roll that left John Campbell, a thirty-two-year-old sailor from Seattle, hanging unconscious in the water at the end of his safety harness. When two other members of the crew attempted to pull him aboard by his tether, he began to slip out of the harness. One of the crewmen grabbed Campbell's hand, but it was too slippery to hold, and Campbell went back into the water, no longer connected to the yacht. He didn't have a life preserver. Regaining consciousness when his head went underwater, he opened his eyes to see that *Kingurra* was being rapidly pushed away from him by the wind. Campbell waved his arms and tried to swim, but he couldn't catch up to the boat. Not knowing that the yacht's engine wouldn't start, he was baffled that the boat wasn't coming back to get him.

The yacht's skipper, a seventy-four-year-old engineering professor named Peter Joubert, had ruptured his spleen, punctured a lung, and broken half a dozen ribs in the roll, but he was radioing for help. Within a few minutes, the police helicopter spotted *Kingurra* and began searching for Campbell. By then, Campbell was out of sight from *Kingurra*. While it was impossible to steer the yacht, the crew kept track of the direction it was moving, and Joubert gave the pilot a bearing back to where Campbell was lost. Miraculously, Constable Barry Barclay spotted Campbell within minutes. Sergeant David Key was quickly lowered to the water, landing just before a wave that looked like a mountain range began to break. Because of the buoyancy of his life jacket, the white water hurtled him along like a cork.

When it was over, he was amazed to find that he wasn't far from Campbell. Swimming to him, he saw that the sailor was in bad shape. His face looked as if it had been run over by a car. After placing the rescue sling over Campbell's head and under his arms, Key raised his hand to signal that they were ready to go up. Then he felt the cable. It was around his legs. If it was still there when it was pulled taut, it would have amputated his leg. Reaching down, he pulled the cable free. But once they were lifted from the water, the winch that was supposed to retrieve the cable stopped well before they reached the helicopter door — and Campbell began to slip out of his harness. Key wrapped his arms around him but knew he couldn't hold him for long. Although Constable Barclay repeatedly pushed the UP button, nothing happened. Finally, on the sixth try, the winch turned and the two men made it inside. It was just in time. After he hugged and kissed his saviors, Campbell vomited salt water and began to slip into shock. His rescuers rushed him to the hospital, where he was treated for hypothermia and several broken bones, including his jaw and cheek.

The passengers in the *Winston Churchill's* rafts needed John Campbell's kind of luck. Now that the crewmen were so close to the water, the waves seemed bigger, and their flimsy rafts didn't appear to be any more likely to survive the pounding than the *Churchill* itself had been. The rafts' outside walls were about fifteen inches high. The floor consisted of a rubber mat. The canopy, which was made of cloth, was held in place by an air-filled tube that arched from one side of the raft to the other. The rafts seemed more like toys than seaworthy lifesavers. And they were already filled with so much water that they resembled the little baby pools that sit in suburban backyards.

Splashing his hand in the water, Lumpy said, "This isn't the way it's supposed to be. Do we have something to bail some of the water out with?"

Lumpy's raft came equipped with a long and narrow nylon supply bag. Unfortunately, though, the only way to find anything inside was to dump out all of the contents. When he did, he found three shrunken sponges, biscuits, plastic containers of drinking water, seasickness tablets, Band-Aids, a mirror, a packet of fish-hooks, and a foot-operated pump that could be used to inflate the raft — but nothing that looked like a bailer. Lumpy tried using one of the sponges, but it picked up very little water. "We can't use those — it's ridiculous," Gould declared. Taking off one of his sea boots, he started filling it with water and dumping it out the opening. Though it was more effective than the sponge, the top of the boot kept collapsing. Beaver contributed one of his boots, which was of a sturdier variety and worked much better.

As dusk approached, the wind was driving rain or spew from the waves — it was impossible to know which — against the canopy with a force that made the raft as noisy as the inside of a kettledrum. But the waves, which were still thirty feet high, were the biggest problem, particularly the breaking ones, which sent the raft bouncing across the water like a beach ball. For some reason, the opening seemed to face away from the direction of the waves and wind most of the time, and the inability to see what was coming added to the anxiety. However, it was even worse when the opening spun to the other side. The crew could then watch the oncoming mountains of water — they looked much bigger when approaching than when leaving — and the breaking waves poured through the opening.

As each wave connected with the raft, Beaver tensed his body, pushing his lower back and feet into the walls, partly in fear but also because he hoped the added rigidity would strengthen the raft. So much was racing through his head that he realized he couldn't think straight. His fear mixed with anger. *This isn't fair*, he said to himself. *These guys have all done dozens of ocean races — and here I am on my first one, sitting in a life raft that no one can find.* Beaver knew the end could come in many ways, but he believed the most likely scenario was that the waves would simply rip the rubber raft into pieces, leaving its occupants with nothing to hold on to. Beaver had never been particularly religious, but he began to say silent prayers. *I don't want to die, God. I'm too young to die. Please, let me live. Please, God, bring us a helicopter.*

Lumpy was focused on the EPIRB. "We've got the EPIRB. We'll get found, and then they'll find the other guys," he said, hoping to convince himself.

In fact, he was worried that the EPIRB wasn't even working. EPIRBs operate best when they're floating in the water because their entire signal is sent upward from that position. When they're inside a boat, some of the signal is deflected in other directions. Therefore, Lumpy asked Winning if he should fasten the EPIRB to a line outside the raft. Remembering what had happened to the line he fastened to the other raft, Winning shook his head. "No, I wouldn't take a chance." The EPIRB remained in the raft.

24

On the *Sword*, the biggest risk was another capsize. The hull and the deck had separated from each other in the back half of the boat on the starboard side, the same area where *Nokia* had crashed into the *Sword*. The gap was big enough to see through and was already admitting water from passing waves. Watching the edges of the deck and hull grate against each other, Dags knew the gap would only expand. And, he thought, if the boat rolled over again, the deck would peel away from the hull like the top of a can of sardines.

The *Sword* certainly felt unstable. It was bobbing sideways across the waves, and some of the breaking waves caused it to lurch to the point where it seemed close to going over. Although it was impossible to steer — what remained of the steering wheel couldn't even be turned — Dags still believed the best way to avoid another roll was to keep the *Sword* from becoming broadside to the waves. Some boats carry large drogues, parachute-like sacks that can be released from the bow or stern so they drag against the water to keep a vessel pointing into the wind and waves, but the *Sword* didn't have one. Dags was searching for a substitute. Before the rigging was pushed over, he had thought about tying it to the bow so it could act as a giant drogue. He had never heard of anyone using that technique, but he was planning to try it until he decided that it made more sense to simply use the anchor, a proven method. It was attached to three hundred feet of chain and line, and after Dags threw it off the bow, the boat seemed more stable: the rate of drift slowed and the nose of the boat generally aimed into the waves.

Sitting in the cockpit, Dags tried to reconstruct what had happened to Glyn. By then, he had a pretty good idea. Before the capsize, the boom, attached to a metal fixture, still had the mainsail wrapped around it. Together, the boom and the sail would have offered a substantial amount of resistance to the water during the roll, enough that something probably had to break. The Spectra line Dags used to tie the boom to the fixture was virtually indestructible. Therefore, the force must have torn the fixture itself from the deck — freeing the boom to swing from one side of the cockpit to the other. The boom would have smashed into Glyn like an enormous baseball bat, bursting the stitching in his tether and hurling him over the side. The blow, which must have also destroyed the aluminum steering wheel, was probably the reason Glyn couldn't swim.

Dags, who knew the same bat would have struck him if he hadn't gone to speak to Brownie, was left to ponder several haunting questions: *Could I have somehow made Glyn change course or give up the wheel? Would Glyn still be alive if we had removed the boom from the mast rather than tying it to the fixture? Did the fixture fail to hold the boom because the accident with* Nokia *had weakened the deck?*

For most of the *Sword*'s crew, there wasn't much to do other than brace themselves for the next wave, so they were lying in bunks or on the floor of the cabin. Like Dags, Kooky was absorbed by regrets and what-ifs. In particular, he was thinking about a device that could have saved Glyn — the marine rescue-line throwers his company manufactured. Some of them could propel a line for one thousand feet. Every year, Kooky sold hundreds of line throwers to commercial shipowners. He had thought about making a version that could be used on private yachts, but he hadn't gotten around to it.

Kooky's continued calls for help over the radio still hadn't been acknowledged. If the EPIRB was working, rescuers would know the boat's location, though they wouldn't know that Glyn had been lost or anything about the *Sword*'s condition. It was all too easy to imagine a scenario that would lead to total disaster. Evidence of the yacht's structural weakness was everywhere. The top of the cabin was wobbling so much that it looked as if it could collapse at any time. Cracks ran through it, some of them extending from one side of the boat to the other. The remaining section of the steering wheel had punched a hole through the deck underneath it, and water poured through the opening even after Brownie tried to close it by stuffing a sleeping bag into the gap. On the starboard side, the bulkheads were cracking away from the hull. One or two large waves could roll over the stern and fill the cabin until the yacht lost buoyancy. Even more likely, Dags thought, the damaged cabin top, or even the hull itself, would simply collapse.

Depending on the angle of the yacht, some parts of the cabin floor were still covered by several inches of water. Without enough buckets, Simon Reffold was bailing with a drawer. Normally, he could simply toss the water into the cockpit, and it would flow into drains and out of the boat. But given the hole beneath the steering wheel, any water in the cockpit just leaked back into the cabin. Therefore, Simon Reffold had to pass the drawer to Dags, who then dumped it over the side.

Since a vessel's buoyancy is also affected by its weight, Andrew Parkes suggested that the *Sword*'s now useless sails be jettisoned. Brownie agreed, although he couldn't resist telling the sailmaker, "You would say that," as eighty thousand dollars' worth of sails went over the side. Although the sails were heavy, air trapped inside the bags kept them from sinking. Brownie wished they had thought to throw them into the water when Glyn went overboard.

Although no one was steering the yacht, Dags remained on deck so he could be on the lookout for other vessels. There hadn't been any since Glyn was lost, but a little after 6:00 P.M. he spotted a white-hulled sloop. "There's another yacht," Dags yelled into the cabin. "It's coming our way."

Glyn had been in the ocean for about an hour. Given the difficulty he had had keeping his head above water, it was probably too late for the other yacht to do anything to save him. On the other hand, Dags knew that a yachtsman named John Quinn had survived for more than five hours in the water during the 1994 Hobart before he was spotted by a passing cargo ship and picked up by another vessel. In addition, the other yacht could have used its radio to tell the outside world about the *Sword*'s desperate condition. When Brownie came on deck, he initially thought the other boat was the *Winston Churchill*, but then he recognized it as the *Margaret Rintoul II*, a classically designed, forty-eight-foot sloop. He could see two figures in the cockpit, both wearing yellow rain jackets.

Nigel Russell and Andrew Parkes fired a barrage of flares — including five red parachute flares, which, after they reached their maximum altitude, were held in the sky by small parachutes to increase the chances of their being sighted. They also set off a standard red flare and three white ones along with an orange smoke flare. While the pyrotechnics burned, Dags and Brownie frantically waved and screamed toward the yacht, and Kooky shouted into the VHF radio.

"White boat, white boat, this is the *Sword of Orion*. We have been dismasted — and we have lost a man overboard. We are four hundred meters to the east of you. Come in please."

"They're coming toward us," Nigel Russell said just after he launched the last flare. But the *Rintoul* hadn't changed its course. In fact, the distance between the yachts was increasing. The *Rintoul* hadn't even made radio contact with the *Sword*, which, given its lack of a mast, would be easily recognized as being in distress. Either the *Rintoul*'s crew somehow didn't see the *Sword* or its flares or they had decided against trying to help. To Dags, the second possibility seemed as impossible as the first. But given the lack of plausible alternatives, the *Sword*'s crew considered an enraging theory: were the *Rintoul*'s crewmen looking the other way so they could continue racing? Did they want to win so badly that they were willing to risk sacrificing the lives of fellow sailors? It would be hard to imagine a more monstrous violation of maritime tradition, but half an hour after it appeared, the *Rintoul* was out of sight.

Nautical convention and international law require ships to do whatever they can to help vessels in distress. Only when a would-be rescuer would endanger his own crew is he excused from this responsibility, although there are many examples of mariners doing just that. During around-the-world races, solo yachtsmen have gone hundreds of miles out of their way and knowingly sailed into dangerous storms to save fellow competitors.

The *Sword*'s crew knew a yacht-to-yacht rescue in those conditions was probably impossible. But they couldn't understand why the *Rintoul* didn't at least communicate by radio. It could have provided the same kind of information relay that the *Sword* had offered *Team Jaguar*. Planes and helicopters could have been dispatched to search for Glyn and to determine whether the *Sword*'s crew required immediate assistance. If the *Sword* were to sink later, its crew would have had a much better chance of survival.

"I can't believe it," Dags declared. "How could they not stop? They had to see us."

"Of course they saw us," said Carl Watson, who used to crew on the *Rintoul*. "We saw them — they had to see us. They just couldn't be bothered."

Richard Purcell, the *Margaret Rintoul*'s owner, was a tough-minded construction contractor who loved classic sailing yachts. He was just a teenager when he first admired the *Margaret Rintoul*, which was launched in 1968, and he dreamed of being its owner long before he could afford it. Like the *Winston Churchill*, the *Rintoul* had graceful lines and a handsome mahogany interior. After Purcell bought it in 1988, he replaced the teak deck and had worked to keep the boat in immaculate condition ever since. The 1998 Hobart was the *Rintoul*'s twenty-first Hobart. Only one other yacht had done as many.

Purcell, a solidly built forty-seven-year-old with a full head of blond hair and a thick mustache, was slouching against the front of the *Rintoul*'s cockpit, where he was somewhat sheltered from the wind, when he spotted a flare. It was about 6:15 P.M. No one else on his yacht saw it.

"I just saw a flare," he said to Bill Riley, a fifty-eight-year-old pharmacist who was steering. "And there's a dismasted yacht." Pointing in the direction of the *Sword*, Purcell asked, "Can you see it?"

Riley turned around for a few seconds, but he was afraid to take his eyes away from the waves any longer. "No," he said,

"I didn't see anything." Assuming that he would be turning the *Rintoul* around to go toward the other boat, he added, "We'd better get some more guys on deck."

Shouting below to Colin Betts, the *Rintoul*'s navigator, Purcell said, "I've just seen a flare and a dismasted yacht. Get on the radio and give *Young Endeavour* our position."

Turning back to Riley, Purcell asked, "What should we do?"

"You're the skipper. It's your call."

Purcell, who had sailed in four previous Hobarts, fully understood that he was obligated to help a yacht in distress unless it would put his own crew in unreasonable danger. But he was frightened. He was remembering the storm he had sailed into near Australia's southeastern corner on December 15, 1979. He had been taking his first yacht, a thirty-seven-foot sloop, from Melbourne to Sydney so it would be there in time for that year's Hobart, when the wind built to more than sixty knots. Purcell was relatively inexperienced then, so he had hired two professional mariners for the trip. Even so, he shook uncontrollably for much of the night, certain that the waves would capsize and sink his yacht. The boat survived, but a few days later he learned that *Charleston*, another thirty-seven-foot-long yacht that had been crossing Bass Strait that night, had disappeared without a trace. *Charleston* had been just ten weeks old. Built of Tasmanian pine and cedar and reinforced by an interior metal frame, it had been owned by Glyn Davies, whose family had owned Hobart's leading newspaper, *The Mercury*, until Rupert Murdoch bought it. Davies and four other crewmen, who also were heading to Sydney for the start of the Hobart, were never seen again.

Except for that night almost twenty years earlier, Purcell had never seen waves like the ones that surrounded him when he spotted the *Sword*. He thought he was lucky to have lived through the last time, and he was reluctant to press his luck. The *Rintoul* weighed seventeen tons, but changing course would be extremely dangerous, particularly since its engine had broken down the previous night. He wasn't sure that by the time he turned his boat, he would even be able to find the other yacht. And if he did, he couldn't imagine how he could be of assistance. The most likely result of turning around, he concluded, would be two yachts in trouble.

"We could lose a man over the side," Purcell said to Riley.

Riley, a veteran of twenty-one Hobarts, was thinking the same thing. Step-by-step, he had been going through the procedure for turning the boat. At least one man would have to go on the forward part of the deck, where the waves were sometimes crashing so hard that Riley thought it quite possible the man would be washed overboard. Even so, Riley was shocked by what Purcell said next.

"Continue on this course. There's nothing we can do for them."

As Riley stood there, stunned, Purcell shouted below. "Colin, give *Young Endeavour* our position, but tell them we aren't going to assist. It's too fucking dangerous."

Riley had always had ambivalent feelings about Purcell. When they met for the first time, not long after someone recommended Riley as a helmsman, Purcell's first words were "You better be fucking good." However, while Riley was put off by Purcell's rough style, he eventually came to enjoy racing with him. Purcell's decisions about selecting sails and picking courses were almost always correct. Riley also liked the way Purcell made definitive decisions and stuck with them.

But this decision, Riley thought, was a terrible mistake.

In 1980, Riley was at the wheel of another yacht that had seen a flare. It was just after midnight in a different long-distance race, and he immediately turned his boat and headed off to help. Over the radio, his crew learned that there was a man overboard. Several other yachts had already been searching the area, but Riley, whose boat was the only one that hadn't turned on its engine, was the only one to hear screams from the man in the water. Within minutes, they pulled the missing man on board.

In 1998, Riley instinctively thought the right thing to do was to turn toward the vessel in distress. But since he had told Purcell that it was his call, he thought it wouldn't be fair to then question it. He didn't have to. From the distressed look on Riley's face, Purcell knew what his helmsman was thinking. "It's my decision," Purcell said. "And that's it. We're not going to have any heroes."

A few minutes later, the *Rintoul* was hit by a set of three particularly large waves. If someone had been on deck when they hit, Riley realized that there was a good chance he would have been lost. To himself, Riley said, *Purcell may have been right after all. It's not what I would have done, but he might have saved a life.* Having declined to help Purcell decide what to do, he now felt compelled to say something.

"I agree with your decision."

When Colin Betts turned on the radio to call Lew Carter, there was so much traffic, much of it related to *Team Jaguar*, that he held off from breaking in. It was about 7:15 P.M., an hour after Purcell had sighted the flare, when Betts reached Lew Carter on *Young Endeavour*. "Lew, it's Colin Betts on the *Margaret Rintoul II*," he said before he gave Carter the *Rintoul's* latitude and longitude from an hour earlier. "We've seen a flare from a yacht that was about a half mile from our position."

"Thanks for that," replied Carter, who didn't hear Betts say anything about the yacht being dismasted.

Betts didn't think to turn on his VHF radio, which probably would have enabled him to speak to Kooky. He monitored the HF radio to see if Lew Carter tried to call him back, but after about thirty minutes, he turned it off. The *Margaret Rintoul* went on its way.

25

Steamer's raft was carrying too much water. A funnel-like opening in the canopy was part of the problem. Steamer wasn't sure
whether its purpose was to enable the passengers to see outside
or to gather rainwater for drinking, but the water contained too
much seawater to be potable and was arriving in a steady stream
that couldn't be stopped except by squeezing the tube shut by
hand. As on the other raft, a sea boot, Gibbo's, was thought to
be the most promising bailer. John Dean and Michael Bannister
took turns using it.

For everyone on the raft, the biggest fear was capsizing. If
the waves could turn the *Churchill* on its side, they clearly could
flip a raft. Bannister thought the best way to reduce the danger
was to slow down the raft as much as possible. Surveying what
remained from the supply pouch — somehow, most of the contents had disappeared — he found a small drogue that he thought
might provide a degree of stability. "We'd better get this thing in
the water," he said. The drogue was fastened to the raft by a thin
nylon cord, but when Gibbo dropped it into the water, the cord
became entangled with a line that circled the inside of the raft and
was attached to the canopy.

Alarmed, Steamer declared, "We have to fix this — or it's
going to rip the canopy off."

Gibbo and Bannister had retrieved about twenty feet of the drogue's nylon cord when the canvas suddenly filled with water and the cord began to pull away. Bannister let go immediately, but Gibbo, afraid the cord would slice through the raft when it became taut, hardened his grip and continued to pull. It would be like reeling in a big fish, he thought. But he was quite mistaken. The force of the water was tremendous, and by the time Steamer used a knife to cut the interfering line inside the raft, the drogue's cord had torn through Gibbo's flesh, deep enough to reach bone. Gibbo was angry with himself and furious with the raft. *You're supposed to be our salvation*, he said with silent outrage, *our protection from the sea — but now you're attacking me!*

Horrified by the damage to Gibbo's hand, Steamer was nevertheless pleased with the drogue. He believed it cut the raft's speed in half and provided some stability. But ten minutes later, the drogue's cord snapped, and the raft resumed its frightening pace.

The breaking waves, which sounded like locomotives as they approached, set off a worrying chain reaction. When the white water first hit the raft, the boat accelerated and canted forward. Then, as the raft seemed to submerge into the wave, its floor would buckle into a V shape, sometimes so steep that the passengers' heads hit one another. The raft frequently felt as if it could fold over onto itself like a book. At other times, it seemed as if the raft was about to be upended. The rough ride made the quarters seem even more cramped.

Everyone's back was up against the outside of the raft in a way that enabled their heads to rest on the top of the wall. Legs were crossed over and under one another's, and when the raft was thrown by one particularly large wave, the pile of limbs rose and fell — mostly on Steamer's legs, which were at the bottom of the heap. The impact ripped several tendons, and Steamer was afraid one of his artificial hips might have been damaged. "Ah, fellas," he groaned. "This is no good. We have to rearrange ourselves." They moved their legs so they were parallel to one another, packed like sardines in a can. Once that was accomplished, Steamer asked Dean to search the supplies for anything that looked like a pain-killer. He couldn't even find aspirin.

26

For the *Sword of Orion*'s crew, being ignored by the *Margaret Rintoul* was like a kick in the teeth. Their morale, which had begun to recover as their boat seemed less likely to sink, plummeted to a new low. Kooky kept trying to hail the *Rintoul* by radio even after it disappeared, repeating his words so many times and so frantically that Carl Watson, afraid that Kooky wouldn't be understood, suggested that he take a break. Kooky readily agreed. Although he had become a virulent tobacco hater after he gave up cigarettes several years earlier, he bummed one from Brownie.

Watson guessed that the VHF radio had just a few miles of range. He was sure the *Rintoul* would have heard it, but he doubted that another boat would come close enough anytime soon. It was just before 7:00 P.M. when he finally heard a faint reply to his steady chorus of Maydays. It was from Neil Boag, the pilot of the civilian search-and-rescue plane who thought he had spotted the *Winston Churchill* an hour earlier. Checking a handheld GPS, Watson gave Boag a position to help him find the *Sword*.

"As soon as we're near you," Boag said, "set off a flare."

When Dags, who was on deck, heard the plane a few minutes later, he fired an orange smoke flare, the only remaining flare of any kind. Since the wind was still blowing at close to fifty knots and the waves were still mountainous, he worried that the yacht and smoke would be invisible to the plane, so he also attached several strobe lights to the deck. In fact, the plane flew out of the murky sky and into view almost immediately. As it began circling overhead, the quality of the radio's reception improved dramatically.

"Do you need a life raft?" Boag asked.

"No, we don't need a raft," Watson responded. "We've stabilized the yacht somewhat."

"What is your condition?"

"We have been dismasted and we've lost a man overboard — a British resident named Glyn Charles."

Boag also had some bad news. "You are too far from land for a helicopter rescue. Can you give me an estimate on your rate and direction of drift?"

"We're probably moving at about four knots to the north."

A few minutes later, Boag, who had contacted AusSAR, came back with some encouraging words. "You're mostly moving in the right direction. In a few hours, you should be close enough for one of the Navy Sea Hawks to get to you. We'll log your position and stay in touch."

Boag, who was flying two to three hundred feet over the water beneath a ceiling of clouds that was just four hundred feet above the ocean, began searching for Glyn. However, he quickly concluded that there was no chance of finding anyone with such limited visibility.

Overhearing the radio, Andrew Parkes said to Dags, "I hope the boat doesn't break up before a helicopter gets here." Parkes was particularly concerned about the way the cabin's ceiling was flexing up and down. He was sure it had gotten worse, and he knew the ceiling provided more than shelter. By connecting both sides of the hull, it also played an important structural role. Dags too was nervous about the movement, so he pulled out the spinnaker pole, hoping to use it as a prop. With a saw, he cut it into two pieces and placed one of them between the floor and the cabin top, making the roof much more rigid.

As the sky darkened, Watson suggested that the crew have something to eat. "There's not much we can do now," he said. "Why don't we heat a couple of meat pies." The oven and stove burners were still working, so Dags made a pot of coffee and found a dry box of ginger cookies. Kooky suggested that it was time for a round of Sustagen. Everyone had something to eat but Kulmar. He was sitting alone in the bow compartment, an area that was partially separated from the main cabin by a bulkhead, still not talking. As the rest of the crewmen gathered, Brownie and Dags recounted what happened to them during the roll. Brownie talked about falling off the ladder, and Dags described what it was like to be underwater. They mentioned the topic dominating everyone's thoughts — Glyn — only fleetingly until Simon Reffold finally forced the issue. "Given what happened to Glyn," he said, "shouldn't we work out what we're going to say?"

"There's nothing we could have done about it," Kooky replied. "And we can't worry about it now. We have to concentrate on keeping ourselves alive."

After a pause, Kooky, speaking in a softer tone, added a few more words. "I don't think he suffered very long. The rest of us are going to be okay. Dags is going to keep the boat together, and Carl will stay on the radio. We're going to be rescued soon, so let's try to relax."

"It's just so weird," Nigel Russell said. "I didn't really know him, and now he's gone."

It was hard to know what else to say.

Dags wasn't interested in Kooky's Sustagen. He wanted a more potent cocktail and suggested to Brownie, "Maybe I should get the medical kit out." The rum was no longer a secret, and it was mixed with Sustagen as well as Coke and also consumed straight from the bottle. Rather than objecting, Kooky asked for a shot. The rum seemed to lift everyone's spirits, except for Kulmar's. But by 11:00 P.M. the crew was silent. The yacht was still pitching wildly against the waves, yet everyone was so exhausted that they were falling asleep.

Only Sam Hunt was too restless to lie down. He had bailed more water than anyone, and continued to do so throughout the night until he stopped to make a slumber-destroying announce- ment. "I've bailed vomit. I've bailed piss. But this is fucking ridic- ulous," he blurted with a strange sort of poetry. "I'm not going to bail anybody's shit." Hunt's bucket had captured a pair of break- fast sausages. Discovering the actual source of Hunt's outrage provoked the night's only real outbreak of laughter.

Afterward, silence returned, and Dags felt cold and emotion- ally drained. All of his clothes, what he was wearing as well as what was in his duffel bag, were soaked and impossible to dry. Rather than suffer alone, he climbed into the same narrow bunk that Andrew Parkes already occupied. "Don't get the wrong idea," Dags said, "but I'm freezing. If it's all right with you, maybe we should hold on to each other."

"Yeah, that sounds okay to me," Parkes said. He was lying on his side, facing away from Dags, who wrapped an arm around his friend's chest. As their bodies melded together, Dags felt reas- sured by the human contact. After a while, Parkes felt comfort- able enough that he took Dags's icy hands into his own, which were much warmer. "This way," he joked, "I know your hands aren't going to go anywhere else."

27

Larry Ellison knew he was heading into a terrible night. He usually enjoyed sailing in the dark. He believed evening wind was more consistent, he liked looking at the constellations, and he thought the overall atmosphere was serene. But at dusk on Sunday, the wind was coming from the southwest at close to sixty knots, and he knew he wouldn't be seeing any stars. To Ellison, the wind didn't even sound like wind anymore. It was more like a high-pitched siren, and it had an otherworldly quality that he found disturbing.

"In the Whitbread we had wind like this, and we had waves this big — but it never lasted this long," T. A. McCann said to Joey Allen.

"How much longer can it go on?" Allen asked.

"Who knows? We already know we can't trust the weather forecasters. This isn't anything like what they were talking about."

Sayonara had been designed for both inshore and offshore racing. Therefore, it wasn't perfect for either. At the bow, for example, two holes enabled rigging to pass through the deck. For inshore racing, these holes made it possible for the jib to be held lower to the deck, increasing the sail's surface area. But in rough seas, when the bow plunged into waves, submerging under several feet of water, the holes, each of them the size of a quarter, seemed to admit water like a fire hydrant turned on full. Hamish Pepper, a twenty-eight-year-old member of Team New Zealand, was trying to reverse the flow. Pulling a long hose that was connected to a pump, he was trying to suck out hundreds of gallons of water near the front of the cabin.

Jabbing the end of the hose to the bottom of the hull, he found something worse than water: a raised bubble on the hull's inside skin. It was oval in shape, a foot high and six inches wide. Showing it to Mark Turner, a Kiwi boatbuilder who was known as Tugboat, Pepper said, "Look at this. I think there's some delamination around here."

Tugboat wasn't surprised. He was already monitoring several other areas of delamination. "Yup," he replied with contrived flippancy, "she's breaking up." In fact, Tugboat was more worried about the way the bulkheads were beginning to separate from the hull.

The critical balancing act in designing racing yachts is to minimize weight without sacrificing seaworthiness. Fiberglass hulls and aluminum masts were revolutionary steps. Their durability and the costly facilities that are required to build boats with higher-tech materials are underlying factors in the disappearance of many small-scale boatbuilders during the past few decades. The *Winston Churchill*, which weighed twenty-five tons, was built in a family-owned yard that had closed many years earlier. *Sayonara*, which weighed just twenty-three tons even though it was 50 percent longer than the *Churchill*, was built by one of the survivors, Auckland-based Cookson Boats. Because of its focus on racing yachts and its investment in cutting-edge computer and manufacturing equipment, Cookson attracted business on a global basis.

To make the inside and outside surfaces of *Sayonara*'s hull, sheets of carbon-fiber fabric were laid into a mold and impregnated with resin, compacted to eliminate pockets of air, and then heated inside an enormous oven. The mast was produced with a similar process by another Auckland firm, Southern Spars. A carbon mast has two benefits: first, it weighs 25 percent less than an aluminum one; second, carbon is stiffer than aluminum, and the energy that would be absorbed by a more flexible mast instead goes to driving the boat. The benefits have a price: *Sayonara*'s mast and rigging cost more than $300,000, while an aluminum mast-based rig would have been less than $200,000.

Some yachtsmen believe the trend toward lightweight yachts has gone too far, that boats like *Sayonara* and the *Sword of Orion*, which rely on finlike keels with bulbs at their bases rather than much larger traditional keels for stability, capsize too easily and are more like oversize Windsurfers than oceanworthy vessels. For the Hobart, most yachts were required to have "limited positive stability" of at least 115 degrees, meaning that if they tipped up to twenty-five degrees past horizontal, they would turn back upright rather than capsize. Regardless of standards, some yachtsmen believe it is impossible to build a truly stable vessel without a substantial keel. On the other hand, it's also true that wooden yachts like the *Churchill*, which carry formidable keels, are only as seaworthy as their weakest plank — and the sea is relentless in finding weakness.

Even on *Sayonara* the risks were real. Since it was sometimes impossible to maintain a grip on anything when waves poured over the deck, safety harnesses and tethers were needed to keep the crew from being washed over the side. During the multi-month Whitbread Race, only once had T. A. McCann fallen and been saved by his tether; in the previous twenty-four hours, it happened to him twice. McCann had been lucky: on each occasion he remained on board. When a wave captured *Sayonara* crewman Curtis Blewitt, he was washed under the lifeline and into the water. Thanks to his tether, he was hanging against the port side of the hull, his head held above the water while the rest of his body scraped across the wave tops.

"Come on, let's get him back up," Allen screamed.

With help from T.A., Allen leaned over the rail, grabbed Blewitt's harness, and, struggling against the rushing water, lifted him back to the deck. Afterward, Blewitt, another Whitbread veteran, laughed hysterically, although no one was sure whether it was because of his sense of humor or delirium.

Once again, the wind strengthened to the point that the mainsail had to be reefed. This time, just when Chris Dickson turned the yacht into the wind to reduce the pressure against the sail, a wave poured over the side. Phil Kiely, who was getting up from the rail, didn't see it coming. Losing contact with everything but his tether, the water lifted him several feet above the deck. When he fell back down, the side of his right foot landed first. Kiely collapsed in a heap near the center of the cockpit. Looking down, he thought his sea boot had come partly off his foot because it was at a right angle to his leg; but when he reached down, he felt that his foot was still in the boot and realized that the bones in his leg and foot were no longer joined. Afraid of blacking out, he hugged the drum of the central utility winch and waited for the pain to hit.

T.A. also had a problem. He was trying to pull the front edge of the sail down, but it refused to budge. Something was caught. The bottom section of the sail was held to the mast by five "cars," metal devices that were sewn to the sail and slid up and down a metal track that ran along the backside of the mast. In fact, there were three tracks, which were supposed to be lined up with one another, allowing the cars to slide freely. However, the middle section, which was about two feet long, had gone out of alignment, and the cars were stacked above it, about five feet higher than where the boom was joined to the mast. Realizing that he would have to force each car from one track to the other, T.A. climbed up the mast so he could stand on the boom. With one hand clutching the mast, he tried to coordinate moving each of the cars with Robbie Naismith, who was in the cockpit. But no matter how hard T.A. pushed or pulled, he couldn't get any of the cars into the middle track. Desperate, he used a winch handle to hammer one of the cars, which only caused the middle section of track to begin peeling away from the mast.

"Stop — don't pull," T.A. shouted to Robbie.

"This is a fricking mess," screamed Joey Allen, who was near the mast. "We're going to have to take the track off."

Every task was hard in sixty knots of wind, even twisting a screwdriver against the twenty screws that held the middle track in place. Once all of them were undone and the track was removed, Allen and T.A. had an even more difficult job — moving each of the cars from the top track to the bottom one by hand. Even though the boat was heading directly into the wind, there was enormous tension against the sail, pulling it and the cars away from the mast. Allen and T.A. knew they might not be able to keep hold of the cars, but they didn't have a choice. Stepping up onto the boom, Allen tried to move the first one. Flying out of his hand, it whipped into his forehead, carving a deep gouge. As his vision darkened, reaching a point where all he could see was a single black dot, he was sure he would go unconscious. Seeing Allen's eyes rolling upward, T.A. screamed, "Don't go out now! We need you."

Allen stayed conscious, but T.A. quickly replaced him on the boom. After he wrestled the first car into the lower track, he had the second one in his right hand. His left thumb was resting on the top of the bottom section of the track. Naismith was helping pull the car down by yanking at the inboard reefing line when a car that T.A. thought had already slid into the track sliced into his thumb.

"No — go back up!" T.A. cried. There was so much blood, he thought his thumb had been severed from his hand, but he still managed to get the car onto the lower track. In fact, his thumb was only cut, and while he wrapped it with electrical tape, Allen managed to get the last three cars into the bottom track.

Ellison, who was watching T.A. and Allen from the cockpit, was in awe of what they were doing. "This is impossible," he said to Dickson. "How much of the track is a problem? Can we fix it? Or can we sail without it?"

"It's only part of the track. It won't stop us from sailing."

But the sail suffered during the confusion. While it was flailing about, a tear developed near the back edge of the fabric about twenty feet above the boom. Given the rip and the force of the wind, Dickson decided that the mainsail had to be dropped altogether. "If we don't get it off," he shouted, "it's going to disintegrate."

When Justin Clougher scrambled to find a position where he could reach up to pull at the sail, he saw a crumpled person next to the winch.

"Who is that down there?" Clougher asked. "Are you hurt?"

During the battle with the sail, Kiely, anxious to stay out of the way, hadn't done anything to draw attention to himself. "Yeah," he said. "It's my ankle."

"You can't sit there when we're taking the sail down," Clougher said, unaware of the seriousness of Kiely's injury. "Get back to the steering wheel; nobody can step on you there."

Kiely dutifully slid toward the stern, still not complaining. As soon as the mainsail was tied to the boom, Clougher and T.A., who had both been trained as medics before they sailed in the Whitbread, carried Kiely downstairs and lifted him into a bunk. Afraid they would further injure Kiely's foot by taking his sea boot off, they cut it free with a pair of scissors. Just as Kiely had thought, nothing but skin and tendons connected his leg and foot. Clougher did his best to strap Kiely into the bunk. The only pain reliever on board was codeine, but Kiely had already resolved that he would not — no matter how he felt — be responsible for ending *Sayonara*'s race.

Ellison, told by T.A. what had happened, got down on his knees next to Phil's bunk. "I'm okay," Kiely claimed.

Ellison looked sympathetic, but bedside manner wasn't one of his strong points. "Just remember," he said, "it was your idea to come on the race."

"Don't worry about me. There's no way I'm not going to be on the boat when we cross the finish line."

Bringing the sail down was such a messy maneuver that Joey Allen decided to take a head count. When the system of watches was functioning, it was relatively easy to keep track of who was on deck. But so many crewmen were sick and unable to stay on deck that there was a much greater risk that someone could go missing without being noticed. Coming up one person short, Allen mentally checked off names until he came to Frizzle.

"Where's Frizzle?" Allen yelled. "Has anyone seen Frizzle?"

He frantically searched the deck and then the cabin. Mark Rudiger pushed the MAN OVERBOARD button on the GPS and joined the search. A few minutes later, Frizzle was found, sleeping on the floor of the cabin, partially hidden beneath the empty sail bag he was using as a blanket.

Phil Kiely wasn't the only injured crewman. Bob Wylie, one of the mainsail trimmers, cracked several ribs when he fell against a winch. Dave Culver, a Californian who had sailed with Dennis Conner in the 1992 America's Cup, had a deep cut in one of his thumbs. He had no idea how it happened. Tugboat sprained his ankle, although he continued to hobble around the cabin so he could monitor the delamination.

For the rest of the night, the wind held at about sixty knots, and *Sayonara* carried on with only its storm jib, which with only 340 square feet of surface area, was its smallest sail. Even with just a tenth of *Sayonara's* usual sail area up, the yacht was still moving at close to ten knots.

Rupert Murdoch was following the race as best he could. Late Sunday night, an editor on the night desk of the *Daily Telegraph*, News Corporation's largest circulation paper in Sydney, picked up his phone and heard Rupert's familiar voice at the other end. "Do you know where *Sayonara* is?"

"Last time they checked in, they were still out in front — but it's the worst weather anyone can remember."

"Good," Rupert chortled, somewhat missing the point. "It sounds like it's character-building."

PART IV

ADRIFT

28

At 11:12 p.m. Sunday night, an official at Australian Search and Rescue named David Cole contacted Neil Boag by radio. Cole and his colleagues hadn't heard anything about the *Winston Churchill* since Boag's plane reported seeing it five hours earlier, so Cole wanted to question Boag about what he had seen. It didn't take long to discover that a mistake had been made. Boag said the vessel he had seen looked like a modern yacht that had been dismasted. Cole was sure that no one would consider the *Churchill*'s design to be modern, and he didn't believe it had been dismasted.

The *Churchill* was promptly returned to the priority list. Not much could be done at night, but a P-3 Orion was immediately instructed to fly to the area where Lieutenant Commander Galletly had wanted to search, and then head in the same direction of the current, dropping high-intensity flares along the way. The hope was that the Orion would elicit response flares from the *Churchill*'s crew, but none were seen.

At midnight, several AusSAR officers gathered to develop a much more extensive search, to be implemented at first light. Based on the rough position Winning had provided and estimates for the subsequent impact of the wind and current, AusSAR's potential search area was enormous, by one calculation 150 square miles. Hoping to refine its efforts, AusSAR asked a helicopter to drop several traceable buoys to gauge the current's direction and speed. In the meantime, it divided the largest possible area into smaller plots and organized the logistics for an operation that would involve three layers of aircraft: air force P-3 Orion planes at the highest, helicopters at the lowest, and fixed-wing aircraft in between.

While the planning continued, Brian Wiley, a senior search-and-rescue coordinator, called one of his colleagues in Hobart, Sam Hughes, and instructed him to ask the CYC officials who had assembled there to consider calling off the race. AusSAR was running out of planes and helicopters. Several CYC officials met to discuss the request but decided that the fleet was already in the storm. Changing course wouldn't help. Sorry, they told Wiley, but it was too late.

During most of the night, Richard Winning's raft was buffeted by torrential rain. Beaver demanded answers. "Is anyone going to come for us? Did anyone get our Mayday?"

"I spoke to the helicopter pilot," Winning said. "The communication was garbled, but we have the EPIRB. They'll find us."

Beaver had one more question: "Are these waves going to tip us over?"

That possibility, unspoken until then, had been uppermost on Bruce Gould's mind, too, although he saw no sense in talking about it. "Beaver, you're going to get through this shit fight," Gould said. "You haven't done enough bad things in your life yet. There's no way in the world you're going to die out here."

With the heavy cloud cover, there was no moon or stars, so it was impossible to see the waves either before they arrived or after they had passed. While the breaking ones sounded like rolling thunder as they made their way toward the raft, others arrived without warning. Just before nightfall, one of the quiet ones lifted the raft and began to break at the same time. Captured by the white water, the raft hurtled along on what seemed like an endless rocky road. The raft's walls flexed as if they were made of Jell-O, bodies bounced against one another like bumper cars, and when the ride was over, the raft was upside down. Four men were underwater, trapped inside the raft by its canopy, entangled with one another, unsure what was up and what was down. Lumpy's face was jammed down against the canopy of the raft, he felt bodies on top of him, and he was certain — absolutely certain — that he was about to drown. Beaver was doing a handstand, with his hands resting against the canopy, yet at first he didn't realize he was underwater.

Within seconds, however, everyone regained enough sense of balance that their heads found the pocket of air created by the interior of the inverted raft, where they gasped for breath. There were only ten inches of space between the water and the floor of the raft. Thanks to a small waterproof flashlight that Lumpy had, there was enough light to see the terror in everyone's eyes. Even Winning was frightened to his core. Until then, convinced that everything would be all right if he just followed the principles he had been learning since he was a child, he had been a model of calm and confidence. But having never been trained in the use of life rafts, he was unprepared for this.

Beaver was frantic. "What are we going to do? What are we going to do?"

Whatever it was, it had to be soon. Sensing that it was getting hard to breathe, Winning exclaimed, "We're going to run out of air!"

"That's right!" said Beaver. "There's four of us in this little space. We've got to get out of here — or turn the raft back over."

"Maybe we can all get to one side and tip it over," Lumpy said.

By then, Beaver had calmed down enough to remember something from his commercial-mariners course: a raft is supposed to have a line attached to its bottom, which, if pulled by someone from outside the raft, can return it to an upright position. In fact, he thought he heard a line slapping against the bottom of the raft, which was resting against the top of his head. Almost screaming, he said, "There's a line. You can hear it. What you have to do is go outside and pull on it until the raft turns over."

Everyone was skeptical, if not about the existence of the line, then about the idea that someone could swim outside and pull the raft over without being washed away.

"Yeah, Beaver," Lumpy said. "Are you a good swimmer?"

"Me? No way! There's no way at all."

Cutting off further discussion, Winning declared, "We can't yap about it — we're going to run out of air." Removing his life preserver, which he thought would have prevented him from going underwater, he swam through the opening. Resurfacing outside, he pulled himself partially up the raft's wall so he could see the bottom. From that position, there was enough ambient light to see a line extending between two opposite points on the floor. Assuming that it was the line Beaver had described, Winning, with his knees planted on the side of the raft, reached up for it. He then leaned backward, hoping his weight would be enough to overturn the raft. At first, the only effect was that the floor began to buckle. But then, as the far side lifted slightly above the surface of the water and captured the wind, the raft flipped. "We're going over," Winning shouted as he fell back in the water.

Losing his grip, Winning ended up a few feet away from the raft, but it took just a couple of strokes to swim back. After he hoisted himself though the opening, his face was white. "At least we know we can do that," he said. "But, Christ, I hope it doesn't happen again."

The raft was full of water. Beaver's boot, the one he had been using as a bailer, had disappeared during the roll, so he took off the other one and filled it with water.

The swell of every wave brought new stomach-wrenching fear, the terror that the raft would flip again shared through eye contact rather than words. Lumpy perceived a linked line of emotional defense, one that would disintegrate if he let Beaver know how scared he was. To Lumpy, Winning represented absolute strength, superhuman courage. *I must draw from his strength*, Lumpy reasoned, *so that Beaver can draw from mine.*

Lumpy was also thinking about hypothermia, which commences as soon as the body begins losing heat faster than it can produce it. Although no one was really cold, everyone on the raft had been shivering at one point or another, and Lumpy knew that could be an early symptom. Hypothermia can progress so slowly as to be imperceptible, and he also realized that the crew had begun to exhibit other potential signs of trouble — muscle stiffness, clumsiness, and sleepiness. If their body temperatures dropped low enough, the crew would have difficulty seeing and speaking and would become dangerously disoriented. Hypothermia ultimately causes victims to fall into a coma and suffer fatal organ damage.

Steamer's raft had also flipped. When its five passengers found the air pocket, it was pitch-black. Michael Bannister was the first to speak: "Someone has to go out and right the raft, or we are going to be in big trouble." Jim Lawler immediately volunteered, but then he saw a complication. "To get out there, I'm going to have to take my life vest off."

Steamer knew Lawler, who had sailed in seventeen Hobarts, to be an extremely knowledgeable yachtsman. Having worked as a marine engineer for four decades, he was a senior inspector for the American Bureau of Shipping, the international marine classification organization that determines whether ships are insurable. Lawler, who was fifty-nine, spent his working days evaluating the seaworthiness of everything from cargo ships to passenger liners, making sure, among other things, that they carried required safety equipment.

Steamer, unable to imagine how Lawler could swim outside the raft and turn it over without being washed away, said, "It's too dangerous." After a pause, he added, "Maybe we should stay upside down. The raft seems more stable this way." He had never heard of anyone choosing to ride in an inverted raft, but he couldn't think of any reason not to. With at least one foot planted on the rubber tube that supported the canopy, each man was shoulder deep in water, but it didn't seem uncomfortably cold.

One of the flaws in Steamer's strategy revealed itself when a breaking wave crashed over the raft. It left a puddle on top of the raft's sagging floor, forcing it so far down that it pushed everyone's head partly underwater. By pressing against the floor, they knocked off most of the water, but the episode made them think about the limited supply of air.

Convinced that no one could turn over the raft without being taken by a wave, Steamer suggested using the knife Gibbo had carried from the *Churchill* to cut an opening in the bottom (now the top) of the raft. "If we're happy to stay like this," Steamer said, "let's just put a small slit in the floor so we can get some oxygen."

Only Michael Bannister objected. "I think someone has to go outside," he said. "I'm willing to give it a go."

"Michael, I wouldn't recommend it," Gibbo said. "It's death out there." Gibbo instantly regretted his words as being overly melodramatic, but when another breaking wave pounded the raft, he decided that they were also accurate.

Recognizing that surgery could impair their already unreliable craft, it wasn't done in haste. But once they agreed that the best place for an incision was near the side, where the floor appeared to be reinforced, Jim Lawler carefully pushed the blade through the floor, creating a four-inch slit. When he was done, they gently pushed up on the floor as if it were a bellows and felt an influx of fresh air.

But taking a knife to the raft was a terrible mistake. Less than an hour after the job was done, when a wave hurled the raft right side up and the group tumbled onto the floor, the slit extended halfway across the floor. The opening was big enough that anyone could have slid through the bottom. The oxygen scoop had become a trapdoor.

"We have just got to hang on like grim death," Steamer declared.

Gibbo, who had already decided that the raft's true nature was evil, thought the knife had unleashed a demon — one that could, without any notice, dump him and the others into the sea. His defenses were limited, but remembering his harness and tether, he looked at Lawler and said, "You know, it might be a good thing if I attach this thing to the raft."

"That," Lawler replied, "probably wouldn't hurt."

Later in the night, Winning's raft rolled again. This time everyone knew what had happened, but the violent action and sudden immersion was as frightening as the first time. By the time

Lumpy illuminated the air pocket with his flashlight, he counted only three heads.

"Richard," he screamed.

"I'm out here, son."

Winning, who hadn't put his life preserver back on after the first flip, was already outside the raft, clambering up the wall. From the inside, the others felt the raft bend as Winning tugged on the line. Like the first time, he brought the raft upright quickly. After he flopped back through the opening, Lumpy declared, "That was fucking scary. Is this going to happen all night?"

Glaring at Lumpy, Winning said, "That doesn't even warrant thinking about."

Beaver was deeply shaken. "We can't do that anymore," he declared. "We just can't do it."

Everyone thought they had to do more to support the raft against the biggest waves. "When we have a big one," Lumpy said, "let's really put our weight up against the walls."

Concentrating on reacting as fast as he could to the oncoming waves, Beaver convinced himself that they had developed a reliable defense. "We've got it sorted," he said. "We're not going to go over again." No one shared his confidence, though, and they were sure that Beaver's bubble of optimism wouldn't last for long.

A few minutes later, Winning said he saw a ship through the opening, and he fired a flare. "Look, you can see its light on the horizon," he said. No one else saw anything, though, and Winning later decided that it had been an illusion. There was nothing but storm-filled ocean in every direction.

29

Just after midnight, early Monday morning, a navy Sea King helicopter under the command of Paul "Tanzi" Lea took off from the coastal town of Merimbula and headed toward the *Sword of Orion*. In 1979, Tanzi, then a pilot in the British navy, had retrieved several yachtsmen in the disastrous Fastnet Race. He had emigrated to Australia in 1990 and had switched to the Royal Australian Navy. The weather during the Fastnet had been terrible, but Tanzi, now fifty-three, thought the flying conditions were much worse here. The ceiling of clouds was just four hundred feet over the water, and he was flying at an altitude of two hundred feet, unable to see anything but the driving rain that was hitting the glass in front of his face. An hour into the flight, it was so rough that Dave Hutchinson, who normally operated the winch, was retching from airsickness.

Neil Boag had provided a position for the *Sword*, but when Tanzi arrived there, he didn't see a yacht. Aware that the current and wind had had several hours to carry the boat away, he flew an ever expanding pattern of boxes while speaking over the radio.

"*Sword of Orion. Sword of Orion.* This is Shark Twenty for a radio check," Tanzi said, using his helicopter's code name. "We are in the search area. Please come up on this frequency."

After more than an hour, Tanzi still hadn't heard or seen anything. "We're not getting anywhere," he said over the intercom.
"They've probably drifted a long way. Let's go to the original position and head straight downwind for twenty miles and see how
we go."

"The way we're burning fuel, that sounds like a good idea to
me," said copilot Chris Money.

It was a strategy that depended heavily on chance, but Money
spotted a light just a few minutes after they turned downwind.
"Come left now," he said to Tanzi over the intercom. "Okay, keep
coming left. It's on our nose now." It was 2:35 A.M., and the helicopter was 105 miles from land. As it descended near the *Sword*, aim-
ing a powerful spotlight on the dismasted yacht, Money thought it
looked naked and vulnerable as it pitched from side to side.

"Jesus," he said, "it looks pretty beaten."

Money knew that rescuing anyone in those conditions would
be treacherous. Most of the waves were more than thirty feet high,
and at one point the altimeter indicated that the distance between
helicopter and the water had plummeted from one hundred feet
to fifty, suggesting that a fifty-foot wave had passed. While Tanzi
tried to hold his machine in place against sixty to seventy knots of
wind and gusts as high as eighty-two, Brian "Dixie" Lee, a thirty-
three-year-old airman who was next to the helicopter door,
dropped a smoke flare into the water to give Tanzi a visual point
of reference. Given the wind and waves, it didn't help much.

"This is the *Sword of Orion*," Carl Watson said over the radio.
The helicopter's broadcasts had been audible to him for half an
hour, but those were the first words from the *Sword* to be heard
by Tanzi.

"Okay, *Sword of Orion*. This is Shark Twenty. We've got you.
What's your condition?"

"We're taking in water and require immediate assistance," Watson said before he described how the deck had separated from the hull on the starboard side.

"Okay," Tanzi said. "Can you turn off your EPIRB?"

Tanzi explained that the large number of emergency signals was complicating search-and-rescue operations. But when Nigel Russell went up to the cockpit and pulled the line that held the beacon, there was nothing at the other end. "There is no EPIRB," he told Watson. "The line broke — it's gone."

Hoping to get a better look at the yacht, Tanzi pushed a lever near the right side of his seat forward to reduce the angle of the helicopter's blades, causing it to descend closer to the *Sword*. The helicopter's searchlight projected into the boat through the cracks in the disintegrating fiberglass cabin top to produce a spiderweb of light. Tanzi didn't know much about boats, but the debris on the *Sword*'s deck and the tangle of lines trailing behind convinced him that Watson wasn't exaggerating the danger facing the yacht.

Over the helicopter's intercom, Tanzi asked, "What are we going to do here? Precision hovering over the top is going to be very difficult. And it's way too dangerous to put someone onto the yacht."

The airmen agreed that instead of simply lowering the helicopter's only metal cable to the yacht, they would attach a "hi-line" to the end of the cable. The hi-line is a rope that contains a "weak link" designed to break under pressure. As Tanzi flew over the *Sword*, the hi-line, but not the cable itself, would be dragged over the deck of the yacht so one of the sailors could grab it. If the cable became entangled with the boat, it would have to be cut and the mission would have to be aborted. But if the hi-line got caught, it wouldn't matter, because the weak link would simply give way, leaving the cable undamaged.

At 2:50 A.M., Tanzi radioed the *Sword*. "We don't have a lot of fuel, but the boat is obviously not in a good state. We think we should effect a rescue now. Are you familiar with the hi-line method?"

"I am," Watson replied.

"Okay. Sorry we have to do it this way — but it's too dangerous for us to put one of our guys down."

Tanzi set the radar altimeter to maintain a hover sixty feet above the water and used the control stick between his knees to try to hold the helicopter in place against the wind. Anxious to focus all his attention on flying, Tanzi asked Chris Money to handle the radio.

"Okay, we're ready to go," Money told Watson. "Given the conditions, we should start with a couple of your fittest guys."

"They want two able-bodied men," Watson said to the crew. "Dags and Nigel — you go first. What they're going to do is drag a line across the deck. You grab it — and pull in the line until you get to the sling, which is a harness that you put over your head and under both of your arms. Once you have it on, they'll pull you up."

Kulmar suddenly spoke up, and he was furious. "Who said Dags should go?" he demanded. "He knows the boat better than anyone else. He needs to be here. I should go."

"Dags and Nigel are going," Watson said, amazed by what he believed to be Kulmar's brazen selfishness.

The airmen knew it would be a difficult procedure. In theory, the winch operator was supposed to pay out the cable and hi-line so there was enough slack for the person being rescued to put on the sling while still on the yacht. But given the substantial waves, it was impossible for the winch operator to maintain a consistent amount of slack, and Tanzi couldn't hold the helicopter in place against the gusts. The yacht itself was a moving target. As it rolled up and down waves, it took Tanzi five passes before Dags was able to grasp the line. He retrieved it as fast as he could, but he ran out of slack long before he got to the sling.

Brownie, who was sitting in the cockpit near Dags, shouted, "You have to go in the water and pull in the rest." This wasn't the way it was supposed to work, but Dags didn't see any alternative. Jumping into the water, he started pulling himself toward the sling, hand over hand. Suddenly the hi-line went totally slack. The weak link wasn't strong enough to hold a person's weight against the turbulent water.

At that point, Dags had nothing to hold on to, and he didn't know how — or if — the helicopter could retrieve him. He was already too far from the *Sword* to swim back, and he suddenly realized that he was exactly where Glyn Charles had been. Then it got worse. He could see the helicopter, but the spotlight was no longer aimed at him. He remembered hearing someone from the helicopter telling Watson, "If someone's in the water, we'll get him," but Dags didn't believe that would be true in his case. Right now, he realized, they couldn't even see him. Dags thrashed his arms in the water, screaming and gasping for air, gripped by the certainty that he would drown.

When the spotlight recaptured Dags, Dixie said, "The hi-line is gone. The guy isn't connected to anything."

"Attach another hi-line to the cable," Tanzi commanded, "but take the weak link out." Without the weak link, the hi-line was simply a rope connected to the cable.

Unlike Tanzi, Dixie could see directly below the chopper by extending his head out the side door, and he attempted to direct the pilot to maneuver in a way that caused the line to snake around Dags. It was like a water-skiing boat trying to get a tow-line to a fallen skier, only much more difficult. "Go right twenty feet," Dixie said over the intercom. "Forward five feet ... go right twenty more feet."

Dags was still struggling to keep himself from absolute panic when he saw the cable slicing through the water. The cable provided sudden clarity. Swimming to it, he let it slip through his hands until he had the sling. Determining what to do next was much more difficult. Experienced sailors practice many things, but this is not one of them. Dags knew the sling had to go over his head and under his arms, but it didn't seem large enough. Every time he got the sling into position and tried to insert one of his arms, his head submerged and he was seized by panic all over again. Eventually, with a rush of violent contortions, the sling was snugly wrapped around his chest and under his arms. After he waved toward the helicopter, the cable went taut and he rose out of the water. But suddenly he fell back into the sea, just in time for a breaking wave to crash over his head. Dags concluded that the connection between him and the helicopter had failed again. Exhausted and more than five hundred feet from the *Sword*, he again thought he was about to die.

In fact, Dixie, afraid of what would happen if the top of a breaking wave hit Dags while he was in midair, had intentionally lowered him back into the water. Seconds later, almost twenty minutes after Dags had first entered the water, the cable pulled him upward again, this time steadily all the way to the helicopter.

"Okay, we have one aboard," Money said over the radio to Watson. "We're ready to go for another."

Nigel Russell was next. Having been in the cabin during Dags's rescue, he was oblivious to what his crewmate had been through. Thinking the rescue operation wouldn't be overly difficult, Russell had stuffed some of his personal belongings into a duffel bag. When Brownie saw the bag, he shook his head and said, "No way, mate. You're not taking anything." In fact, Russell's rescue was much easier than Dags's, mostly because there wasn't a weak link in the hi-line. Six minutes after he jumped into the water, Russell was aboard the helicopter.

After Russell, Kulmar, unwilling to wait any longer, declared, "I'm next — I'm out of here," and climbed onto the deck before anything else could be said. But after he got to the back of the yacht and caught the line, he just sat there, still in a state of mental shock and unable to bring himself to go into the water.

"What are we waiting for?" Tanzi asked over the intercom. "We can't spend another fifteen minutes here. If he doesn't want to go in, fine — but we're going to have to leave him there."

Dixie was much more anxious. "Get on the radio," he bellowed to Chris Money, "and tell them this guy has to get in the fucking water."

Money was just as annoyed as Dixie, but he wasn't about to say anything that might be counterproductive. "We need to get moving," he told Watson over the radio. "We're getting quite low on fuel."

On the deck of the *Sword*, Brownie, kneeling next to Kulmar and aware of what the delay meant for the others, was losing patience. "You have to go in the water. You're holding up the queue."

"I can't do it. I just can't do it," Kulmar said as he stared into the darkness. He had pulled in some of the hi-line, but even though there was still plenty of slack left, he was just holding the line in both his hands. "I have a family, I have two little girls at home. I just can't do it."

Brownie finally did the job himself, shoving Kulmar off the side. Trying to sound good-natured, Brownie yelled, "I'll see you back there."

Pulling frantically on the line, Kulmar eventually reached the sling, but then he couldn't figure out how to use it. He put one of his arms through but, utterly exhausted, gave up trying to do anything else. Watching from above, Dixie could see that Kulmar wasn't using the sling properly; however, given the time constraint, he tried to lift him anyway. Almost immediately, Kulmar fell out of the sling and into the water.

"He's lost the line. We've got a real problem with this guy," Dixie said.

Once again, Tanzi dragged the line in an arc around the target, but Dixie saw that Kulmar was again putting only one of his arms through the sling rather than pulling it over his head so it would rest under both arms.

"He's doing it wrong," Dixie said. "This isn't going to work."

Now was not the time for this sort of thing. Holding the chopper in place was extremely difficult, and as it was thrown by a gust, the sling ripped away from Kulmar. Alone in the water with nothing to hold on to, his mind went into overdrive, flashing images of his wife and daughters as well as of Glyn Charles. Like many people who believe they are near death, Kulmar began making promises to God, resolving that he would devote whatever remaining life he might have to being a better husband and father — and that he would never sail another Hobart.

The helicopter was burning 1,000 pounds of fuel per hour. According to calculations Tanzi had made before Dags's rescue, "bingo" — the moment when he had to turn back to land — would come when he had 1,800 pounds left. The needles on three fuel gauges on the left side of the console indicated that they were already down to 1,700 pounds. Although there was some reserve built into the bingo math, the trade-offs and the decisions were becoming desperate. Running out of fuel over the water probably meant death. The helicopter had a flotation device, but it was only capable of slowing the rate of its sinking, theoretically long enough to launch a life raft. However, given the size of the waves, Tanzi thought getting a raft through the helicopter door was probably impossible.

Kulmar had been in the water for twenty minutes. Although he knew he wasn't in the sling the way he should be, he had stopped trying. He wasn't overcome by panic; he simply didn't have any fight left. In a hazy state of semiconsciousness, he said to himself, *At least I'm going to see Glyn.*

From above, it looked as if Kulmar were holding his chin with his hands, as if he had just enough strength to keep his head out of the water. "He can't help himself," Chris Money said. "He's got hypothermia or he's going unconscious."

"Shit!" Dixie exclaimed.

Dixie knew the only hope was for him to go into the water to help Kulmar. He also knew that doing so could have life-and-death consequences not just for Kulmar but for himself and potentially the rest of the helicopter's crew. Not only were they past bingo, but Dave Hutchinson, who would have to operate the winch, was still sick.

"What do you think, Dave?" Dixie asked. "Can you handle the winch if I go down?"

Hutchinson said yes, but Tanzi was reluctant. "I don't know, Dixie. Look at what it's like down there. Are you sure?"

"What else are we going to do? Leave him out there to die?"

It was an option.

Already in his wet suit, Dixie slipped on a pair of flippers and attached the harness he was wearing to the end of the cable. When Hutchinson began to lower him down, Dixie was blasted by the wind and thrown by the movement of the helicopter. Well before he touched the water, Dixie lost sight of his target. Then, hit by a wave, he submerged. When he resurfaced, he caught a glimpse of Kulmar, but they were fifty feet apart. Dixie swam as hard as he could; when he cut the distance in half, he tried to scream over the noise of the helicopter and waves.

"Get your fucking ass over here!"

Kulmar heard nothing. In fact, he didn't see Dixie until they were just a few feet apart.

"Here, mate, I've got you," Dixie shouted, holding the back of Kulmar's life preserver. Kulmar wasn't sure whether what he was seeing was real.

After waiting for a wave to pass, Dixie forced the sling over Kulmar's head. After the two men began to rise from the water, Dixie spoke directly into Kulmar's ear: "We're going to be all right. Are you okay?"

Kulmar still didn't hear anything. He felt his heart pounding fast and hard, and his head felt as if it were going to explode; but his eyes were shut, and he wasn't sure whether he was alive or dead. When he finally opened his eyes and saw the glare of the spotlight, he thought it was the great white light that people see just before they die. Only when he was pulled inside the helicopter did he realize he might be alive. He didn't show any emotions, though. He just said thanks and crawled across the helicopter's rubber-mat floor and rolled onto his side. He heard something about "fuel," but he had shut his eyes again. The only thing he had the energy to do was feel his wrist for a pulse. Still uncertain about his status, he was looking for affirmations of life. Steve Kulmar, the man who had such supreme confidence in himself, wasn't even sure whether to believe the sound of his own heartbeat.

From the front of the helicopter, Chris Money was on the radio to Watson. "We've got him — but we're out of fuel. We're really sorry, but we have to go. Another bird will be out here within an hour. They know exactly where you are."

"I hope they don't come back until dawn," Andrew Parkes said to Brownie. Given how long Kulmar was in the water, he was sure they would be better off staying on the boat.

On the way to the airport in Merimbula, Dags, who was wearing a headset, heard bits and pieces about what had happened to other yachts. Listening to a cacophony of radio traffic, he learned that as many as twenty-two sailors might be lost. He also heard Tanzi talking about the fuel and the amount of salt that was caked onto the engine. When salt adheres to the leading edge of the turbine's spinning blades, it disrupts the flow of air through the engine, causing overheating and a loss of power. Estimating that the helicopter had lost a third of its thrust, Tanzi looked at a map to determine where they would reach the first beach, in case they needed to make an emergency landing. Fortunately, though, he benefited from a powerful tailwind and they made it back to Merimbula in an hour. No one reflected on a strange irony: without the very storm that had forced Shark 20's rescue mission, the chopper may have run out of fuel before reaching land.

30

Steamer's raft flipped two more times Sunday night. In the second inversion, the entire canopy sheared away and the slit extended from wall to wall. Without a ceiling or a floor to contain them, everyone understood how easily they could become separated from the raft. Whether the raft was up or down, there was no safety net. Gibbo began to think of the raft as a wild beast that was deliberately trying to flick human passengers from its back.

Despite the extremely treacherous state of their raft, there wasn't any despair among its crew, at least none that was voiced. In fact, there was little talk of any kind as they careened through the night. Everyone was exhausted, and that was terrifying as well. They were simply too tired to stay awake all the time, but they knew they had to maintain a grip on the raft, so even during catnaps their hands were clenched on lines or the frayed fabric that remained from the canopy.

* * *

Sometime after midnight, an enormous wave, which was virtually silent as it approached, lifted Steamer's raft toward its crest and then began to break. It was the worst possible combination. The five men had received no warning, no signal to tighten their holds. And since they were near the lip of the crest when it began tumbling downward, the raft had a long way to fall amid the speeding piles of water.

Gibbo lost his grip almost immediately. The water was like a tidal wave, pushing his body forward but also twisting it in every other direction, as if he were inside a giant washing machine. Most of the ride was underwater, but it also felt as if he were falling down the face of an endless cliff. More overwhelmed than frightened, there was nothing he could do but gasp for air.

Before the wave arrived, Steamer's left arm had been wrapped around the tube that was designed to support the canopy. The hold that the tube provided made it a choice position; the others had given it to him because of his injured legs. As soon as he felt the wave crashing over his body, Steamer locked onto the tube by using his right hand to grip his left forearm. There was enormous pressure against his body, all of it, he thought, intended to tear him away. He knew he was turning upside down and sideways and that he might not be able to breathe — but his mind was focused on one thing: the need to hold on.

When the wave finally released the raft, Steamer's eyes were so full of salt that he couldn't see anything very clearly, but he feared the worst. Catching a lungful of air and rubbing his eyes, he called out.

"Is everybody here?"

Only Gibbo responded. Still connected to the raft by his harness, he was floating nearby.

The surface of the water seemed remarkably still and was covered by a foamy whiteness that made it easier to see. Looking into the distance, Steamer spotted two human heads bobbing close together about one hundred feet away. One of them was holding a light over his head, and Steamer was sure that it was Jim Lawler, who had been carrying a flashlight. But Steamer couldn't make out whether the figure next to Lawler was Michael Bannister or John Dean. There was no sign of the third man. The distance was already too great for shouted communication, and with the wind pushing the raft much faster than the men in the water could possibly swim, the gap grew rapidly. Gibbo also had a light, and he turned it on and held it over his head, hoping that it would offer some kind of reassurance. But within a few minutes, as the raft left the drifting men behind, Lawler's light disappeared.

Staring across the water, Steamer's eyes filled with tears. In a mournful tone that was just loud enough for Gibbo to hear, he said, "There's nothing we can do."

Steamer and Gibbo didn't say much more about what had happened. They knew they had to come up with a method to protect themselves in the event of another roll. They also knew they should try to keep at least their chests out of the water. The raft was too wide for their feet to reach the other side, so over the next couple of hours, they improvised a system. When the raft was right side up, they sat back-to-back, sitting astride the tube that had supported the canopy, using their legs to prop themselves up against the wall. When the raft was upside down, the tube was underwater, so it offered less support. During those times, Gibbo and Steamer faced each other, using their feet to pin each other's backs against the wall. This was the less comfortable position because it required Steamer to place one of his feet in Gibbo's crotch. Steamer's legs were too painful for him to assume the reciprocal position. Though it was the best method they could come up with, they were flipped two more times before dawn on Monday.

But Gibbo developed more confidence with each capsize. After the third one, he decided that he had gone to war with the raft — and won. Emboldened, he spoke silently to his foe: *If that's the best you can do, then screw you. I'm still here. You're not going to get me.*

For several hours after the three men were lost, Gibbo didn't even consider the possibility that his friends might not survive. It wasn't until sometime after sunrise that he began to weigh their odds. They had been adrift and alone, with only their life preservers to keep them afloat in a punishing ocean. Three men. Three friends. Gone.

31

Adrian Lister, the thirty-five-year-old pilot of a navy Sea Hawk helicopter, had watched the start of the race from the best vantage point in Sydney, a naval base perched atop a bluff near the mouth of the harbor. The base provided a sweeping view of the yachts as they made their way out of the harbor and into the ocean.

At four o'clock on Sunday afternoon, Lister's commanding officer called him at home. "Don't drink that beer," the boss said, explaining that the race was likely to run into a dangerous storm and that Lister might be asked to join a rescue operation. Sure enough, at 2:30 A.M. on Monday, Lister and his crew were flying toward the *Sword of Orion*. It had already been a long day for the airmen. They had been awake for so many hours that their flight required an exemption from mandatory rest rules.

The weather was fine during the first half hour after they left Merimbula, but then the air became increasingly turbulent. Before long, Lister's machine, which weighed ten tons, was bouncing like a car driving down a flight of stairs. Then there was the radar: when it first picked up cells of the storm, it showed them in green. As the clouds thickened, the screen turned yellow, then amber and red before finally going black because the radar wasn't powerful enough to penetrate the thick clouds. Not only was he flying through some of the worst turbulence he'd ever encountered, but he was doing it blindly. Concerned that he might collide with Tanzi's helicopter, Lister made radio contact with the other pilot so they could coordinate their flight paths. Lister also asked Tanzi about his rescue technique. "Did you put anyone in the water?"

"We did, but the conditions were extreme. You'll want to avoid it."

Lister knew night rescues were much more dangerous than daytime ones — he estimated fifty times more dangerous — so he assumed that the *Sword* was close to sinking. With a recent position to aim for, he didn't have any trouble finding the yacht. Arriving overhead at 4:10 A.M., he immediately tried to gather information over the radio.

"Are you sinking?" he asked. "What is your situation? And what are your thoughts about getting off now?"

"We aren't sinking," Carl Watson replied. "The last rescue was very difficult, so we're not sure we want to conduct any more in the dark."

"That's fine with us. We have enough fuel to have some endurance, and it would be a lot safer for everyone if we have some light, so let's wait. We'll do a pass over you every fifteen minutes to make sure you're all right."

Since hovering consumed one thousand pounds of fuel an hour, compared with seven hundred pounds when the helicopter was moving slowly, Lister began flying a large oval pattern. Just after 5:00 A.M., when the sky began to brighten, he turned toward the *Sword*, ready to begin. But in the still-murky weather, he couldn't find it. The helicopter's searchlight was visible from the yacht, though, so Watson radioed instructions. "Go east about a mile."

Daylight provided the helicopter crewmen with their first real look at the sea. The altimeter readings indicated that the waves were more than thirty feet high, but they looked much larger.

"Guys, what do you think?" Lister asked over the intercom. "Are you happy to go into the water?"

"I'm happy to do it," replied David Oxley, the thirty-two-year-old crewman who would go down on the wire. "But let's try something else first."

"That sounds reasonable. Let's try a hi-line without a weak link."

Lister relayed the plan to Watson, but Watson wanted to talk about Kooky. "We have an injured person. What is the procedure for him?"

"We'll get back to you on that."

Kooky, who overheard the exchange, was worried by the noncommittal response. But Lister didn't have a better answer. The helicopter didn't have a stretcher, and even if it did, it couldn't be used in these conditions. Lister decided to start with some of the others.

Watson asked Andrew Parkes to go first. Parkes was glad he didn't have to watch anyone else go before him, because he was sure that would add to his anxiety. He was already nervous enough. Sitting at the back of the boat, waiting for the hi-line, he told Brownie, "I don't think I can do this." But Brownie didn't have to push him off the side; Parkes knew that time was precious, and as soon as he grabbed the line and pulled in as much as he could, he slid into the water. However, when he reached the sling, it wouldn't fit over his head. He was wearing his one-piece survival suit, a garment that appeared to be so watertight that Brownie had stuffed several wallets and mobile telephones down the back of it. The baggage had thickened Parkes's torso to the point that it took several minutes of frantic movements to get the sling around his body. When he arrived at the helicopter, he was so drained that he just stared blankly at the floor.

Sam Hunt and Brownie followed Parkes, and their rescues were rapid, almost routine. Watson, who planned to go last, was more concerned about Kooky than anything else. Using fiberglass batons and nylon straps, Simon Reffold had already fashioned a splint for Kooky's left leg, but Reffold and Watson doubted that Kooky could do what was required. When his turn came, Reffold and Watson virtually carried him to the rear of the boat. Sitting with both legs over the side, Kooky turned his head around to see what was left of his battered yacht. It was the first time he had been above since the roll, and he shuddered at the appearance of the deck. Seeing how cracks extended from one side of the cockpit to the other, he was amazed that it hadn't collapsed. The starboard side of the deck looked as though a bulldozer had scraped away the stanchions and everything else. More than anything, he was shocked to see the mangled steering wheel.

The waves were also worse than he had imagined, leaving his stomach full of stabbing anxiety. But Kooky realized that the *Sword* was close to total collapse, and he was playing a game of lesser evils. Taking a deep breath, he prepared to enter the water just as a terrific wave slammed into the boat, spinning it almost 180 degrees. Kooky, too revved up to pull back, pushed himself off the starboard side of the deck without hesitation. But the wave had turned the boat so much that he entered the water on the downwind side. As a result, the *Sword* was being blown in the same direction he was swimming — and it was moving much faster than he was. A dreadful realization swept those watching: out of control, the *Sword* was headed right for Kooky. As the boat reared up, Kooky put a hand above his head to fend off the hull. His head submerged just as the yacht slid off a wave and slapped down hard against the water. Oxley saw the splash from the chopper. From his vantage point, it looked as if the hull landed on Kooky's head with crushing force.

"Holy shit!" Oxley yelled over the intercom. "He's in trouble. The cable must be under the yacht. This guy could be knocked out."

But Kooky was conscious. The hull had barely missed his head, but the hi-line was already under the boat and was pulling Kooky downward. Opening his eyes, he saw that the line was looped around the rudder. He could see what he had to do — pull himself to the bottom of the rudder, which extended six feet below the surface of the water, and free the line. He used all his limbs except for his injured leg to kick and pull his way down. Once he reached the base of the rudder, he yanked the line downward. After it slipped free, Kooky popped up on the other side of the boat.

"He's out!" Oxley exclaimed. "He looks okay."

Kooky, however, was still far from the sling, and as he gasped for air, he didn't think he had the strength to reach it. The helicopter also was having problems. As Kooky moved downwind, the angle of the cable changed. Eventually, it was almost forty-five degrees to the sea, and following another brutal gust, it snagged on the landing gear on the right side of the helicopter.

"We're caught," Marc Pavillard, the winchman, said over the intercom. "The cable is under the starboard landing gear. I'm going to pay out some more cable to give it some slack. Can you move ahead and to the right?"

The helicopter's maneuver freed the cable, but Oxley and Lister knew that it was almost certainly damaged, perhaps catastrophically. Formed from strands of steel, cables have enormous lifting strength but can be easily damaged when bent. After Kooky got the sling over his head, Oxley, who was wearing leather gloves, pushed the UP button and let the returning cable run through his hand to check for burs. Although he didn't feel any, he wasn't really reassured.

Originally, Lister didn't think he would have enough fuel to remove everyone from the *Sword*. Based on the rate of fuel consumption and fifteen minutes per rescue, he thought he would end up leaving at least two people for another chopper. But after Kooky's rescue, the chopper had more fuel than Lister had anticipated, so he decided to keep going, even if it meant the helicopter had to land on a beach rather than get all the way back to Merimbula. Simon Reffold went next, and he was lifted to safety without incident.

Watson was last. Wearing too much clothing, he had trouble swimming, and when he made it to the sling, he too couldn't get it over his head and under his arms. Putting both his arms through the apparatus, he decided that he couldn't do any better and that he could hold on with his hands.

"He's only half in the sling," Oxley said. "If we lift him, he's going to fall out."

Checking his watch, Lister decided to take a chance. "Let's give it a go. He'll hold on."

Watson's hands were clenched around the cable like a vise. When he reached the helicopter just before 6:00 A.M., his face was drained of color, and he was hyperventilating.

"You look like you're going to have a heart attack," Sam Hunt said.

"No, I'm fine," Watson claimed, although his hands were still tightly clenched and he was wondering whether they would ever work normally again.

Their luck continued as the fuel held up and Lister made it all the way back to Merimbula. Both crews stepped onto the tarmac with an enormous sense of relief. The airmen hadn't had any sleep for more than twenty-four hours. Before they left the airport, though, they told an engineer about the problem with the winch cable and watched as it was paid out onto the runway. When the engineer spotted a bend in the cable, three men gave it a sharp pull, and it snapped in two.

32

On Richard Winning's raft, Monday's dawn brought tentative hope. Fewer waves were breaking, and the yachtsmen believed that so many ships and planes would be looking for them that they would be rescued within a few hours. But the morning also brought more problems. When Lumpy shifted position, water gushed in from where he had been sitting. The floor had developed a six-inch-long rip. Running his finger along the tear, Winning said, "As if we don't have enough bloody problems. There's a puncture kit around here somewhere."

Finding it jammed between the floor and the sagging lower wall, Lumpy read the instructions several times to himself before reading an excerpt aloud: "Make sure the surface is clean and dry before use." Some of the contents appeared to be missing anyway, so he tossed the kit out of the raft. A few seconds later, he asked, "What are we going to do now?"

"Just sit your big fat ass down on it," Winning replied.

Beaver's bubble of hope disappeared. "The raft isn't going to make it," he declared, "and that means we're not going to make it."

But Lumpy's body appeared to stop the inflow of water without worsening the rip, and although he had spent a good part of the night bailing, he suggested that the raft would be more stable if it had more water inside. "You know, when we bail the water down to a few inches — that's when we flip."

"I think you're right," Winning said. "We'll be wetter, but I've never heard of anyone getting hypothermia of the ass."

But despite the repair, as the morning wore on, the disappointment was impossible to mask. "What's happening?" Beaver asked. "Why aren't they here yet?"

"Maybe they think we sunk — and we're gone," Lumpy said.

Winning didn't give a sugarcoated response either. "We gave them a bad position. They don't know where we are." Winning was also concerned about the EPIRB. The device had a telescoping antenna, similar to the kind on automobiles. Sometime during the night, probably during one of the flips, the top two-thirds of the antenna had snapped off, causing Winning to wonder whether it was emitting an adequate signal. "Maybe this thing isn't even working," he said.

"Either it isn't working or the signal is too weak because it's in the raft," Lumpy said. All along, he had thought the EPIRB should be in the water. "They're supposed to work better when they're in the water. Why don't we hang it off the raft? We have nothing to lose."

Winning agreed, and after he tied a polypropylene cord to both the raft and the EPIRB, he dropped it into the water. Within a few minutes, though, the connection somehow failed, and Winning watched the EPIRB float away. The raft was moving too fast to retrieve the signaling device, so it — and with it, a bit more hope — disappeared.

* * *

Bruce Gould had said virtually nothing throughout the morning. He was obviously cold. His arms were folded across his chest, and each of his hands was gripping the opposite upper arm. His head was resting on his shoulder, and Lumpy thought he was beginning to look like a corpse.

Lumpy believed he wouldn't survive unless he stayed awake. He knew that people who die of hypothermia slip into comas after going to sleep. At least in a relative sense, Lumpy had convinced himself that he was in pretty good shape. *Gould is in trouble because he's so thin,* Lumpy thought, *but I'm such a fat load that I'll probably live the longest.* However, a little later, Lumpy lost his struggle against sleep, and dreams transported him to happy memories — friend-filled parties, vacations, and a beach picnic with his wife and two daughters. When he awoke, he pondered his inverted world: instead of waking up from a nightmare to the comforting discovery that everything was okay, his dreams were the only place where happiness lay, and the conscious world was the nightmare.

Urine was one of the reminders of his nightmare existence. The raft included a supply of water — not enough for anyone to really quench his thirst, but enough for a sip every few hours and also enough that everyone, at one point or another, had to pee. They weren't about to try to go outside the raft, so they simply relieved themselves inside their foul-weather gear, by then unconcerned about how low they had sunk. Lumpy was the first to talk about it.

"Sorry, fellas," he said, "I'm going to have to have a piss."

"That's okay," Beaver said. He had come to appreciate warmth from any source. A little later, when Lumpy started bailing, Beaver joked, "Don't get rid of all our warm water."

By Monday afternoon, everyone realized there was a real chance that they wouldn't be rescued before nightfall, and Bruce Gould, deciding he needed to gird himself and the others, seemed to come back to life.

"We can survive another night out here," he declared, "and by tomorrow morning there won't be any waves at all."

Lumpy's mind was wandering. He was imagining what the end would be like if no one came and also trying to understand how he had come to be in such a predicament. He was normally not superstitious, but he had come to the conclusion that the handsome shirt he was so eager to keep may not be such a good thing after all. Pulling it out from a pocket in his foul-weather gear, he held it in front of his chest and looked at Winning.

"You know, I really wanted to have this, but I reckon it's bad luck."

Winning didn't say anything, but the puzzled look on his face made it clear that he didn't have any idea what his young friend was talking about.

"Think about it," Lumpy said. "What's happened since we got these shirts? We've lost our boat, we're in a life raft that's sinking, and there's no search planes."

"All true," Winning replied.

With that, Lumpy threw the shirt into the water.

The hours were passing with excruciating slowness. Beaver asked for the time so often that Gould finally said, "Don't worry about it. It's five minutes after you asked the last time."

The combination of desperate hope and fatigue produced hallucinations. During the day, all four men saw and heard what they believed to be fleets of planes and helicopters. Beaver saw several ships on the horizon, and for a while he believed there were so many planes crossing the sky that there would be a collision. He excitedly pointed to them, but the ships and planes seemed to vanish in the mist. After a while, he stopped talking about his visions — and he had fewer of them.

When Lumpy said he heard a plane at 3:30 P.M., Beaver was dismissive. "No, it's nothing. It's only the wind."

But it was real. Unfortunately, though, the plane was approaching the raft from the opposite side of the opening. By the time Winning used a plastic paddle to spin the raft half-way around, the plane was almost past. It was close enough, however, that he could see that it was a twin-engine, propeller-driven aircraft. He could even read the name of a small commercial airline on the fuselage. He fired a flare, but it was too late. The plane flew onward without any indication that it had seen the flare or raft. "It's a charter plane," Lumpy said. "It's probably going to Hobart, and when they get there, they're going to say, 'We didn't see anything. Don't bother going back in that direction.'"

"That was our lucky chance," Beaver said dispiritedly. "We're in for another night. No one is ever going to find us."

Even Gould seemed to have run out of optimism, asking Winning, "Are you sure they heard the Mayday?"

"Yeah, they heard it," Winning said wearily, "but I'm not sure how good the position was. We didn't have any charts, and the GPS wasn't working."

Scraping for something positive to contribute to the conversation, Lumpy cited the rescue of Tony Bullimore, the British yachtsman who was found and lifted off his yacht 1,200 miles off the coast of Australia after capsizing during a single-handed race around the world. "Well, they found Bullimore, didn't they? How long did that take?"

"A couple of weeks, I think," Winning said.

Lumpy wasn't sure whether Winning's intention was to tell a joke or the truth. In fact, Winning thought he was being accurate, although the actual time was four days.

"We're not going to last that long," Lumpy said.

They were past the point of encouragement. A little later, Beaver, who was staring out the opening, pointed to a bird. "He can't go far from shore. That's got to be a good sign."

Studying the bird, Winning said, "Oh, those. Those birds can fly a couple hundred miles."

Annoyed by Winning's disregard for the crew's fragile emotional state, Lumpy said, "Oh, that's really handy, Richard. Why couldn't you tell him they can only fly a few miles so we can all feel better?"

They returned to listening to the gulp and roar of the sea.

On what was left of Steamer's raft, conversation was almost nonexistent. Most of the words that were spoken were Gibbo's, and he was mostly saying variations of the same thing: "Jeez, I hope the boys are all right."

Gibbo had known Jim Lawler as well as two of his brothers for more than fifteen years. He didn't know John Dean or Michael Bannister nearly as well, but a couple of hours after the three men were swept from the raft, he had begun to feel a spiritual sort of connection with all of them. Closing his eyes, he silently talked to them, as if saying a prayer: *Just hold on for a few more hours. The storm is dying, and someone will be out here to get you soon.*

But Gibbo recognized that there was a good chance that everyone, including Steamer and himself, wouldn't make it. As they did on the other raft, Gibbo believed positive thoughts, occasionally amplified by spoken words, could help. Provoking a conversation with Steamer, however, was almost impossible, which eventually caused Gibbo to vent his frustration.

"You aren't much of a bloody conversationalist, are you?"

Steamer, whose legs were in continuous pain, managed a grunt. He was trying to estimate the rate and direction of the raft's drift. He saw no purpose in trying to come up with things to talk about, and he made a point of letting more than a minute pass before responding to Gibbo. "I'm too busy trying to figure out how we're going to get out of this." Steamer believed airborne rescuers would arrive by 10:00 A.M. He assumed that search planes set out at first light and that it would take some time to get out this far, but he was sure that eventually there would be so many planes in the air that one of them would spot the raft.

His biggest fear was that he wouldn't have the strength to hold on for another big wave. He also noticed that Gibbo's hand, the one that had been sliced open by the drogue's nylon cord, was bleeding, and he worried that it would attract sharks. The east coast of Australia is a hunting ground for several kinds of sharks, most famously great whites. Steamer could imagine a terrible scene: a huge great white — maybe more than one — tearing through the raft, rows and rows of giant teeth clamping down on Gibbo and himself. He tried his best to convince himself that sharks wouldn't come to the surface of such a turbulent sea.

As the morning passed, Gibbo couldn't understand why they hadn't seen any planes. "Why hasn't someone come to get us? I sure hope they activated the EPIRB." Neither man had any answers.

About two o'clock Monday afternoon, Steamer's dour face broke into a smile. "What is it?" Gibbo asked.

Steamer pointed over Gibbo's shoulder to an albatross, which was sitting in the water a few feet from the raft, watching them.

The waves didn't seem to frighten the large bird, which rode up and down for several minutes until it flew to the other side of the raft and faced Gibbo.

"That's good luck," Steamer said.

Gibbo was quick to seize on the glimmer of hope. "It has to be. Where do you think we are?"

That was one of the questions Steamer had been thinking about, and he estimated that they had been moving at three or four knots toward the northeast. "We're probably about ninety miles east of Eden," he said.

Although that was a long way, Gibbo found encouragement in the estimate, as much as anything for its sense of specificity — and he wanted more.

"Do you think we're in a shipping lane?"

"No, Gibbo."

Steamer's weary tone made it clear that he didn't plan to say anything more. Gibbo was annoyed by Steamer's reluctance to talk as well as by his disregard for Gibbo's need for hope, and he took a few minutes to consider how to make the point.

"Well, Steamer, who gets to eat who first?"

By late afternoon, Gibbo had lost his sense of connection to the other three. "It's really looking bad for the boys," he said. Again Steamer said nothing. Both men were dreading the idea of another night on the raft. The waves were only about twenty feet high, and very few of them were breaking, making Gibbo and Steamer much more confident that they wouldn't be washed away. But after twenty-four hours in the water, they were beginning to feel the cold. Steamer was wearing only shorts, a T-shirt, and the top half of his foul-weather gear. Off and on, he had begun to shiver — and he knew it would be much worse at night.

Gibbo had thermal underwear and a fleece-lined vest. His tether, which was still secured to the raft, meant he wouldn't be separated from it, but like Steamer, he was concerned about his flagging strength and even his ability to keep his head from falling into the water. Once again, Gibbo unsheathed his knife, this time to cut two holes in what remained of the canopy, into which he inserted his arms. He hoped the arrangement would hold his head and shoulders out of the water even if he passed out. With Gibbo's arms at right angles to his body and his head slumped slightly to the side, Steamer thought his friend looked as if he had been crucified.

A plane, clearly a real one, was heading toward Winning's raft just after four o'clock. "Richard, we have to get a flare off," Lumpy cried. "It looks like the same plane that passed us before." Winning fired one of their last two parachute flares. It created a bright red light that appeared to hang directly in front of the plane. But then the plane made a right turn away from the raft.

"Bloody hell. You have to be kidding," Winning grumbled. "How could he not see it?"

A minute later, Lumpy believed he heard a changed pitch from the sky. "It's turning. I hear it."

The plane was conducting a box search, passing back and forth over quadrants of the sea like a farmer cultivating a field, and eventually it turned toward the raft. Knowing that Winning had just one parachute flare left, Gould said, "Don't fire the fucking flare until you can put it up his fucking nostril!" Winning did his best, but once again, the plane flew on without acknowledgment.

"He flew right over the top of us," Beaver said in an upbeat tone.

"Michael," Lumpy said, using Beaver's given name the way parents sometimes do when explaining things to their children, "you can't see out the nose of the plane. They didn't see it. Maybe they found the other raft."

Finally, almost twenty minutes later, on its third pass, the pilot saw Winning's raft, signaling so by blinking his landing lights. "They've found us for sure!" Lumpy declared. Beaver was thrilled, although he was already worrying about the next step. "How will they get us?" Once again, Winning dampened hope. "They might send a trawler from Eden." When Beaver asked how long that would take, Winning, who believed they were about one hundred miles offshore, said, "About ten hours."

"That's okay," the suddenly recharged Beaver said. "I can do ten hours."

In fact, a helicopter appeared almost immediately. It hovered for a few minutes, then left. "Maybe they lost us," Lumpy said gloomily. "Maybe we'll have to wait for a trawler." But ten minutes later, just before 4:30 P.M., another helicopter, much larger than the first one, came into position over the raft. When Beaver looked at Lumpy, tears were running down both of their smiling faces.

"We're going home," Beaver said.

Cameron Robertson, a balding forty-year-old, was staring down at Richard Winning's raft from the chopper. He hadn't known anything about the rescue operation until the start of his normal shift at one o'clock Monday morning, when he walked into the barnlike hangar of the civilian air ambulance and rescue service he worked for. The first person he ran into was Peter Davidson, who had been struggling to lift crewmen from *Stand Aside* at the time when Richard Winning broadcasted his Mayday. Davidson briefed Robertson on the massive scale of the search-and-rescue operation and described the sixty-knot winds and seventy-foot-high waves. With that to look forward to, Robertson was unable to sleep. Lying in a military-style bunk, he waited for the helicopter's scheduled 4:30 A.M. departure.

They began the day by rescuing three men from *Solo Globe Challenger*. After a second mission, in which they searched for EPIRBs, Robertson thought he was done for the day; but at four o'clock Stefan Sincich, the chopper's thirty-four-year-old pilot, said they were heading out again to look for a one-man raft that had been spotted by a civilian search plane.

As the helicopter approached Winning's raft, Robertson was sitting at the opening of the large sliding door with his feet resting on the chopper's landing gear. Visibility was much better than it had been in the morning. Robertson estimated that the waves were fifteen to twenty feet high. The wind was blowing at thirty-five to forty knots. From seventy feet above the water, Robertson saw at least two heads projecting from the opening of the canopy. One of them was shining a flashlight upward.

"There's more than one. I think there's three or four," Robertson said to Steve Collins, the thirty-five-year-old winch operator. The basic procedure wouldn't be any different, though, so Collins began lowering Robertson toward the water while also using the intercom to direct the pilot to shift the helicopter's position. "Fifteen feet forward, ten feet toward ten o'clock." After he hit the water, Robertson swam a few feet to the raft and saw that there were four men, all of them animated and smiling. That's an excellent sign, he knew. It meant they probably weren't injured or suffering from hypothermia.

Pulling himself up the side of the raft so he could peer through the opening, he said, "Okay, there's four of you. Are you all right?

"Everyone's fine," Winning said.

"Good. What I want you to do is collapse the canopy and sit on top of it. One at a time, I'll have you go in the water, then I'll put a sling around you. Once you're in it, they'll pull both of us up."

Looking at Winning, he said, "Are you happy to get in the water and go first?"

"Fine."

With a lack of hesitation that took Robertson by surprise, Winning went headfirst through the opening and into the water. Robertson, who had assumed that the sailors would be reluctant to leave the relative safety of the raft, was pleased. He had no trouble putting the sling over Winning's head, and after Robertson flashed a thumbs-up to Collins, the cable rapidly raised the two men from the water. The noise was deafening, but Robertson shouted a question into Winning's ear.

"What boat?"

"*Winston Churchill.*"

"You beauty!"

Robertson was elated by the news. Before the helicopter took off from Mallacoota, the *Churchill* was the number one topic of conversation among the rescuers. After hours of fruitless searching, most of them had concluded that the great old yacht and its crew would never be found. Once they were up to the level of the door, Collins pulled Winning into the helicopter by the back of his sling and directed him to a seat. Without any other delay, he then lowered Robertson back down to the water. Robertson didn't take time to say anything about whom he had rescued, and Collins didn't ask.

Lumpy was next. When Robertson asked if he could swim, Lumpy nodded. But when he entered the water, exhausted and without a life jacket, his head immediately slipped below the surface. After Robertson put an arm around Lumpy's chest and pulled his head up, Lumpy murmured, "I'm okay." However, as soon as Robertson let go, Lumpy began sinking again. When Robertson finally secured him, he responded by throwing his arms around his savior.

"Put your arms at your side," Robertson commanded. "Don't do anything. We'll take care of you."

When Lumpy was pulled into the helicopter, he was totally elated and still eager to shake hands and say thanks, but Collins was just as stern as Robertson. "Right. Sit down over there. Don't move." Lumpy's euphoria was punctured by the harsh military-style discipline, and when he looked at Winning, his spirits sank even further. Lumpy thought his friend looked terrible, much older than his years and totally drained. "Oh, Richard, what have we done?" Winning just shook his head.

Back in the water and swimming toward Gould, Robertson was suddenly frightened. Gould was just a few feet away, and he appeared to be poised to throw his arms around his rescuer. Like Lumpy, he was simply bursting with gratitude. Robertson, knowing that an embrace from a panicked swimmer can be fatal, gave himself a margin of reaction time by paddling a couple of feet in the opposite direction. Gould instantly understood Robertson's standoffishness, and he dropped his arms and waited for Robertson to put the sling in place. At that point Gould attempted another hug and suffered another rebuff. "Put your arms by your side."

Beaver, alone on the raft, wasn't worried anymore. He marveled that such a small and decrepit craft had saved his life. Whether the raft capsized didn't matter now. As Robertson descended, Beaver, unsure whether he should enter the water, pointed to his chest and then the water. Robertson vigorously shook his head and raised the palm of his right hand. When he climbed on top of the raft, collapsing the canopy, Robertson, who judged Beaver to be remarkably cool and collected given what he must have been through, explained that they would be lifted to the helicopter directly from the raft.

It wasn't until Beaver was inside the chopper that Collins asked, "What vessel are you from?" He too had been hoping that this was the *Winston Churchill*'s crew, but he had not had time to ask. To the good news, he exclaimed, "Sensational!" He then passed the word to Sincich, who exchanged a high five with his copilot and radioed the information to AusSAR. Handing a pen to Lumpy, Collins then asked him to write down their names. Lumpy tried, but his fingers were numb and incapable, so he named the crew verbally.

"Has the other raft been found?"

All four *Churchill* crewmen were asking the same question. Telling them no, Collins watched their smiles dissolve. Almost immediately after that, though, they began insisting that they knew that the other raft was okay, and their optimism infected the airmen.

Though most communications with AusSAR had to be relayed through a radio operator, Sincich wanted to talk directly to someone at the agency, so he used a cellular phone as soon as he was in range. He passed on the names of the *Churchill* survivors he had picked up and then proposed a follow-up mission that AusSAR immediately approved: "We can't do anything at night with this helicopter, so why don't we drop these guys off — and go back out as soon as we can? We can trace a course from where the boat sank and where we found this raft. Maybe we can find the other one before dark."

In the back of the helicopter, Lumpy reached into his jacket pocket and pulled out a packet of biscuits and the last few containers of water. For the first time since the start of the race, Beaver was hungry. "I'm really hanging for a biscuit," he said, his youthful swagger seemingly resuscitated. Munching on one of the dry wafers, he said, "Wow, we can binge on these."

As soon as the helicopter set down at an airport in the small coastal town of Mallacoota, Sincich began preparing to head out again. Once they were back in the air, Steve Collins reminded the pilot that some of the guys in the first raft had flashlights around their necks, a potentially crucial asset with dusk approaching. Sincich passed the information on to a Royal Australian Air Force P-3 Orion that was already raking the skies near where Winning's raft had been found.

Several Red Cross volunteers greeted the survivors from Winning's raft at the airport and took them to a nearby community center, which had been turned into a hostel for sailors and their rescuers. On the way, Lumpy asked one of the volunteers whether she thought his wife would know that he had been missing. "You have got to be kidding!" the volunteer exclaimed. "The whole world knows you've been missing. There's not a person in Australia who hasn't been on the edge of their chair praying for you."

Lumpy and Beaver went directly into a shower room, not bothering to remove their clothes until they were under hot water. Lumpy was so exhausted that he was leaning against the wall for support, but he and Beaver agreed that they had never enjoyed a shower more. "Mate, now what we have to do is go to the pub and have a steak and a beer," Beaver announced, virtually intoxicated by the thought. It was a very long shower — neither of them wanted to get out — and before they got dressed, one of the volunteers, who had overheard Beaver, produced four steak sandwiches.

After devouring two of them, Beaver called his father. Beaver still lived with his parents, and his dad had spent much of the previous night in his son's bedroom, gazing at a matching pair of cabinets that contained photographs of Beaver on a variety of boats and more than a dozen sailing trophies.

"I gave up hope for you," his dad said over the phone. "I thought you were gone."

A few minutes later, Beaver's desire for a beer was realized as he and the rest of the crew gathered around a fireplace in the community center. Beaver felt pleasantly light-headed after just a few sips. Lumpy, still cold in spite of the shower, was slurping a cup of hot soup. *This is ridiculous,* he thought. *It's the middle of summer, I'm sitting next to a fire with a bowl of soup, and I'm still freezing.* The crew talked about the other raft, trying to boost their hopes by reminding one another that it was superior to the one they had been on.

33

Larry Ellison spent most of Monday night in his bunk, too seasick to do anything else. Sunday night had been terrible, but the waves were even steeper on Monday. During the previous twenty-four hours, he, like most of his crew, had been badly seasick and hadn't eaten anything.

Lachlan Murdoch was holding his own. He had never sailed in weather as bad or been so seasick, but his strategy was simply to tough it out. He was trying to show up for all of his watches and, unlike several of the professional sailors, had missed only one. But he knew how easily the race could turn disastrous. At first, the damage to the boat had added to the sense of danger and excitement that he had always craved. He didn't feel that way anymore. Sitting in the cockpit, he noticed that the housing for one of *Sayonara's* two compasses was developing cracks. Every hour or so, something else came apart, and the cumulative list worried him. He was also concerned about his right hand, the one he had hurt Saturday, which he thought had become infected. Going below after his watch was over, he saw that all the bunks were taken. Searching for space on the floor, he held on to whatever he could as he stepped between sails and bodies. When the yacht fell off a wave, he grabbed one of the carbon-fiber bulkheads for support. It kept him from falling, but it didn't provide much reassurance. It felt hollow, not unlike cardboard or balsa wood. Sayonara *may be the world's fastest maxi*, Lachlan thought, *but it wasn't built for nights like this.*

Lachlan's specific fear was that the yacht would capsize. With that in mind, he selected a small opening on the floor near the steps, thinking he could make a quick escape if he had to. It wasn't a good choice, though: when he lay down, he was tortured by a steady drip of water.

Unable to sleep, he returned to the deck before it was his watch's turn again. Donning his safety harness, he sat in the cockpit, not far from the steering wheel. It was dark, and he didn't talk much. Even the simplest conversation took too much energy. Lachlan was conflicted. On the one hand, he was silently berating himself. *Why would anyone in his right mind do this? This is absolute lunacy.* But at the same time, he also recognized that he was likely to do another Hobart. This was pushing him to the limit, and there was something thrilling about that. Lachlan Murdoch wanted to show the world — and himself — that he was tough enough for anything. Well, *this* was as tough as it gets.

The rest of Lachlan's thoughts were focused on the basics — the weather and how much longer the race would take. One of the things he was trying not to think about was seasickness, but every wave set off a cycle of nausea-inducing motions. After several false alarms, he leaned over the side of the boat. Failing to compensate for the wind, his vomit flew directly into the face of Robbie Naismith, who was steering.

"Ah, Lachlan," Naismith said, "I think I'm going to have a sympathy chuck."

Embarrassed, Lachlan patted Naismith on the shoulder and said, "Sorry," feeling too lousy to add anything more. *At least it's raining,* Lachlan said to himself as he used his good hand to wipe his face. The rain was so heavy that it quickly rinsed him clean.

A little later, Lachlan wondered what would have happened if he had been racing his own boat this year. In 1997, half of his crew were serious sailors, but the others were friends who had spent little time on the water. The nonsailors included the owner of a small advertising agency, a film director, and an Internet entrepreneur. The people who knew the least about sailing had the most leadership experience, and Lachlan thought that kind of combination could have been deadly.

"If we had conditions like this last year," he told Mike Howard, "I would have lost the boat."

When Ellison saw Zan Drejes pumping more water from the hull and noticed how bloodshot his eyes were, Ellison said, "What a bunch of dumb shits we are to call this fun."

"Just you wait," Zan said. "You'll look back on this race with pride, and you'll be out here again someday."

Ellison didn't have an audible comment, but to himself he was adamant: *There's no fucking way I'm ever going to be here again.*

34

The sky was almost dark on Monday evening when Steamer saw the big P-3 Orion. He waved an arm with as much vigor as he could manage, but the plane continued on a straight-line course until it began circling a point a couple of miles away. "I reckon they've found the other raft," Steamer muttered. But that hope for the others was balanced by the prospect of another night on the raft. "It looks like it's going to be a long night for us," Gibbo concluded. A little later, though, the Orion broke from its pattern and headed directly toward Steamer and Gibbo. Steamer aimed his flashlight at the plane, and it was spotted by an airman named John Flynn. When the Orion's landing lights flashed a reply, Steamer had something to say.

"Gibbo, we're in luck."

Shane Pashley had joined the navy when he was sixteen. At thirty-four, he was an athletic petty officer whose left calf was tattooed with an image of a panther battling a snake. He had been attached to a helicopter squadron for nine years, and he had already plucked ten people from the sea. As he watched the start of the race on television from a plaid couch in the living room of his tidy house, which sat next to a cow pasture more than one hundred miles south of Sydney, he told his wife, Kay, that there was a good chance their Christmas holiday would be interrupted. She was annoyed, though not surprised. It had been the same story for five of the previous six years. Kay understood that rescuing people was part of Shane's job, and she kept a scrapbook filled with newspaper articles and letters attesting to his good deeds. One year he plucked Isabelle Autissier, the famous French solo sailor, from the Southern Ocean after her yacht was dismasted during an around-the-world race. Still, Kay had been hoping for an interruption-free holiday.

The bad news came early Monday morning when Pashley and his Sea Hawk helicopter, a sophisticated machine that carries enough fuel to fly 150 miles an hour for four hours, were called into action. On its first mission, it was assigned a ten-square-mile search area, where it swept back and forth across the sea until it landed for refueling on the *Newcastle*, the frigate that had rushed south from Sydney. Descending into the bowels of the ship to the officers' mess Monday night, Pashley helped himself to a cup of coffee, which he placed on a slip-resistant rubber place mat. A large television set, held in place by a vise-like steel bracket, was tuned to a news program. Pashley heard that it had been almost thirty hours since the *Winston Churchill* issued its Mayday and that its second raft still hadn't been found. *Those guys,* he said to himself, *will have to be incredibly lucky to survive.*

Moments later, he was called to the chopper. AusSAR had asked Rick Neville, the pilot, to fly back to shore. However, shortly after takeoff, Neville heard that a nearby P-3 Orion had spotted something, possibly a life raft. Closer to the location than any other helicopter, Neville diverted from his original course. It was just after 10:00 P.M., and the sky was overcast and dark as Pashley, lying on the helicopter's floor with his head extended out the open door, scanned back and forth across the black water, seeing nothing until he caught a glimpse of a phosphorous candle that the P-3 Orion had dropped. Seconds later, he saw a speck of light and finally, with the help of the Sea Hawk's searchlight, the life raft. As the helicopter descended, he saw two human shapes. Over the intercom he said, "It looks like two guys sitting in a wading pool."

To Gibbo, the helicopter looked like a flying saucer. In fact, it was equipped with lots of futuristic equipment, including a radar-driven altimeter capable of maintaining a constant distance between the helicopter and the surface below. Neville set the device for sixty feet, and turned a switch that enabled Lieutenant Aaron Abbott, who was operating the winch, to fine-tune the helicopter's horizontal position with a handheld control. Once they were almost directly above the raft, Pashley was lowered toward the sea. He dipped in and out of two waves before he fully entered the water about twenty feet away from the raft, which was being blown away by the wind as well as by the chopper's downdraft.

Within the navy, Pashley's informal job descriptions included "tea bag" and "shark bait," and sharks were what he was thinking about as he swam toward the raft and tried to climb aboard.

"Watch out — there's no floor," Steamer yelled.

Not hearing the warning, Pashley splashed through the hole where the floor used to be. As he put his arms over the side and saw that the two men who were supposed to be on the raft were mostly in the water, clearly accessible to sharks, he said to himself, *I guess I don't have to worry about being eaten.* He was also amazed that these relatively old men had survived on such a pathetic life raft.

"Are you okay? Any injuries?"

"No, no," Steamer lied, shaking his head in spite of the pain in his leg. "But you better take Gibbo first. He's hurt his hands."

Immediately after Pashley placed the sling around Gibbo's torso, the two of them were violently yanked from the raft and pulled across the surface of the water as if they were trout being reeled in by a fisherman. As they ascended, they were hit and swallowed by a wave. Reappearing, they were finally lifted out of the water but rose only a few feet before something else went wrong. The helicopter suddenly lost altitude, dumping both men back into the sea. Watching from the raft, Steamer thought, *This can't be the way it's supposed to happen.* Neville was thinking the same thing. The helicopter was too far upwind, and the men had been dropped back into the water because the radar altimeter, apparently overwhelmed by the changes in the height of the sea, had failed. Neville attempted to reset the device, but it still didn't work. Below, two men desperately tried not to drown. The only thing left to do was for Neville to hold the helicopter in place manually. And he had to do it now. While the helicopter bounced violently in the turbulent air, Gibbo and Pashley were pulled up the rest of the way.

Without a working radar altimeter, Neville decided that it was too dangerous for Pashley to go back into the water. Instead, he instructed the crewmen to lower the sling into the water, hoping that Steamer could figure out what to do. Steamer was on his own.

When he saw the unmanned cable, Steamer wasn't worried. Since he had suggested that Gibbo be taken first, Steamer thought they must have decided that he was in pretty good shape. *And I am*, he said to himself. *All I have to do is pull the sling over my head. No problem.*

The sling landed next to the raft, and very quickly Steamer wrapped it around himself and signaled above with a thumbs-up. But as the winch began to raise him, Pashley saw that Steamer was pulling the raft up with him. Something was tangled. Lowering Steamer back into the water, Pashley waited a few seconds until he saw the raft blow away, obviously no longer a problem, before beginning to lift Steamer again. But when Steamer was twenty feet above the sea, he fell out of the sling and plummeted back into the water. Either he hadn't put the sling under both of his arms or he didn't have the strength to keep it there. Whatever the case, Pashley feared that Steamer was too weak to manage on his own.

"Should I let him try it again or should I go back in the water?" he asked Neville.

"Let's let him try one more time on his own."

Pashley dropped the sling back into the water, and once again Steamer seemed to have no trouble getting into the sling. This time he was lifted to the chopper without incident.

"Who are you?" Pashley asked

"I'm John Stanley — and that's John Gibson. We're from the *Winston Churchill.* Did you get our other raft?"

Almost shouting into his ear, Pashley told Steamer that everyone on the other raft was safe. Although Steamer had pretty much given up hope for the other three men, his own rescue infused him with optimism. "They have to be nearby," he said. "They're probably a few miles from where we are on the same track you've been running on." Gibbo claimed to know exactly where they were. Demanding a map, he wasn't satisfied until he was told that other aircraft were already searching the area. Steamer, who was thinking about what a relief it was not to have to hang on to the raft anymore, told Pashley that he had had nothing to drink since he abandoned the *Churchill* twenty-nine hours earlier. Both men drank a lot of water. To reduce the risk that they would go into shock, Pashley tried to keep Steamer and Gibbo awake by engaging them in conversation, but before long they had both passed out.

When the helicopter arrived in Merimbula, one of the nurses who greeted it asked Gibbo if he had hypothermia.

"Don't be ridiculous," he responded. "All I need is a cup of tea."

In fact, he and Steamer were so weak that they had to be half carried to a waiting ambulance, which took them to a hospital. They were bruised and nearly broken, but safe.

35

Shortly after dawn on Tuesday, *Brindabella*'s jib ripped into pieces, and the top third of the sail became entangled in the rigging. Until it was removed, there was no way to put up a replacement. Despite thirty knots of wind, Andrew Jackson, called Jacko by everyone on the crew, immediately volunteered to climb the mast. "I'll have to bear away to make a more stable platform," said Bob Fraser, who was at the wheel. He didn't have to tell anyone what that meant for the race. Bearing away from the wind meant heading north. *Sayonara* was only a few miles ahead, but for as long as it took Jacko to go up the mast, free the sail, and come back down, *Brindabella* would be traveling back toward Sydney.

In fact, though, Fraser wasn't thinking about the Hobart. He was remembering what had happened two years earlier when Billy Rawlings went up *Brindabella*'s mast during another race. While he was high above the deck, the hull hit a wave and Rawling's head crashed into the mast, knocking him unconscious. At that point, he turned upside down and was suspended head down from the bosun's chair. As he swung back and forth like an out-of-control pendulum, it looked as if he would either fall out of the chair or hit his head again before he could be brought back to the deck. In the end, he was safely lowered and he recovered, but the crew — Fraser among them — never forgot what it was like to watch him dangling.

"I want you to get up there quickly and get down even quicker," said Steve Byron, Snow's nephew and the man who would control the halyard that would lift Jacko from the deck.

Jacko had climbed the mast many times, but never in such a turbulent sea. As he was hoisted, he tried to keep a grip on the mast while also looking upward, attempting to determine exactly where the problem was. When he was about eighty feet above the deck, he saw that the leech line, the drawstring that was supposed to run along the back edge of the sail, was wrapped around the forestay, a cable extending between the top of the mast and the bow. Although reaching the rod was difficult, once he got to it, Jacko didn't have any trouble cutting the line with a small knife and pulling the section of the sail free. The impact on *Brindabella*'s position, however, was devastating. During the forty-five-minute exercise, *Brindabella* traveled seven miles north while *Sayonara* moved nine south, giving it an additional sixteen-mile margin.

On *Sayonara*, Tugboat was tapping at the hull near the bow early Tuesday morning, trying to judge how weak it had become. Watching him, Bill Erkelens saw that the blisters were continuing to grow and asked, "Are these okay?"

"No, they're not!" Tugboat replied. "This is about the worst place there is to have delamination. We can't keep doing this for much longer."

Finding Dickson, Erkelens told him, "We're going to have to do something different. We have to slow the boat down."

Although Dickson had been very seasick, the idea of doing anything but flat-out racing repulsed him. "So you're saying we have to quit," he snarled.

Erkelens was also annoyed. Dickson's tone made it sound as though he was blaming him for the delamination. "No," Erkelens said, "but we should probably idle back ten percent or change our course a bit."

When Frizzle came back on deck to take *Sayonara's* helm, he too thought something had to be done to reduce the pounding that the hull was taking. He knew they were on the most direct course to Hobart, but he thought they should turn toward Tasmania to seek calmer water. Frizzle, who worked for Incat, a leading builder of high-speed ferries and Tasmania's biggest employer, had been working with boats for most of his life and had a keen appreciation of their limits. Summoning Rudiger to the cockpit, Frizzle told him, "I think we should think about making a change here. We're still going square into these waves, and it's putting the boat under enormous strain."

"I know what you're saying," Rudiger said, "but this is still the fastest course to home. I think we have to hold it for a few more hours."

Frizzle wondered whether the navigator recognized just how dangerous the sea was. "You only need one freak wave," he pointed out. "If we landed badly, we could be in big trouble. If we tacked toward land, we'd stop crashing into the waves."

"I still think it's too early — but I'll talk to Dickson and Larry."

Ellison, who was still in his bunk, was ready for a change. Seasickness and his fear that the hull would collapse had robbed him of his usual winning-is-everything zeal. Before Rudiger had a chance to talk to him, Ellison peered from his bunk to see Tugboat, who was on his hands and knees, using a Magic Marker to draw circles on the inside of the hull.

"What the hell are you doing?" Ellison asked.

"I'm marking the spots where we're getting delamination."

With a tone of incredulity, Ellison bellowed, "What?"

"The bow has been delaminating for quite a while, and there's quite a few problem areas. The boat could stay together for a while longer, but we're in pretty bad shape. I think we should be thinking about finding some calmer water."

"Fuck —that's it!"

This is a complete fucking nightmare, Ellison added to himself. He already knew about the delamination near the bow and how the bulkheads had separated from the hull. Off and on, he had also considered the possibility that the boat could come apart and he could die, but he had mostly pushed those thoughts from his mind. Just as he had to Melanie in the Botanic Garden on the morning the race started, he told himself that the perception of danger was much greater than the reality. The numbers were substantially on his side, he reminded himself. Thousands of people have sailed in Hobart races, but very few have died. *I'm on a perfectly maintained yacht with the world's best crew. Other boats may be in danger, but not us.*

But now, the circles that Tugboat was drawing were all too real.

Ellison had entered the race to test himself as a yachtsman, and the results were in. *I wanted to see how I stacked up,* he said to himself. *Well, I've found my answer. This is way past my limit.*

Ellison often played a role in major strategic decisions. His favorite example occurred a few months before the Hobart during the Newport to Bermuda Race. Having decided to take a different course than the other maxis, *Sayonara* had fallen behind all of them. Ellison argued that they should turn toward a formation of clouds that might produce better wind. *Sayonara* did change course, but a couple of hours later there still wasn't much wind. Ellison insisted on pushing on, taking *Sayonara* even farther from the rest of the fleet. "It's just like business," he told Dickson. "If you've gone this close to the edge, it's pointless not to go all the way." Ultimately, *Sayonara* did find better wind. Picking up thirty miles on the other boats, it finished second rather than last among the maxis.

By the time Ellison climbed out of his bunk and onto the deck, he had already resolved that *Sayonara* was going to stop crashing off the waves, regardless of what that meant for the race. He knew that *Brindabella* hadn't reported its position during the last sked — making it impossible to know where it was — but he didn't care. In fact, he was remembering a conversation he had with George Snow in 1995. *Sayonara* had won a short race a couple of days before the start of that year's Hobart. Afterward, Ellison and Snow, who came in second, chatted during a cocktail party at the CYC. First, Snow offered his congratulations. Then he talked about the big race and made the point that it's sometimes difficult even to complete the race. "The thing about the Hobart is that in order to win, you have to finish."

Rudiger was in the cockpit when Ellison arrived there. "Where are we?" Ellison asked.

"About seventy-five miles off the coast of Tasmania."

"I want to tack the boat so we head toward land and stop falling into elevator shafts."

"We don't know where *Brindabella* is. I'm not sure it's the best thing for the race."

Ellison was angry. "I'm not sure sinking is the best thing for the race, either. Tack the fucking boat."

The relief was immediate. During the next hour, the weather also improved. Patches of blue sky developed toward the south. Rudiger was still concerned about *Brindabella*, however, until he saw a photographer's helicopter flying toward Hobart from the north. He assumed it had come from taking pictures of the other maxi, meaning that it was behind *Sayonara*.

But the relief of a calmer passage and the likelihood of victory was countered by the bad news Rudiger had begun to hear on a small AM/FM radio. Listening to commercial radio stations, hoping to get a report on *Brindabella*'s position, all he heard was information about abandoned boats and lost sailors. For Rudiger, the news about the *Winston Churchill* was a particular shock. When he was admiring it the night before the race began, he told a friend that it would be the best boat to be on in bad weather because of its weight, big keel, and deep cockpit.

"I knew it was bad, but this is terrible," Joey Allen said when he heard the news. "Can you imagine being on one of those little boats?" Justin Clougher was doing just that. Two of his brothers were racing on smaller yachts.

Several crewmen knew Glyn Charles. T.A. was trying to imagine what it would be like to be in the water and know you're not going to be rescued. Hamish Pepper couldn't understand how such a top-notch sailor could be lost. "I don't get it," he said to Brad Butterworth. "He's such a fantastic sailor. Of all the people who could be lost, it doesn't make any sense that it would be him." Pepper, who had become friends with Glyn when they were both competing at the Atlanta Olympics, had met up with him for a drink at the CYC a few days before the Hobart began. "I really don't want to do the race," Glyn had said, "but the owner is paying me good money, so I'm going to do it."

Ellison was stunned by the idea that people were dying. Even though he had been worried about his own life, he had never really accepted that it could be snatched away at any time. In the past, he had sometimes tried to find some good in this hard truth by attempting to convince himself that life's fragility and beauty are inextricable, telling friends that was why his backyard was full of cherry trees, which bloom for just a couple of weeks. But if he appreciated nature's cycle of passages, Ellison couldn't stand the thought of his own death — particularly at sea. "This is supposed to be fun," he said to Butterworth. "You're not supposed to die doing it."

And he wouldn't. When *Sayonara* entered the Derwent River for the last leg of its journey to Hobart, it was ahead of *Brindabella* and all the others. The fifteen-knot breeze seemed gentle, there were no waves, and the sun was shining. Ellison sat on the rail, studying the bank of the river, where dramatic rock formations were bordered by purple heather. It reminded him of Scotland, and the contrast made him philosophical. "Life is the only miracle," he said to Steve Wilson, who was sitting next to him on the rail. "It's so beautiful — and it's so very, very brief." Watching the banks, Ellison was almost overcome by the realization that his boat could have ended up like the *Winston Churchill*. "We've been pushed to the absolute end of our endurance. It's crazy. It's too much for me. I'm never going to do this race again."

"That's what you said last time," Wilson said.

Ellison knew he had said the same thing after the 1995 Hobart, and he meant it even though he was very proud of being the first boat to finish that year. The trophy he received, the only prize he had ever put on display, had a prominent place in *Katana*'s main cabin. But this was different. "This time I'm serious," he told Wilson. "You couldn't pay me to do it. Never in a thousand years will I do this race again."

Sayonara crossed the finish line just after eight o'clock Tuesday morning — two days, nineteen hours, and three minutes after the race began. Although it was well behind *Morning Glory's* record time, it was almost three hours ahead of *Brindabella.*

At the end of most Hobarts, a flotilla of two or three hundred boats greets the victor, but fewer than fifty came out to see *Sayonara.* As in other years, a kilt-clad bagpiper was standing on a launch just after the finish line, producing a mournful drone. To Ellison and the rest of his crew, it sounded unspeakably sad. Most of them had tears in their eyes. Joey Allen was trying to think about his fiancée and how much he was looking forward to their upcoming wedding, but he felt as though he was heading to a funeral. In a way, he was. The awards ceremony had already been canceled, and CYC officials were already making plans for a memorial service on New Year's Day.

As soon as *Sayonara's* sails were lowered, the crew started the engine and gathered in the cockpit. Ellison wanted to talk. Never before had he recognized the extent to which his crew could do things that he could not, and he said thank you in the humblest tones the crew had ever heard. "When you have a chance, take a look in the mirror. You should be very proud of what you see. In extraordinarily difficult conditions, you managed to find what was necessary to bring us in safely. You've done a fantastic job, and I'm enormously grateful. We won the race — but let's remember that there's been a lot of tragedy out there. We should be thinking about their families and thinking about our own families more than anything else."

It was a very humble Larry Ellison — a Larry Ellison that Silicon Valley probably will never see — that stepped off his boat to stand in front of several microphones that had been set up on the dock reserved for the first boat to arrive in Hobart.

"We're all pretty choked up," he began with a trembling voice and tears running down his cheeks. "And this is a tough crew. I'd like to acknowledge them. Guys were knocked down over and over again, and they kept getting up and kept getting back to work to do what was needed to keep the boat in one piece and keep all of us alive. This is not what racing is supposed to be. Difficult, yes. Dangerous, no. Life-threatening, definitely not. I'd never have signed up for this race if I knew how difficult it would be. No race I've ever done has been anything like this. It was like sailing through the eye of a hurricane. The seas were enormous, and the wind made noises we'd never heard before. We just want to pay tribute to families who lost sailors who were in this race. Our prayers go out to the search crews and the people who are still in the water. We hope they can all be found."

Ellison wanted to leave. Less than an hour after he came ashore, he was on his plane, heading toward Antigua. "What the crew did is incredible," he told Melanie. "We're not allowed to have heroes anymore, but I find my heroes on the boat." Not long after that, Ellison was sound asleep.

PART V

WAKE

36

George Snow was at the helm when *Brindabella* approached a dock near *Sayonara*'s. Niree Adriaanse, the wife of crew member Erik Adriaanse, was waiting for her husband, and by the time they threw their arms around each other, both had burst into tears. "Are you okay? Is anything broken?" Without waiting for a response, Niree used her hands to search for broken bones. As she did, she noticed that Erik's whole body was trembling. That had happened only twice before — at the births of their children, Alice and Jack.

For *Brindabella*'s crew, the post-Hobart partying always began on the boat. In 1997, when *Brindabella* had the winner's dock, the crew was there for several hours. This year, the party dissolved in less than two. It was different on Wednesday, when Snow took his crew to what had become an annual lunch at Shipwright Arms, a large pub on a hill above Hobart. "We are just bit players in the dramas that happened out there this year," Snow said at the beginning of the lunch, "but there are people in this room who did things that don't happen in normal life. It's very hard to ask someone to put their life at risk, but some of you did just that. What Jacko did up the mast was incredible. I want to thank all of you for doing a remarkable job."

Lunch was never an adequate description for *Brindabella's* gathering. It always carried on for hours, and 1998 was no exception. The crew, along with their wives and girlfriends, arrived at noon. At first, they were reluctant to mount a full-scale celebration, but that changed over time. Sometime after sunset, most of the crew had stripped off their shirts and had taken to the dance floor. Bob Fraser's wife, Sue, the sister of tennis great John Newcombe, had been to a lot of celebrations, but never one as wild. She understood how they felt but was also a bit embarrassed. "I hope you don't think they're being disrespectful," she said to a pair of Hobart residents who had wandered into the party. "They're just celebrating being alive."

Richard Winning didn't hear what had happened on the other raft until Tuesday morning, when a television reporter, who assumed he already knew, asked, "How do you feel about losing your mates?"

"What the fuck are you talking about?"

Winning felt as though he had been punched in the gut. Walking away from the reporter, he went to find his other crewmen, who were still sleeping. His face, drained of color and turned downward, told almost the whole story. Desperate to know more, when they heard that the helicopter crew that rescued them was about to land, they rushed to meet it. Seeing the downcast group through the chopper's window, Cameron Robertson tried to imagine their feelings. Walking over to talk to them, he was particularly worried by Winning's demeanor. He was shifting his weight from one leg to the other, and his face was twitching involuntarily. Robertson pulled him aside from the others and did his best to tell him that what had happened was the result of forces beyond anyone's control. But Winning wasn't really listening.

"I was responsible," he insisted. "I was the skipper. It was my boat."

Later that day, Winning and the others drove to Pambula Hospital, where Steamer was being treated for hypothermia, a broken ankle, and ripped muscles. By the time they got there, Gibbo had been flown to a larger hospital in Canberra and Steamer had already identified bodies belonging to Jim Lawler and Michael Bannister; they had been found by a helicopter and brought to the hospital, where doctors were unable to determine precisely when they had died. After gathering around Steamer's bed, the four men from Winning's raft listened to a tale even more harrowing than their own. "We were amazed that the others had died," Winning said afterward, "and even more amazed that Steamer was one of the survivors."

New Year's Day in Hobart was just like the afternoon the race started. The sky was a brilliant blue, the air was warm, and there was a gentle breeze. Richard Winning had fallen asleep in his hotel room about an hour before the start of the large outdoor memorial service that had been planned for three o'clock. Awakened just fifteen minutes before the ceremony, he quickly dressed and rushed to Constitution Dock, where the service was to be held. On the way there, someone asked, "What are you going to say?"

"What am I going to say? I'm not going to say anything." Winning hated speaking in public. But as he made his way to the service, he saw something that seemed remarkable. Four planes flew overhead in a formation known as the "missing man," and Winning, watching them, suddenly changed his mind. *What was I thinking?* he asked himself. *I have to say something.*

A short while later, standing on a podium in front of more than two thousand people — sailors and their friends and families along with local residents and tourists — Winning spoke about how he had raced with Michael Bannister and John Dean since they were teenagers. "May their loved ones find some comfort in the knowledge that these men died doing something they loved." Then he recited a couple of lines that he had remembered just before he stood up. Although he thought they came from the Bible, they are actually part of an age-old seafarers' prayer: "The sea was so vast, and the ship was so small. Man and everything made by man is finite."

Representing the *Sword of Orion*, Steve Kulmar spoke about Glyn Charles. "What you saw was what you got. No politics. Just this wonderfully direct manner. You always knew where you stood. The sailing community will miss you, Glyn."

Hugo van Kretschmar, the CYC commodore, who had dropped out of the race after the radio on his yacht broke, had the job of presiding over a club in mourning. "The bond of the sea is so strong that all sailors feel your loss," he told the assemblage. "We will miss you. We will remember you always. We will learn from the tragic circumstances of your passing. May the everlasting voyage you have now embarked on be blessed with calm seas and gentle breezes. May you never have to reef or change a headsail in the night. May your bunk always be warm and dry."

Six sailors died in the fifty-fourth Sydney to Hobart Race. Of the 115 boats that started the race, just forty-three made it to Hobart. Seven were abandoned. Five sank. But it could have been much worse. More than twenty sailors were washed off their yachts, and fifty-five had to be pulled from the water by helicopters and rescue ships. It was easy to imagine how many of those rescues could have gone tragically wrong.

After the service, six wreaths, each containing white daisies and red roses, were set to drift down the Derwent River.

Merrion Charles, Glyn's sister, as well as Anne Goodman, his girlfriend, and Julie McCollum, one of Glyn's cousins, had flown to Hobart for the service, and they joined the *Sword*'s crew for dinner a few hours later. "I hope you don't mind," Julie said partway into the meal, "but we would like you to tell us more about what happened." One by one, the crew described the capsizing and what occurred afterward. More than anyone else, the three women wanted to hear from Dags, and after dinner the four of them went for a walk, strolling past some of the handsome stone warehouses near the waterfront that had been converted into restaurants and art galleries.

After listening to Kulmar's description of Glyn's straightforwardness, Dags suspected he would want them to know the truth. On the other hand, the women obviously adored Glyn, and they had such great regard for his skill as a sailor that Dags thought they might not accept the idea that Glyn could have done anything wrong. In the end, Dags was very specific in describing how the wave turned the boat over and how the boom must have thrown Glyn into the water as it swung across the deck. He also explained why he was unable to swim to Glyn.

Dags stopped short of talking about Glyn steering the boat. *What's the point?* he thought. Sailors could draw lessons from what happened. For his girlfriend and relatives, it was different. All they had were memories, and Dags saw no purpose in spoiling them. Even this sanitized version of what happened was too much for Goodman, who left the group and went back to her hotel. The other three met up with the rest of the *Sword*'s crew at the Customs House, a pub near the waterfront where photographs of classic sailing vessels cover dark wood-paneled walls. The Customs House has always been one of the most popular watering holes among Hobart yachtsmen, and some of them were trying to recapture a bit of the raucous celebratory spirit that follows most races.

Shortly after Dags ordered a round of beers, he saw an angry-looking Richard Purcell moving through the crowded bar toward the *Sword*'s crew. The survivors had been discussing the *Margaret Rintoul* for most of the day. In racing terms, it ended up doing very well, finishing first among boats in its class and eighth overall on corrected time. Some members of the *Sword*'s crew were convinced that Purcell really did ignore their calls for help because he was more interested in racing, particularly after they heard about a television interview he gave soon after he arrived in Hobart. In it, Purcell bragged, "I have been in seas three times as big as that. It wasn't scary. It wasn't scary to me. We got what we wanted. We were ready for it."

Purcell headed straight to Carl Watson. "You'd better watch what you say about me."

"I haven't said anything that wasn't true," Watson replied. "You fucking saw us — I know you did — and you kept on racing. Ten people could have died because of you."

"That's right, I saw you. We didn't stop because we couldn't do anything to help you. It was my decision — and I'd do the same thing tomorrow."

That was enough to set off an escalating round of pushing and shoving, the beginnings of a brawl. Brownie and his girlfriend, Barbara Devlin, were sitting on bar stools near Watson, and when Barbara was shoved off her stool and pressed against the bar, Brownie's usual calm was replaced by fury. Slamming the top of his glass of beer against the edge of the bar, he held the jagged remnants of the glass, ready to slash Purcell. Before events got completely out of hand, Nigel Russell grabbed Brownie's wrist and seized the glass. Kooky also stepped into the fray, using one of his crutches to defuse the confrontation by whacking both Purcell and Watson.

Afterward, things settled down, albeit without Purcell, who angrily strode out of the pub.

A few days after the race, Lachlan Murdoch flew to Fiji, where he had rented a house for a long-planned vacation with his fiancée and father. During long walks on the beach, Lachlan tried to describe what the race had been like. He also showed them where the skin on his hands was pinched away. But he tried not to talk about the race too much. He was afraid it would sound as if he was bragging, and he also knew that his dad preferred talking about the future rather than about the past. But during the week-long vacation, Lachlan realized he was still suffering because of what happened. The skin under both of his eyes had swelled up into what looked like a pair of welts. That had never happened before, and he was sure it was the result of some form of unresolved stress.

To Sarah O'Hare, it seemed obvious that Lachlan should find another form of recreation. "There's no reason for you to do that race again," she said.

"I'm sorry," Lachlan replied, "but I'm going to."

For Lachlan, the inexplicable need to live on the edge remained. For others, there would be no return to anywhere near Bass Strait.

On a Sunday a couple of weeks after the funerals for their lost mates, the *Churchill*'s surviving crewmen gathered at Richard

Winning's house for lunch and to talk about what had happened, partly to enhance their own understanding but also because of what they knew would be an intensive investigation into the race by the coroner of New South Wales, the state that includes Sydney.

Australia's coroners, who are trained as lawyers and act as judges, have vast powers. They can borrow police and hire consultants to pursue broad-ranging investigations, hold public hearings, make criminal indictments, and issue recommendations aimed at preventing similar deaths. The Hobart inquest was certain to have a high profile, with potentially enormous consequences for several parties. If the coroner determined that the weather bureau provided grossly inadequate forecasts or that the CYC should have canceled the race or that skippers were irresponsible, civil lawsuits would almost certainly follow.

Richard Winning didn't believe he had any legal vulnerability. By then, he had heard about what Mega Bascombe said he saw near the *Churchill*'s bow on the morning the race started, but Winning was certain that whatever it was had nothing to do with the *Churchill*'s sinking. "We could have lost some putty, but that wouldn't have made any difference," he said. "There's no way that any caulking came out." Winning, along with Steamer, believed the *Churchill* sank because of damage near the keel, not the bow. Even so, Winning was dreading the inquest.

He knew that Jim Lawler's widow, Denise, had hired a lawyer and that he was asking questions about the *Churchill* and its crew. The other families had never even suggested that Winning might have been at fault. In fact, when Michael Bannister's son, Stephen, heard that Denise Lawler had hired an attorney, he wrote a letter to her. "What possible reason can drive this anger that you have toward Richard Winning to sue him?" the typewritten note began. "Only the weather was to blame, if anything, and no sailor was going to back down from the challenge of the Sydney to Hobart Race, even in the conditions of 1998." In the conclusion of his letter, Stephen wrote: "I have spoken to Nathan and Peter Dean, and they totally agree and support everything I have said. You should rethink your stance and contemplate what your husband would really want. Would he ever want to sue a friend?"

At Winning's house, the crew attempted to reconstruct what had happened and agree on a time line. While the *Churchill*'s crew and their wives helped themselves to cold chicken and rice salad, Bruce Gould's wife, Pru, who worked as a nurse, initiated a roundtable discussion, asking each of the sailors about his emotions. It was exactly the kind of thing Winning hated. "I think all this contrived stuff is a waste of time," he said later. "The idea that we should all get together and relive the whole thing every two weeks is ridiculous." By the time dessert was served, Winning had left the room and was in another part of the house, filling out a questionnaire that the CYC had sent to every skipper.

Finding him, Gibbo asked, "Shouldn't we all help you with that?"

With a hint of reluctance, Winning said, "Sure."

After Gibbo summoned the rest of the crew into the room, Winning started reading from the list of 101 questions about the crew's experience, the weather they went through, injuries and damage to the boat, and descriptions of everything that went wrong. At first Winning took a perfunctory, almost cynical, approach. But an engaging discussion quickly developed, particularly when it came to the wave that knocked down the *Churchill*. Before they finished, they went back to the first questions to add more detail to their answers.

Every survivor was troubled by particular aspects of what had happened. Gibbo was haunted by a singular thought: *If I had just turned on the engine, the bilge pump might have stopped the boat from sinking. Or at least it might have slowed the process long enough to enable Winning to radio a more precise position, one that would have led to our being rescued before three men were lost.* Gibbo, of course, was being unfair to himself. He didn't turn on the engine because he had decided that he should let the more senior crewmen make the important decisions. And in fact, Steamer could have started the engine before he untied Winning and Dean. Those realities, however, did nothing to lessen Gibbo's gnawing sense of guilt, and he had raised the issue with Bruce Gould during the lunch at Winning's house.

"That's ridiculous," Gould declared. "That boat was taking on water so fast, it was going down no matter what. The bilge pump wouldn't have made any difference. None."

But Gibbo wasn't fully persuaded by Gould's words, in part because of a conversation he had had with Steamer several weeks earlier. As he had with Gould, Gibbo explained why he believed he could have prevented the deaths. After hearing Gibbo's theory, Steamer responded with a horribly inconclusive word.

"Maybe."

Over and over, Richard Winning had run though the events of the race, trying to think of what he could have done differently. He never really blamed himself, though. "Fault is one thing. Responsibility is another," he said. "It wasn't my fault, but I was responsible. The fact is, it was my boat, and I came back without a third of my crew."

Soon after the race, Winning told friends he would never sail again. But several weeks later, he claimed that he didn't mean what he had said. "That was a political statement," he said. "It was a political statement to please my wife. I'll get another boat — and if anyone will go with me, I'll do another Hobart."

Steamer stopped working at Winning's boatyard after the Royal Yacht Squadron, Sydney's toniest yacht club, offered him a better-paying job as the manager of its yard. Around the club, Steamer was a living legend. Everyone knew who he was, and when they saw him hobbling around the docks, they couldn't help but wonder about how he had survived. Steamer knew what they were thinking. "Everyone is a bit amazed," he said. "And it makes me think that I have a purpose — telling people what happened, so they might learn something about what you have to do when you're at sea."

Like Winning, he wasn't about to let the experience diminish his love for sailing or get in the way of future Hobarts. "I put the whole thing together — I lost a lot — but I found this fabulous sport when I was a kid, and I know I'll never find anything on land that compares."

37

In June of 1999, the CYC released a 166-page report based on its own investigation of the race, which concluded that "no one cause" was responsible for what went wrong. The age or design of yachts wasn't the issue, the report said, nor was any lack of ocean-racing experience or the club's management of the race. "The report finds that the race organization, safety requirements, eligibility requirements, and attitudes of skippers and crews are not fundamentally flawed in any way," Commodore van Kretschmar told a large group of journalists who had gathered at the CYC for a press conference.

The facts weren't quite that straightforward. The club's investigation revealed that *Business Post Naiad*, a yacht on which two men died after it capsized, didn't meet the CYC's own stability requirement. *Naiad*'s entry application, which was accepted by the CYC, had made it clear that its stability index was well below the CYC limit. Therefore, if the club had enforced its own rules, the *Naiad* would have been disqualified and two deaths would have been prevented. Although club officials worried that they would be asked about their acceptance of the *Naiad* during the press conference, no one picked up on the issue.

Instead, van Kretschmar explained the disaster more generically: "Quite simply, in my view, part of the fleet sailed into unexpectedly extreme conditions." While he acknowledged that competitors should have known more about meteorological language — like the difference between *gale* and *storm warnings* — he pinned most of the blame on the weather bureau. "The forecasts were misleading or misinterpreted by competitors and organizers," he asserted, because the bureau "failed to give a clear impression of the extreme conditions to be expected." Like nearly everyone involved with the race, he refused to accept the bureau's contention that yachtsmen should have understood that gusts could exceed average wind speeds by 40 percent. (In fact, a survey of competitors undertaken by the CYC for the report indicated that nine in ten thought winds would be "slightly stronger or slightly less strong than forecast.") Clouds Badham, whose assessment of the bureau's forecasting was incorporated into the club's report, acknowledged that gusts exceed average wind speed, but he estimated that the actual ratio during the race was probably less than 20 percent. He suggested that the bureau "latched onto" the larger ratio only to cover up what he considered to be mediocre forecasting.

Before the report was issued, club officials had resolved that they wouldn't talk about the *Margaret Rintoul* other than to say that they would ask a protest committee to investigate whether Richard Purcell was guilty of "gross misconduct" under the international rules of sailing, an offense that could lead to his being banned from sailing competitions around the world. "The rules of yacht racing," the commodore said at the press conference, "are quite specific in terms of the obligation to render whatever assistance they can safely provide to a yacht that is in distress. Not dissimilar at all to not stopping after a car accident."

Helping yachtsmen in distress was something van Kretschmar felt very strongly about. During a race in Sydney Harbor a couple of years before the 1998 Hobart, the commodore's son, Matthew, fell off his yacht *Bashful* after it broached in thirty-five knots and went out of control. Van Kretschmar kept his eye on his son while the rest of the crew prepared to turn the boat around. At first, van Kretschmar wasn't worried. Although his son wasn't wearing a life jacket, he was a good swimmer and seemed to be relaxed. Then a wave washed over Matthew's head, and he started flailing his arms. The yacht was already about one hundred yards away, but van Kretschmar stripped down to his shorts and dove in. After a few strokes, when he stopped to see if he was going in the right direction, he saw that Matthew was in full panic. At that point, his father swam as hard as he could. When he got to his son, he was utterly spent. During the next twenty-five minutes, several boats passed within forty feet of the commodore and his son as they struggled to keep their heads above the two-foot-high chop. Each yacht appeared to be about to turn to help, but none of them did. To van Kretschmar, it looked as if each one had decided that the next boat would do the job. By the time his own yacht arrived, the two van Kretschmars were close to drowning. The commodore never forgot the fear and anger he felt as he watched yachts that might have helped continue racing.

But Purcell was enraged by the commodore's comments at the press conference, particularly the comparison with a driver's obligation stop after an automobile accident. Although van Kretschmar used the analogy to answer a question about the nature of a sailor's obligation to help another vessel, Purcell viewed it as an outrageously unfair personal attack. After all, unlike a car driving down a highway, the *Rintoul* didn't have a motor and was contending with a violent sea. "I made a decision that there wasn't anything we could do for them," Purcell said after the press conference, "and that I had an absolute responsibility to protect the safety of my own crew." By the time van Kretschmar apologized for the remark, it was too late. Purcell had already hired a team of high-priced lawyers, not only to defend him before the protest committee and during the coroner's inquest but to prepare a defamation suit against the commodore and the CYC. "It's preposterous," van Kretschmar said. "Apart from that one comment from me, which, if you take it out of context, doesn't seem very nice, he has nothing to stand on."

The CYC report recommended a number of rule changes, all of which were approved by the club's trustees. In future Hobarts, when a yacht experiences winds greater than forty knots, it will be required to tell the rest of the fleet about the weather it is experiencing, just as Kooky did in 1998. There will be mandatory seminars on weather forecasting and safety equipment. Yachts are to carry more accurate EPIRBs — ones that identify the yacht they are on — and one for every life raft. Every yacht has to have a handheld VHF radio, and every crewman will be made to carry a strobe light or a powerful flashlight. No one under the age of eighteen will be able to crew.

Adhering to the traditions of ocean racing, the CYC upheld the principle that decisions about whether to abandon a race should remain with skippers. After all, van Kretschmar believed, skippers are almost always in the best position to determine whether their yachts and crews can handle the conditions. The club, he added, would only postpone or cancel a race if the weather was already dangerous at the time of the start. There were precedents for delaying races. In the United States, the Newport to Bermuda Race was delayed for a day in 1982, and in 1993 one of the legs of the Whitbread was held back. But Martin James, one of the CYC's trustees and the owner of *Team Jaguar*, the yacht that had been dismasted, insisted that changing the start of a race because of weather must be a last resort. "We regard this as a fundamental tenet of our sport. If the club is left with the responsibility of canceling the race whenever there is a risk to any yacht, that would destroy the sport of yachting."

While van Kretschmar acknowledged that the CYC's changes were incremental, he claimed that the collective impact would be substantial, leading to changes in the way offshore races were conducted everywhere. He argued that the story of what happened in the 1998 Hobart, precisely because it was made memorable by tragedy, would magnify the lessons and also increase the focus on safety. In fact, yacht clubs around the world did cite the 1998 Hobart as they adopted new safety requirements, held additional safety classes, and increased the enforcement of existing rules. "There is no simple answer to preventing this from ever happening again," van Kretschmar said. "I believe, however, that the experiences of 1998 will be recalled forever by all future competitors as a stark reminder of the unpredictable and awesome force of the sea."

There was no doubt that the Hobart itself would survive. "The Sydney to Hobart Race is part of our way of life," Australian prime minister John Howard proclaimed. "These people have lost their lives following a sport that they love. It's a tragedy, but there are many tens of thousands of Australians that are keen sailors and yachtsmen, and they will go on. I'm quite sure that those who have been touched by this tragedy would want them to go on."

38

Kooky wasn't about to give up his dream of winning the Hobart. Even as he flew back to Sydney after being rescued, he was thinking about the next boat he would buy. Three weeks after the memorial service, he invited his crew to his house for pizza and beer. "I'm not going to slow down," he told them. "If I quit now, this will be the last thing I remember about the *Sword*. I intend to buy a new boat — and I'm going to call it the *Sword of Orion*." Dags and Brownie tried to tell Kooky to take some time off, but he was like a bulldozer. "I'm either going to move quickly or I'm going to stop — and it's not in my nature to stop," he said afterward. "If you don't get back on the horse, the fact that you didn't will always be there. You'll be crippled. I still expect to win the Hobart someday."

Steve Kulmar was not invited to rejoin the crew. He had enraged the *Sword*'s crew by telling a reporter from the *Sunday Telegraph*, a British newspaper, that he had pulled the crew together and organized the rescue effort after Glyn Charles was lost. The others understood that Kulmar had been suffering some kind of shock in the hours after Glyn was lost, but most of them were unwilling to forgive him for claiming a hero's role after he insisted on being rescued before the others.

In fact, Kulmar didn't step on a boat for several months after the race, and he said he would never back away from his resolution never to do another Hobart. "I've had a lifelong love of sailing — an intense love — and that makes it even worse," he said several months after the race. "I was absolutely shattered by doing what I love more than anything else. There's no way I'll do another Hobart or any ocean racing in darkness."

In many ways, Kulmar had become a bitter man. Given his long ocean-racing experience, he believed the CYC should have asked him to play a leading role in its investigation into the race. He wasn't offered one, and when officials refused to give him a copy of the report before it was published, he resigned from the club. Kulmar's anger was also directed at Richard Purcell and the crew of the *Margaret Rintoul*. "They're like the oxygen-starved people who climb over half-dead people so they can make it to the top of Everest," he said. "I think Purcell should sell his boat and retire from racing for the rest of his life."

Kooky, with an enhanced appreciation for the importance of having a cohesive crew, knew he had to move quickly to avoid losing his core group to other skippers. Buying a high-performance, forty-foot yacht, he resumed an active racing schedule as soon as he could, boasting that he would race in the 1999 Hobart.

Dags wasn't sure whether he wanted to do another Hobart with Kooky. In August, Dags joined the *Sword* for the Hamilton Island Race Week, a regatta near Australia's Great Barrier Reef, nine hundred miles north of Sydney. Just being on the new *Sword* brought back vivid memories of what happened on the old one. After one day of racing, Dags sat in the cockpit with tears in his eyes as he talked about how difficult the previous eight months had been. The new *Sword*'s cockpit was so similar to the old one that he couldn't stop thinking about the day the *Sword* capsized.

"Glyn was cold and scared, and he wasn't thinking straight, but what was I supposed to do?" Pausing to use the sleeve of his T-shirt to wipe his eyes, he added, "I have to put this behind me so I can sort my own life out. Everyone else on the crew has moved on, but I can't."

Late that evening, after Kooky had gone to bed, several members of the crew discussed whether they would sail the next Hobart on the new *Sword*. Andrew Parkes had already made it clear to everyone that he would not. "I made a deal with God," he said. Sam Hunt said he was also reluctant. "I'll do another Hobart," he said, "but not on this boat. It's just too small." Brownie said he would do at least one more Hobart but wasn't sure he wanted to go on the new *Sword*, either. "I don't trust the boats anymore," he explained. "And the new boat is lighter and less stable than the first one."

A couple of months before the 1999 race, Dags told Kooky that he had firmly decided against doing the Hobart on the *Sword*. Kooky tried to change his mind, but Dags wouldn't budge. Not long after that conversation, Dags was offered a chance to sail on a sixty-foot, Danish-owned yacht named *Nokia*. (Although it had the same name as the yacht that collided with the *Sword* in 1998, the two yachts had nothing in common other than a mutual sponsor.) This *Nokia* was a dream come true for Dags: its owners hoped to put together a campaign for the next Whitbread Round the World Race, which had been renamed the Volvo Ocean Race. For Dags, crewing on *Nokia* would bring him much closer to his dream of competing at yachting's highest level, so he eagerly accepted the invitation. He became its bowman and one of four Australians on the multinational crew.

* * *

Larry Ellison never even considered entering the 1999 Hobart. He described his feelings in a speech to members of San Francisco's St. Francis Yacht Club after the 1998 race: "*Sayonara* is perfectly maintained, it probably has the world's best professional crew, but we were at the limits of our ability to keep everything together," he said. "We felt like sending out a radio call and saying, 'Everyone go home. This is just insane.' This is not what sailboat racing is supposed to be about."

Only eighty yachts entered the 1999 race. Some yachtsmen stayed home because of what had happened a year earlier. Others planned to take family vacations to celebrate the Millennium. In the days before the race, strong winds were forecast but they were expected to be much more favorable than in 1998. In fact, a few hours before the start, Clouds Badham rushed between his client yachts, excitedly predicting that the fastest boats could do what had long been considered impossible — finish in less than two days. "This is the one," he declared. "I've never prepared a more exciting Hobart forecast. You're not going to see a weather pattern like this for another fifty years."

Clouds's forecast was spot on. As in 1998, *Brindabella* was locked in a battle to be first across the line, this time with *Nokia*. The wind, blowing out of the northeast at up to forty knots, enabled both yachts to surf south at record-breaking speeds, but *Nokia* had a crucial advantage — a water-ballasting system that enabled two and a half tons of water to be pumped from one side of the boat to the other, providing as much weight as thirty crewmen sitting on the rail. No one had ever taken advantage of a loophole in the eligibility requirements to enter a water-ballasted yacht before — and never before had the extra weight been so important.

The breathtakingly rapid trip south wasn't enough to erase memories of the 1998 race. At 2:05 P.M. on the second day of the race, about the time when yachts had begun to get in trouble in 1998, Dags was sitting next to *Nokia*'s nav station when Lew Carter, who was again serving as the radio operator, swallowed hard and said, "What I'm about to say is more difficult than sailing into a forty-knot headwind. Please join me in a moment of remembrance for our crewmates lost a year ago. It seems not to matter whether we knew them or not. The bond between us, as sailors, is so strong that we all feel the loss, and it hurts us to recall the loss of Bruce Guy, Phil Skeggs, Glyn Charles, Jim Lawler, John Dean, Mike Bannister. We will miss you always and remember you always."

Dags eyes filled with tears even before he heard Glyn's name. "I'm always thinking about that day," Dags told one of *Nokia*'s crewmen. "I've thought about it every day since it happened. The only difference today is that we're out here."

Nokia finished in one day, nineteen hours, and forty-eight minutes, smashing Hasso Plattner's record by more than eighteen hours. *Brindabella* finished less than an hour later to become the fastest unballasted yacht to complete the Hobart. For Dags, it was the best possible outcome. *Nokia*'s skipper, impressed with Dags's performance, invited him to join the crew in Europe for a series of races there.

Kooky and the new *Sword* had a frustrating race. Brownie was the only returning member of the 1998 crew. For much of the race, the *Sword* was in first place on the basis of corrected time. But the wind direction changed dramatically after *Nokia* and *Brindabella* arrived in Hobart, leaving the *Sword* and most of the smaller yachts to battle gale-force head winds. The *Sword* ended up in seventh place.

EPILOGUE

On the morning of March 13, 2000, Coroner John Abernethy entered his courtroom and sat down at the center of a long, elevated bench, where he was flanked by thirty-two black binders, each crammed full of evidence that had been accumulated during the fourteen months since the race. From the bench, Abernethy, a bearded man with the commonsense manner of a rural magistrate, looked out over a rectangular room with stained beige carpeting, furniture that looked as though it had been acquired many years before, and institutional-gray brick walls. Directly in front of him, behind a long table, sat more than a dozen dark-suited lawyers representing most of the people and organizations that might be blamed for the deaths that occurred during the race. During every day of the five-week inquest, the CYC and the weather bureau were each represented by at least two attorneys. The other chairs were filled by a revolving cast, including legal representatives for Richard Purcell, Kooky, Lew Carter, Richard Winning, and Jim Lawler's widow.

Behind the lawyers, several chairs were reserved for family members of the sailors who had died. Penny Dean and her two sons, Nathan and Peter, were present on several days, as were Denise Lawler and Shirley Bannister. Anne Goodman had made the trip from England. Because Glyn had been paid by Kooky, she believed that he could be liable for failing to provide a safe working environment. Each morning she unpacked a laptop computer, plugged it into the wall, and then sheathed the wire with a strip of adhesive tape to make sure that no one would trip over it. During the inquest, she typed notes and snippets of testimony. At lunch and coffee breaks, she kept to herself, rarely talking to anyone other than Penny Dean and two police detectives who had investigated the race for the coroner.

Richard Purcell had been dreading the inquest. More than anything, he was worried that a tape of the television interview he gave soon after he arrived in Hobart — the one in which he bragged about having sailed through waves "three times as big" — would be played to discredit his claim that it had been too dangerous to turn toward the *Sword of Orion*. The stakes were high: if the coroner concluded that the *Margaret Rintoul* had been capable of doing something that might have prevented Glyn Charles's death, Purcell could face criminal charges. For that reason, he had hired one of Australia's most prominent litigators, Alex Shand, to represent him.

When Kooky sat in the witness box, he asserted that the *Rintoul* should have done more. "If they had stopped, it would have meant the search for Glyn Charles could have been commenced" sooner than it was, Kooky said. If he had been on the *Rintoul*, he added, "the first thing I would have done was tuned in to the second radio channel. I would have found out what their situation was. I would have reported their position — and that it was dismasted. They only said they saw a flare — nothing else."

Coronial inquests can have the quality of a legal free-for-all in which blame is passed around like a hot potato. Every attorney is given a shot at questioning each witness. When it was Shand's turn with Kooky, he attacked with the ferocity that had made him a legend among Australian barristers. First he challenged Kooky's qualifications as a skipper by criticizing him for waiting so long to retire from the race. "For some hours," Shand said, "you were frozen in indecision." Kooky defended himself by blaming the weather bureau, saying it hadn't provided enough information about the location of the low-pressure system. "I was concerned that if we went to the north that we would go back into the storm," he said. After a pause, he added, "That's what happened."

Kooky later submitted a statement to the coroner that expanded upon that point and claimed that the bureau was directly responsible for Glyn's death because of its failure to provide more details about the storm. "Had the information been made available," Kooky said in the statement, "the decision to turn back would not have been made, the *Sword of Orion* would have sailed into better weather, and the roll which resulted in Mr. Charles' death would not have occurred."

The weather bureau appeared to be an easy target. Clouds Badham had testified before Kooky, and he too criticized the bureau for failing to pinpoint the location and trajectory of the low. "They said, 'There's a low in Bass Strait,'" Clouds said as he looked toward Richard Stanley, one of the bureau's attorneys. "Well, hell, you can tell them where it is. It's not a secret."

Stanley rejected Clouds's criticism as well as Kooky's attempt to blame the bureau for Glyn's death. Claiming that the forecasts were "substantially accurate," Stanley argued: "There has been an attempt by Mr. Kothe to fabricate evidence to justify his decision not to turn around earlier."

Alex Shand wasn't interested in the quality of the bureau's forecasts. What he wanted was for Kooky to portray the actual conditions as being so extreme that it would have been unreasonable to expect the *Margaret Rintoul* to turn toward the *Sword*. When Kooky failed to provide the sort of answer Shand was looking for, he placed two clenched fists on his hips as if he were a gladiator. With tones of contempt and outrage, he demanded, "Will you answer my question, and answer it directly?"

When Kooky ultimately acknowledged that "it was pretty horrible," Shand removed his fists from his side and snarled, "That took you a while, didn't it?" (The coroner, aware that Purcell was preparing a defamation suit against the CYC, appeared to be troubled by Shand's brutal approach and by the way his courtroom might be being used for agendas other than his own. "How does this help me?" Abernethy demanded of Shand. "It may help you somewhere else. I can't see how it can help me.")

When Purcell took the stand, Alun Hill, an attorney who assisted the coroner by playing a prosecutor-like role, noted that failing to help a boat in distress is "probably the most heinous thing a sailor can be accused of." Purcell agreed and went on to describe his decision not to turn back as "one of the hardest things I've ever done." But because the *Rintoul* was contending with fifty knots of wind and thirty-foot waves without a working engine, Purcell declared, "Mr. Hill, we were battling for our lives at that particular time."

"That's not what you said on television," Hill interjected. The moment Purcell had feared had arrived. After Hill asked the court staff to play a videotape of Purcell's interview, a jocular and prideful Purcell, his nose still covered with pasty white sunscreen, was projected onto a large screen in front of the courtroom. While everyone else watched the tape, Purcell turned his head downward. When it was over, he claimed that he had been in "fantasyland" when he gave the interview.

The coroner accepted most of what Purcell had said. Given the conditions at the time, Abernethy said, "I have no issue with the decision not to go back to the boat's assistance." The coroner was troubled by the *Rintoul*'s failure to make radio contact with the *Sword*, but Purcell said that wasn't his responsibility. "I wasn't thinking about the radio," Purcell said. "I left that job to Colin Betts," the *Rintoul*'s navigator.

Betts, whose testimony was punctuated by long pauses, claimed that he simply never thought of turning on the VHF radio. He said he turned off the HF radio soon after he reached Lew Carter because he wanted "to conserve power and also to let the guys that were resting try and get some rest." Hill, who noted that Betts had been racing since 1955, appeared to find his testimony difficult to accept. Hill appeared to be even more skeptical when he questioned Betts as to why he hadn't told Carter that the yacht Purcell had seen was dismasted. Betts said he had. Hill said a log of the conversation with Lew Carter didn't include any such information.

Most of the testimony from the *Winston Churchill*'s survivors focused on their struggle to stay with their rafts amid the enormous waves. Steamer, who testified with his usual calm confidence, said no one from the *Winston Churchill* had heard anything about what Mega Bascombe had seen near the yacht's bow on the morning the race started. Nevertheless, Steamer dismissed the possibility that the defect had anything to do with the yacht's sinking. The boat had been out of the water and standing in a prominent position at Richard Winning's boatyard for several days prior to the race, Steamer said, asserting that any serious problem would have been noticed. "Fifteen tradesmen would have walked by it at least four times a day," he said, adding that the only thing that could have been missing was a "cosmetic piece of putty."

As with the *Margaret Rintoul*, the most troubling questions dealt with radio communications. Steamer was unable to offer any explanation for the *Churchill*'s failure to give its position during the 2:00 P.M. radio sked on the day it sunk. It was a crucial issue. By the time Lew Carter called the *Churchill*, it was about 3:00 P.M., a bit less than two hours before the *Churchill* fell off the wave and began to sink. If someone on the yacht had provided a precise position during the sked, AusSAR may have realized that the yacht Neil Boag spotted couldn't have been the *Churchill*. And with an accurate and fairly recent position, it would have been possible to focus the search on a relatively limited area, increasing the likelihood that the rafts would have been found before the night when Michael Bannister, John Dean, and Jim Lawler were lost.

The court had to break for lunch before Steamer had completed his testimony. At a nearby pub, he couldn't have been more relaxed as he sat down with Gibbo, who had been in the courtroom all morning, and ordered a steak sandwich and a beer. The mood changed dramatically when an obviously agitated Richard Winning sat down between them. Winning was alarmed by the questions about the missed sked. "There's been a sea change!" he declared. "All of a sudden, they're trying to make it look like we didn't know what we were doing."

"I don't see it that way," Gibbo said. "Are you really worried?"

"Yes, I'm really worried!" Winning snapped. His specific concern was that no one could explain why Lumpy, who as the navigator was supposed to report the *Churchill*'s position, hadn't done so. "They're trying to make it look like we put our most inexperienced man in an important job — and that he didn't know enough to do it."

Gibbo tried to reassure Winning, but it had no effect. Winning left the table and called his own lawyer, asking her to be in court for the afternoon session. In fact, although he didn't say so, Gibbo was also concerned about the missed sked. Prior to the inquest, he hadn't even known about the lapse, and as he began to appreciate its potential significance, he wanted an explanation.

Lumpy offered one when it was his turn in the witness box. He testified that he had monitored the radio during most of the sked — but that at 2:30 P.M., not long before the *Winston Churchill* was called, he was so tired that he asked John Dean to take over and report the *Churchill's* position. Lumpy said he then climbed into a bunk and went to sleep.

Dean's widow and sons were outraged by the suggestion that he had failed to do such a critically important job. Dean, of course, was unable to represent himself, but the coroner sought to do so in his final report, stating, "I can be certain on the evidence that I have that if John Dean was asked by Paul Lumtin to radio *Winston Churchill's* position as required by the sked, then he would have done so."

On Friday night, a couple of hours after the inquest ended for the week, Gibbo and a group of friends gathered at the Sydney Amateur Sailing Club for a twilight race. It was a perfect evening. As Gibbo guided his yacht toward the center of Sydney Harbor, not far from where the starting line for the Hobart had been, the breeze was steady and warm. It was one of those nights when everyone who was on a boat, even those who had never been outside Australia, was absolutely certain that Sydney is the world's greatest city. It was also the kind of night that reminded Gibbo of everything he loved about sailing. A big part of twilight races is the camaraderie, and everyone had opened a can of beer before the starting gun.

Inevitably, though, after it was fired, some of the conviviality was displaced by the urge of competition. With Gibbo's son, also named John, at the helm and Gibbo suggesting tactics, the rest of the crewmen did their best to trim the sails as the sun set and the sky turned from a brilliant blue to shades of pink. After the race was over and the crew returned to the clubhouse, the race committee had calculated the results according to each yacht's handicap-adjusted time. Gibbo was declared the winner.

After a celebratory bottle of red wine was poured, the conversation turned to the inquest. "It's a terrible thing for sailing," Gibbo said. "No one's to blame for what happened. The weather bureau did the best job it could. So did everyone on the *Churchill*. Richard Winning didn't do anything wrong. In fact, he's a hero: going outside that raft and turning it over — that's what heroes do."

In the cove, the yachts eased back and forth, swaying in the calm water. Beyond was a harbor, and beyond that an ocean. Since men had first gone to sea, that water had attracted them. For thousands of years, men like Gibbo and his son had set out to play, to explore, and to prove themselves against the sea. Some never came back and others would keep returning. Many were unable to articulate exactly why they felt so drawn to the waves. Sitting there, sipping wine and remembering, Gibbo had no words for it. Yet the pull remained, as powerful as ever.

AFTERWORD

Several months after the original edition of this book was published, I was asked to speak about it at a dinner at Australia's Royal Sydney Yacht Squadron. Like the CYC, the Squadron has a long-established commitment to competitive sailing, but it has a very different feel to it. For one thing, it's more elegant. At the dinner, an immaculately polished silver trophy was placed at the center of each of the large round tables at which guests would sit. All of the survivors from the *Winston Churchill* were sitting at a table near the front along with Shirley and Stephen Bannister. John Stanley, who I had never seen in anything but casual clothes, was wearing a dark suit. Beaver was wearing a tie and jacket.

I was nervous. Having made the same presentation throughout the United States, I knew the words would roll out with almost unthinking ease. I had also brought a guaranteed crowd-pleaser: the book's cinematic twin, a CNN documentary that is also called *The Proving Ground*. It focuses on the same boats as the book and contains some riveting footage. But this would be the first audience that knew more about the race than I did — people who had been there. I was also worried that someone who didn't like the way he was portrayed would initiate a confrontation that would mar the evening. Paul Lumtin was sitting directly in front of the podium. Like the coroner, I didn't believe Lumpy's claim that he had asked John Dean to report the *Churchill's* position during the radio sked not long before the yacht sank, and I knew Lumpy was angry that the book reflected this.

In fact, my presentation was followed by a lively but rancor-free discussion of various aspects of the race and the steps that have been taken to prevent similar tragedies in the future. Lumpy said nothing. After most of the guests left, Steamer, Beaver, and I went to the Squadron's wood-paneled bar to catch up over pints of Victoria Bitter.

But I left Sydney feeling unsatisfied: I wanted to know what had happened to the other people I had written about. Therefore, during several subsequent trips to Sydney I spoke to all of the survivors from the *Churchill* and the *Sword of Orion*. I also went to see Larry Ellison who told me how his trip to Hobart had led to his pursuit of sailing's ultimate prize, the America's Cup.

Gibbo didn't mention it during the dinner at the Squadron, but he was then developing a series of lawsuits against the CYC, the weather bureau, the life raft manufacturer — and, more surprisingly, Richard Winning. Gibbo had persuaded the three women whose husbands had been lost from his raft to become plaintiffs, and he was also drafting a suit in which he would himself be the plaintiff. The suits blamed the weather bureau for failing to communicate the severity of the forecasted weather, the CYC for allowing the race to continue after the storm warning was issued, and the life raft company for making an inadequate craft that could not be "righted without exposing the occupants to danger."

The lawsuits faulted Winning for deciding not "to withdraw from the race and seek safe harbour or divert course" and for neglecting "to instruct each of the crew occupying the raft as to the correct and efficient procedure to be employed to right the raft in the event of capsizing." The suits also cited Winning for having "failed to alert the CYC of the yacht's correct position during the mayday call made at about 4:30 p.m. on 27 December 1998." Gibbo's suit demanded that Winning compensate him for "post traumatic stress disorder, depression, and insomnia."

Gibbo told me he had struggled over his decision to bring the suits. "The last thing I wanted was to be seen as suing anyone or anything related to the Hobart, but I ended up concluding I had to do it," mostly for the sake of the widows, he said. The widows of course had suffered, financially as well as in ways that could never be adequately compensated. When I went to see Shirley Bannister at her home, she said, "For me the first year was just about surviving. The second year was about nurturing. Since then, I've been trying to move ahead in little baby steps. I even have a date every once in a while, but it's hard — I lost such a good one…"

But the survivors from the *Churchill*'s crew were troubled by Gibbo's legal actions. "If it's a way of getting some money to the widows, I guess it's a good thing," Bruce Gould said, "but I hate doing it this way. Litigation takes on a life of its own and ends up hurting people." More than anything, the survivors were unhappy that Gibbo had brought an action of his own against Winning. Paul Lumpton put it this way: "I understand the widows' position — they've been left wanting. But Gibbo hasn't been left wanting. He's just trying to jump on the gravy train."

Gibbo disputed that. "I'm in a unique position in that I was there, and I have the legal skills and the experience to make sure that the litigation doesn't go off the rails. For that reason I have to be involved." This was not entirely true. He could have helped the widows find a lawyer other than himself. And he could have pursued suits on behalf of the widows without filing one of his own. By representing them and himself, he would have the kind of multiple roles lawyers generally seek to avoid because of the conflicts they create. After all, in addition to being both a lawyer and a plaintiff, he would almost certainly be called as a witness. And having publicly praised Winning for his heroic work to upright the raft he was on, Gibbos's own words could be used to discredit his testimony to the potential detriment of his clients.

Gibbo said he still regarded Winning as a friend, and he claimed the legal action was nothing more than an effort to obtain money from Winning's insurance company. "This has nothing to do with my relationship with Richard," he said. "I'm not suing Richard — I'm suing his insurance company."

Winning didn't see it that way. While he acknowledged that his insurer would cover the costs of litigation and, if it came to it, a judgment or a settlement, he viewed the suits as a terrible betrayal, and the prospect of a trial loomed like an endless black cloud. "It's going to be adversarial and damn acrimonious," he said. "Given the time that's passed, it's going to be difficult to remember things, and they'll be doing everything they can to trip me up."

Other than the families of the crewmen who died, few had suffered more than Winning. In addition to the burden of having lost three friends, his beloved yacht had disappeared and, it turned out, so too had his love for sailing itself. In spite of what he had said about wanting to buy another boat and entering a future Hobart, he had done very little sailing since 1998. Of the Hobart, he said, "At this point I don't have any interest in it." Winning's closest friends found that difficult to accept. "I know what makes him tick," said Lumpy. "It's water and wind — and that will never change."

It was not until 2005 — when the lawsuits were settled out of court with terms that were not disclosed — that Winning restarted his nautical life. He began by crewing on a friend's boat. Then he purchased a fifty-year-old, wood-hulled sailboat. Forty feet long, it rarely left Sydney Harbor. Winning said he probably would not compete in another Hobart, but he was onboard the radio relay vessel that accompanied the fleet during the 2010 race.

Memories of the 1998 race were a frequent presence for all of the survivors. When I went to Bruce Gould's house for dinner, his seventeen-year-old daughter Felicity proudly announced that she had just finished a year-long science project — a pump that could send air to the occupants of an inverted life raft. The idea for the project was hers, but the inspiration had obviously come from her father's experience, and she had consulted with him about the details. Each conversation transported him back to the raft, and memories came back at other times as well. "I think about the raft capsizing at the oddest times — in the gym, in a meeting, when I'm sailing, or when it's raining." But that did not deter Gould from entering Hobart races. He sailed in several after 1998, and he too was on the radio relay vessel in 2010.

Steamer was sailing more than ever. For much of his adult life, he had reminisced about what he believed to be the sport's good old days — a time when sailors built their own boats and spent more of their time on the water. In attempting to resurrect some of that, he had organized several regattas for a class of high-performance, eighteen-foot-boats that had been sailed in Australia since the 1890s. "If you can sail an eighteen-footer, you can sail anything," he declared. "And they can put the fun back into the sport."

When I met up with Beaver on the beach in Manly a few years after the race, he said he still occasionally woke up in a cold sweat and that it was always because he was dreaming about the Hobart. "A couple of nights ago when we had a heavy rainstorm I kept thinking about what it was like to be sitting on the back of the *Churchill* watching the wind indicator hit fifty knots." But Beaver was eager to sail to Hobart again. And although he was installing air-conditioning systems for a living, he ultimately hoped to become a professional boat captain. As we watched waves march toward the beach, he admitted that he did not know how the 1998 race had affected him. "It left me with a weakness somewhere inside of me — but I also I think I'm more confident, more headstrong than I used to be. If I'm sailing offshore and the waves are crashing over the deck, I'm less hesitant to go to the bow. I think it's because I've made it through something most people have never seen."

Beaver committed suicide in 2008. He had been diagnosed as bipolar some years earlier and had broken up with a girlfriend just before it happened. At a funeral service attended by more than three hundred, Steamer gave the eulogy. He remembered the "enthusiasm and infectious smile" he had noticed back when Beaver was piloting a yacht club launch. "I saw a bit of myself when I was at that age. We are going to miss you."

All of the *Sword of Orion*'s survivors continued sailing except for one — Kooky. Not long after he completed the 1999 Hobart aboard the "new" *Sword*, he sold it. He said the leg injuries he suffered when the first *Sword* capsized made it impossible for him to continue racing. He was still involved in sailing through a new business venture — he started a website that provided news about Australian racing — but he seemed happier writing about the competitors more than being one. "I still enjoy being around boats and seeing my old crew," he said, "but my sailing days are over."

Having put the 1998 Hobart behind him, Kooky said he felt sorry for those who had not, namely Richard Purcell, who had continued to pursue his defamation suit against the CYC with dogged determination. Purcell told me he was still devoting much of his time to the effort and had paid more than a quarter million dollars in legal fees. "It's had a huge cost on me, physically and mentally, and it's stretched me to the absolute limit financially." Purcell predicted that the CYC would be forced to reimburse him for his legal fees and to pay at least half a million dollars in damages. "When I finish with them, everyone will see how they conspired to hurt me." Six years after the race, Purcell got much of what he wanted when the club agreed to pay him an undisclosed amount of money and to issue an apology in which it said it had never meant to suggest that Purcell was guilty of "gross misconduct for failing to render assistance to the *Sword of Orion*."

Other than Purcell, the most embittered person I spoke to was Steve Kulmar, who said some of his unhappiness stemmed from my book. He said my description of how he demanded to be lifted from the *Sword* before the others was false — and he was extremely angry about it. "I got off the boat before the others because no one else was brave enough to do it," he declared. "They wanted someone to get in the water at three a.m., and I was the only one who had the guts to go."

I told Kulmar that the book's account was consistent with what each of the *Sword*'s eight other survivors had told me, but I promised to question each of them again. When I did, they all said Kulmar's account was completely at odds with what happened, although no one accused him of lying. "There's no doubt in my mind that Steve *thinks* he's telling the truth, but he's just wrong," said Andrew Parkes. Kooky agreed, saying, "He just has his own reality."

Kulmar also told me he remained deeply affected by Glyn Charles' death and said that was why he had temporarily stopped sailing. "After the race, I promised my wife that I would take some time off, but now I'm getting back involved. Unlike everyone else on the *Sword*, I've been sailing since I was eight. It's always been a part of my life and it always will be."

Dags was also still sailing, but he had given up trying to make a career out of it and had taken a job with a construction company. "I needed to make a better living," he explained. Nigel Russell and Simon Reffold were still spending their weekends crewing on high-performance yachts, although Russell had a new hobby — flying helicopters. Inspired by the one that rescued him, he had earned a pilot's license. Adam Brown, Carl Watson, and Sam Hunt were also crewing for some of Sydney's most competitive race boats. Andrew Parkes was working as a yacht broker and participating in harbor races almost every week, but he had consistently rejected invitations to sail to Hobart. "I've never felt any need to 'get back on the horse again,'" he said. "As a matter of fact, I think it takes as much conviction to say no as it does to say yes."

Larry Ellison had also not wavered from his no-more-Hobarts vow. With the America's Cup, he said, "I decided to focus on a more technical and less life-threatening form of sailing."

It would not have happened without *Sayonara*. In April 2000, Ellison was sitting in a bar in Antigua with several of its crewmen after a maxi-yacht competition. Tony Rae, a veteran of both *Sayonara* and Team New Zealand, which won the Cup from the United States in 1995 and again in 2000, mentioned that several members of Team New Zealand were likely to abandon the squad to join foreign-sponsored Cup contenders. Ellison was shocked. It seemed impossible that men who had brought so much glory to their proud little nation would consider switching sides.

"So you're saying that if I had a team you could sail on it?" Ellison blurted.

As Rae confirmed what he had said, a history-changing idea was born. For the man who was named for Ellison Island, the idea of bringing the Cup back to America was irresistible. When Bill Erkelens joined the group a few minutes later, Ellison declared, "Bill, we're going to the America's Cup."

A couple of months after that, Ellison went to Newport where *Sayonara* was preparing for the start of the Newport Bermuda Race. He was not going to be onboard. He was there to recruit sailors for the thirty-first competition for the Cup, slated for 2003. His targets included members of *Sayonara*'s crew as well as those from other top boats. From J.P. Morgan, the Vanderbilts, Sir Thomas Lipton, and more recently, Ted Turner, the Cup has always attracted very wealthy men. *Katana*, Ellison's 244-foot motor yacht, was in Newport's harbor to signal Ellison's where-withal. Loaded with luggage belonging to *Sayonara*'s crewmen as well as some of their girlfriends, *Katana* set out for Bermuda a few hours after *Sayonara* crossed the starting line. With its two diesel engines plus a gas turbine, *Katana* could travel at better than twenty-eight knots, so it was there in plenty of time to greet potential members of Ellison's Cup team at the finish.

Several other billionaires were also vying to attract sailors for their Cup campaigns, including Craig McCaw, the telecom-munications entrepreneur whose syndicate was later backed by Microsoft cofounder Paul Allen; Patrizio Bertelli, the head of Prada, the Italian fashion house; and Ernesto Bertarelli, the head of Serono, Europe's biggest biotechnology company. (Hasso Plattner, Ellison's archrival on the maxi-yacht racing circuit, did not have a team of his own but he became a major contributor to Team New Zealand.) Thanks to the billionaire contenders, who became known in sailing circles as "The Bees," the total amount of money devoted to the 2003 regatta would exceed $700 million.

Tony Rae ended up rejecting offers from Ellison as well as McCaw and Bertarelli to stay with Team New Zealand. "The money I was being offered was great — it was out of control — but in the end I decided that I wanted to help keep the Cup in New Zealand. To jump to a team that wanted to take the Cup away from New Zealand just didn't seem right." Ellison did hire several of the others who were aboard *Sayonara* for the 1998 Hobart, including Chris Dickson, Mike Howard, Robbie Naismith, Mark Turner, and Bob Wylie. Ellison also hired Paul Cayard, an America's Cup veteran who had been *Sayonara's* professional skipper before Dickson.

Unlike the other Bees, Ellison said he would take time away from his job to train as a member of the sailing team and that he would take the wheel during races. Peter Holmberg, who became Ellison's lead helmsman after Dickson and Cayard were both sidelined, told me, "It will work because Larry is smart. He has great concentration and he hits the target speeds. We're quite confident that he won't jeopardize the result for a bit of a thrill."

Having harnessed cutting-edge technologies to build Oracle, Ellison said he would do the same thing to develop the boat he would sail for the Cup. The process would involve thousands of decisions about the shapes of the hull and sails, the structure of the mast, and hundreds of other variables. Once the basic design was settled and two boats were built, they were equipped with more than sixty electronic sensors that evaluated equipment as well as sailing techniques. Some of the campaign's 140 full-time employees would turbo-charge the analysis by using Oracle's database software to isolate various factors and identify the best possible options. "The problem in the past was that we collected lots of data but we weren't very good at processing it," said Erkelens, who managed the campaign on a day-to-day basis. "Now we're gathering even more information, but we know what to do with it. It's a real competitive advantage."

Ellison ended up spending $120 million on his campaign, but it was not enough. He was knocked out of the competition by Bertarelli (who had heard about the possibility of defections from Team New Zealand before Ellison and hired several of its stars). Bertarelli's team then defeated New Zealand to return the Cup to Europe for the first time since a yacht called *America* won the first competition back in 1851. The next races took place in Valencia, Spain, in 2007. Ellison invested even more money in that campaign, although when I asked the amount, his response was almost offhanded: "a couple of hundred million dollars." But once again, his team was eliminated and the Swiss squad came in first.

Two days later, Bertarelli announced the rules for the next competition. The victor has always had a degree of leeway in setting the ground rules — one of the reasons the New York Yacht Club had been able to maintain its 132-year winning streak — but Bertarelli took things much further than ever before. Under his rules, he could reject or eject competitors and select the umpires who judge races.

Ellison was outraged. The protocol was the first thing he talked about when I went to his Malibu beach house to ask about his Cup efforts. "When I first read the protocol, I thought it was a joke," he said. "They could disqualify us at any point in time for any reason — and the umpires would work for them. I mean, I could be the leading scorer in the NBA if I could get the referees to work for me!"

After Bertarelli refused to alter his approach, Ellison filed a lawsuit in New York where the Deed of Gift that governs the competition is registered. The two men, who had once been friends, were soon locked in a bitter grudge match. One of the lowest points came when Bertarelli told a Swiss newspaper that Ellison was "a loser." That was something I decided to mention to Ellison. He was sitting in the sun on a comfortable outdoor sofa on a deck just above the beach when I did so. The first evidence of his reaction was in his posture. He went from a semi-reclined position that allowed his bare feet to rest on a coffee table to stiffly upright. Then he repeated Bertarelli's words. Twice. The first rendition was soft, almost a whisper. The second was louder. The tone obviously reflected anger, but I also detected an element of how-dare-he disbelief. Then, for several seconds, he said nothing as he stared into the waves. I wondered if he was considering his response or thinking about what else he might do to ensure that Bertarelli ended up the real loser. Finally, he looked at me and started laughing. "You know, you have to either get angry or laugh," he said. But he did not leave it at that. "If I'm a loser, why won't he come out and sail against us with fair rules?" he demanded. And he brought the conversation back to Bertarelli's comment a few minutes later, saying, "You don't look good making statements like that. It makes him sound like a frustrated child." Later on, he added more: "I think it says a lot more about him than it says about me."

Ellison made it clear that he would do whatever it took to win, and while the litigation was underway he took a major step by hiring Russell Coutts, who had been Team New Zealand's skipper in 1995 and 2000 and Bertarelli's in 2003. By then, the tide was already flowing in Ellison's favor. He would prevail in a series of courtrooms and, in February of 2010, on the water. Once he was awarded the Cup, he announced that the next regatta would take place in San Francisco in 2013.

Ellison said he would modernize the competition to attract more interest. He started by developing design parameters for a new class of Cup boats: seventy-two-foot catamarans that would be powered by solid, wing-shaped sails and be capable of speeds greater than thirty knots. With much faster boats and the possibility of capsizings and crashes, the Cup was likely to make a profound step away from its roots as a competition among like-minded gentlemen toward something closer to an extreme sport. Media coverage would also change with the use of onboard cameras and microphones as well as the kind of high-tech graphics that have become common in other professional sports.

After I heard about the extent of Ellison's plans, I suggested that his involvement in the Cup, his victory as well as his innovations, could end up becoming his most enduring achievement, more so than even Oracle Corporation. Ellison did not disagree. "Oracle could just disappear someday," he said. "The America's Cup will not."

Meanwhile, at the CYC and other yacht clubs around the world, the 1998 Sydney to Hobart Race continues to affect the way ocean races are organized. "There's a formality that wasn't there before," said Hugo van Kretschmar, the CYC's former commodore. "Everything is fully documented, there are more rules, more training, crisis committees, and dry runs. There are a lot more burdens on everyone, but the 1998 race showed that it's all sensible stuff." Yet van Kretschmar, like most yachtsmen, said the changes would not eliminate the risks.

"Of course it will happen again," said Richard Winning. "All the red tape and regulations won't stop it from happening. If you're in the wrong place at the wrong time, you're gone."

ACKNOWLEDGMENTS

I could not have written this book without the exhaustive cooperation of its subjects. During the ten trips I made to Australia, each of the survivors from the *Winston Churchill* and the *Sword of Orion* submitted to lengthy interviews and endless follow-up questions. *Sayonara*'s and *Brindabella*'s crews were no less helpful. George Snow not only described his experience during the Hobart but showed me what maxi-yacht racing is all about by giving me several opportunities to join his crew. Larry Ellison found time to answer all of my questions, beginning over a marathon lunch in the backyard of his home in California, as did Lachlan Murdoch, during interviews in Sydney and New York.

In addition to reconstructing the events of the race, each yachtsman did his best to remember his words and feelings at the time. It is probably worth noting that the quote marks in the book surround only words that at least one person remembered saying or hearing. Unspoken thoughts, some of which are recorded in italics, are the product of questions such as "What were you thinking when that happened?"

Some of the book's subjects died during the race. I interviewed family members of each of them, and I am deeply grateful for their willingness to invite me into their homes to share memories and photo albums.

Patrick Sullivan, the former regional director of Australia's Bureau of Meteorology, did much more than explain the bureau's role during the race: he patiently educated me in the complicated science of weather. Roger Hickman, the Cruising Yacht Club's rear commodore, helped me clarify a number of complicated issues. John Abernethy, the coroner of New South Wales, provided me with several hundred pages of materials from his inquest, including the transcripts of police interviews that were conducted soon after the race. Alan Kennedy, the multitalented journalist who covered the race and its aftermath for the *Sydney Morning Herald*, was the closest thing I had to a colleague while I was researching the book, and he provided me with a number of important assists. Two of my actual colleagues, Paul Steiger, the managing editor of the *Wall Street Journal*, and John Bussey, its foreign editor, played an even more fundamental role by granting me the leave I needed to complete the book.

David and Andrée Milman made several helpful introductions during my first trip to Sydney and provided me with spectacular accommodations during almost all of my subsequent visits. Equally important, their enthusiasm about the project, conveyed over many wonderful meals, offered daily reassurance that this was a book worth writing. At various stages, several other friends — Reginald Chua, Adam Glick, Denise Scruton, Doug Sease, Harry van Dyke, and Tim Zimmermann — read the manuscript with pencil in hand. Each of them had an important impact.

The book also benefited from an all-star cast of professional editors and publishers. Larry Kirshbaum and Maureen Egen, the skippers at Time Warner Trade Publishing, and Michael Pietsch, Little, Brown's publisher and editor in chief, repeatedly demonstrated why they are the best in the business. Steve Lamont, the book's meticulous copyeditor, ensured that the manuscript was free of errors, and Elizabeth Nagle helped me gather photographs. Vicki Flick, Michelle Kane, Jessica Napp, and Cathy Saypol promoted the book with entrepreneurial enthusiasm. I am grateful to Patrick Gallagher and Paul Donovan of Allen & Unwin, the book's publisher in Australia, for their editorial guidance and hospitality and also for trusting an American with a subject so important to many Australians. I'm also thankful to Nicholas Pearson of Fourth Estate, the publisher in Britain, particularly for the storytelling advice he began providing even before he acquired the book.

And then there are Sarah Burnes and Bill Clegg, without whom there would have been no book. It was Sarah, a gifted editor and an accomplished blue-water sailor, who conceived of the book. It was Bill, my friend and agent, who told Sarah that I should write it. From the very beginning, they have offered the kind of unwavering support and wise counsel that every author needs. Finally, after Sarah left Little, Brown to launch an exciting new literary agency with Bill, Geoff Shandler picked up the ball and succeeded in managing a seamless transition as well as in making his own very substantial contributions to the final product.

G. Bruce Knecht
Hong Kong

ABOUT THE AUTHOR

 G. Bruce Knecht is a former senior writer and foreign correspondent for the *Wall Street Journal*, where he wrote about the banking and publishing industries and pursued various investigative projects. Before joining the *Wall Street Journal*, he wrote for *Dun's Review* magazine and the *Los Angeles Herald Examiner*. His articles also have appeared in the *Atlantic Monthly*, the *New York Times Magazine*, the *Independent (UK)*, *National Review*, *Barron's*, *Conde Nast Traveler*, *SAIL*, and *Men's Journal*. He is also the author of *Hooked: Pirates, Poaching and the Perfect Fish*. A New Jersey native, he earned a bachelor's degree from Colgate University and an MBA from Harvard University and was a Reuters Fellow at Oxford University. An avid sailor, Knecht raced across the Atlantic Ocean in 2005 aboard *Mari-Cha IV*, the yacht that broke the 100-year-old transatlantic race record. He is currently at work on a new book that will describe the design and building of a very large yacht.